D0303206

This study, based on the Bampton Lectures delivered in the University of Oxford in 1992, examines what is often called the crisis of modernity, with reference not only to modernity but to modern culture in general. Problems of social, theological, and philosophical thought are traced back beyond the Enlightenment to the very roots of Western Christian theology. A response to these problems is essayed by constructively developing conceptual possibilities to be found in ancient and modern theology of the Trinity.

THE ONE, THE THREE AND THE MANY

God, Creation and the Culture of Modernity
The Bampton Lectures 1992

COLIN E. GUNTON

Professor of Christian Doctrine,
King's College, University of London

CAMBRIDGE
UNIVERSITY PRESS

Published by the Press Syndicate of the University of Cambridge
The Pitt Building, Trumpington Street, Cambridge CB2 1RP
40 West 20th Street, New York, NY 10011-4211, USA
10 Stamford Road, Oakleigh, Melbourne 3166, Australia

© Cambridge University Press

First published 1993

Printed in Great Britain at the University Press, Cambridge

A catalogue record for this book is available from the British Library

Library of Congress cataloguing in publication data

Gunton, Colin E.
The One, the Three and the Many: God, creation and the culture of modernity /
Colin E. Gunton.
p.   cm.
Incudes bibliographical references and index.
ISBN 0 521 42030 X (hardback). ISBN 0 521 42184 5 (paperback).
1. Theology – 20th century. 2. Christianity and culture. 3. Trinity – History of
doctrines – 20th century. 4. Modernism.
1. Title.
BT28.G86   1993
231'.044 – dc20   92-34659   CIP

ISBN 0 521 42030 X hardback
ISBN 0 521 42184 5 paperback

TAG

Contents

ix

Preface

The writing of all books involves a process of discovery. What happened in this case was what began as a study of culture became both that and a study of the doctrine of creation. The reason is that the human activity we call culture takes shape in the context of what is sometimes called nature. The created world provides the framework within which human activity takes place. Because, however, a salient feature of the culture we call modernity is its confusion about the nature of that relation, a study of our world that would probe its roots will soon find itself running up against the broader question of the character of the world within which that activity takes place.

The writing of all books also involves a process of conversation. Even for those who prefer to write in cloistered calm away from all direct human contact, there is the wisdom of the sources to be consulted. This book has gained from an immensely wider process of conversation. First drafts were read to the weekly seminar of the King's College, London, Research Institute in Systematic Theology, and I have many of its members to thank for comments which have strengthened the argument. I am as always particularly grateful to Christoph Schwoebel, whose careful response to all my writing means so much to me. My wife and our elder daughter have also read and commented on much of the material, and the dedication of the book is a small token of what I owe to them, and not only in this connection.

This book, however, is unlike most others in that it was written to be delivered as the 1992 Bampton Lectures in the University of Oxford, and it is in that connection that I have many other debts of gratitude to acknowledge, not least for the opportunity given me by the electors to return to my first university with what is, in effect, a report on a process of thought which first began to take shape there many years ago. One major debt is to Geoffrey Nuttall, through whose initial encouragement I came to take on the lectureship. The second is to the University of Oxford, for the kindness and hospitality of whose representatives I cannot speak too warmly. Finally I would thank Alex Wright of the Cambridge University Press for his patience and encouragement, and for the contributions his readers have made to the process of writing and rewriting.

King's College, London
July, 1992

Introduction

When William Morris said that 'Modernism began and continues, wherever civilisation began and continues to *deny* Christ',[1] he indicated that salient aspects of modern culture are predicated on the denial of the Christian gospel. The reason for this is in part to be found in the direction that Christian history has taken. For all of its unifying vision, the era of Christendom was dearly bought, that is to say, at the expense of certain dimensions of the Christian gospel which became effectively submerged. But in reacting against Christendom, the modern world has bequeathed equal and opposite distortions of human being in the world. It is for that reason that I am attempting in this book neither to react against modernity nor slavishly to follow its lead. Modernity is like all cultures, in being in need of the healing light of the gospel of the Son of God, made incarnate by the Holy Spirit for the perfecting of the creation. But it is unlike some in that the distinctive features of its plight derive from its rejection of that gospel, albeit for some understandable reasons. The gospel will therefore not be served by the mere denunciation of modern rejection, but by probing how it came to happen. Christianity is indeed offensive to the natural human mind; and yet it is often made offensive by its representatives for the wrong reasons. This book is offered in the hope that it will illumine both the gospel and the modern condition, so that a continuing dialogue between them may take place.

[1] Cited by Peter Fuller, *Theoria. Art, and the Absence of Grace* (London: Chatto and Windus, 1988), p. 139.

I

As the argument developed over more than a year, it became increasingly evident that this work is a theology of creation as much as, if not more than, a theology of culture. Part One can be understood as a seeking of the roots of the modern crisis of culture – its fragmentation and decline into subjectivism and relativism – in an inadequate exegesis of the opening chapters of Genesis and the other biblical focusings of creation; Part Two as an attempt to draw out some of the implications for culture and our understanding of the world of a more explicitly trinitarian approach to the texts. The importance of Irenaeus in all this is considerable, for his straightforwardly trinitarian construction of the act of divine creation, in some contrast as it is to the later more sophisticated but also more Platonizing approaches, provides not the answers so much as the essential clues for the reshaping of the tradition that is necessary alike for Christian theology and for culture, oppressed as they both are by varieties of gnosticism.

Three main features of the doctrine of creation require to be emphasized in revision of the form it has often taken in the past since it was shaped by the Platonizing minds of Origen and Augustine. They represent rather different ways of interpreting the biblical orientation on creation from those of the two Fathers, and are as follows:

1. Creation is one and not dual. In a number of places in Augustine, the Genesis account is taken as indicating a double creation, first of the Platonic or 'intellectual' world, second of the material world made in imitation of the (created) eternal forms. The effect of the dual interpretation has led to the depotentiating of the Bible's affirmation of the goodness of the whole world, in favour of a hierarchy favouring the immaterial against the material creation. It also had the effect of tying the doctrine of creation to a belief that species were created as timeless and unchanging forms, a belief that made theories of evolution more difficult to engage positively during the nineteenth century. This book is in part an analysis of the damage that resulted long before Darwinism became an issue, and a proposal for an alternative approach. The general point is that a dualistic or Platonizing doctrine militates, despite its in-

tention, against an affirmation of the true plurality and diversity of creation.

2. Human being in the image of God is to be understood relationally rather than in terms of the possession of fixed characteristics such as reason or will, as has been the almost universal tendency of the tradition. By this I mean that the reality of the human creature must be understood in terms of the human relation to God, in the first instance, and to the rest of creation in the second. The relation to the remainder of creation itself falls into two. In the first place, to be in the image of God is to subsist in relations of mutual constitutiveness with other human beings. In the second place, it is to be in a set of relations with the non-personal creation.[2] The human imaging of God is a dynamic way of being before God and with the fellow creature.

3. There is a continuity within discontinuity between the human and the non-human creation. The continuity derives from the fact that the human race is, like the non-human creation, created. As John Zizioulas has argued, in teaching us of this the theory of evolution is salutary for Christian theology. 'A blessing in disguise as we might call it, Darwinism pointed out that the human being is by no means the only intelligent being in creation ... Thus Man was thrown back to his organic place in nature ... '[3] The discontinuity is not that one part of the creation is rational, the other not, but that the one is in a particular form of relation to the other: that known as dominion, which should be understood as a responsibility under God for the proper perfecting of created things.

There is a relation between the way the doctrine of creation was formulated in the West and the shape that modern culture has taken. It is far from being a simple matter to elucidate, but has much to do with the way in which all three of those stresses were in some way neglected. It led to what I shall call the contradictions of modernity. If, in the following chapters, the

---

[2] I have sought to explicate some aspects of the relatedness involved in *Christ and Creation. The* 1990 *Didsbury Lectures* (Exeter: Paternoster Press, 1993).

[3] John D. Zizioulas, 'Preserving God's Creation. Three Lectures on Theology and Ecology. I', *King's Theological Review* XII (1989), 1–5 (4).

words paradox and contradiction are used from time to time, the reason is to be found in the odd character of the modern age. On the one hand, the age, or aspects of it at least, arose out of a failure of the doctrine of creation, as the reader will see. On the other hand, the opposite could also be said, that aspects of modernity took their direction from the very success of the doctrine. At any rate, as these lectures have been written, revised for delivery and again revised for publication, the conclusion has become inescapable: that modernity, in its greatness and its pathos, has a queer and what could be called dialectical relation to that most central and neglected of Christian doctrines.

The relation between the doctrine of creation and modern science has long been the subject of debate and speculation, but the direction of the discussion was changed with the publication in 1934 of the article by Michael Foster that will be referred to in the body of the book. Whatever be the outcome of the debate recently renewed on the basis of the article, it is no longer possible to accept what was for long the received view, that science arose in the teeth of Christian theology. In many respects, the relationship is far more positive. That, however, is not to deny that much modern culture did take shape in contradiction of some Christian teaching, for modernity is far more than science: it is also modern art, literature and philosophy, and indeed most of the distinctive forms that culture, including theology, has taken in recent centuries. It is in the juxtaposition of the two opposing streams that the root of modernity's oddness is to be discovered.

In order to develop a theological account of modernity, I have in each of the first four chapters taken a sounding in different aspects of the ideology and practice of modernity. The soundings were suggested by the concepts which will provide the framework for the second and constructive phase of the project, so that the critical part of the book has been shaped in advance by the later constructive development. What kind of description of the modern condition is, then, being essayed? It is not primarily a genetic or causal account, a neutral description of how and why modernity came about, that is being sought. To be sure, causal influences will be suggested and analysed, but the centre of interest is to be found in the kinds of attitudes, ideologies and forms of action that are characteristic of the era we call modernity, within which are to be included some of those which are described as postmodern. Indeed, the continuities and essential community of interest between the modern and the postmodern are of far more interest for a theology of modernity than the naive assumption that something truly new is happening in the reaction against modernism.

To the four soundings of modernity in the first phase of the book there correspond four constructive essays in the second. The shape of the whole is chiastic, because the reconstruction takes its orientation from the final chapter of the first part, in which the intellectual outcome of modernity, with its decline into various relativisms and subjectivisms, is charted. The rebuilding begins with an essay at a theory of meaning and truth which seeks to avoid the pitfalls both of the antiquity against which modernity rightly rebelled and of the catastrophic outcome of its rebellion. The proposal is one in which, with the help of Coleridge, I call for a transcendental enquiry that avoids the weaknesses both of the ancient (Platonic) and modern (Kantian and Hegelian) approaches. On its basis, I seek in the final three chapters to pick up some of the pieces left lying at the end of the first three. In the third chapter were traced some of the deficiencies of the modern treatment of relationality as they were revealed in certain modern conceptions and use of time. Correspondingly, the sixth chapter is designed, with the help of a theology of relation in time and space made possible by the economy of creation and salvation, to develop an account of how things can be understood to be related to each other in time and space.

In the second chapter were described some of the roots of the modern world's difficulty in treating particularity, both human and worldly; in the seventh there is an answering attempt to develop a way of dealing with the particularity of things that does not reduce them, as do so many of the pressures of modern life, to a bland homogeneity. In some ways, the proposals in this chapter are among the most important of the work. Most of the things in the book have been said elsewhere, or in similar ways, but not, I think, what is attempted there, the transcendental development of the concept of *hypostasis*. In the first chapter the scene was set by showing how the opposing alternatives for thought and social order presented by Heraclitus and Parmenides have left to Western thought a legacy of a dialectic in which the rights of neither the one nor the many are adequately sustained; in the final chapter a vision is sought of a trinitarian sociality in the light of which we may understand something of who we are and what is the world in which we are set.

There is a number of supporting theses which form threads running through the fabric of the argument. One is that antiquity and modernity are remarkably alike in having a defective understanding and practice of what I call relationality. Both eras, in the main streams of their thought, play the one against the many, or the many against the one, in such a way that the rights of both are often lost. Both eras have difficulty in giving due weight to particularity, both in developing a truly relational account of what it is to be, in large part because they are in thrall to a doctrine that the one, but not the many, is of transcendental status. A second thesis is that modernity tends to displace God from the transcendent to the immanent sphere, so that the locus of the divine is to be found not in a God who is other, but in various aspects of this-worldly reality. I argue that the displacement is damaging and sometimes demonic in its outcome, because only where relatedness is held in tension with genuine otherness can things, both human and divine, all be given their due. A third thesis is that the fragmentation of the realms of truth, goodness and beauty – a fragmentation begun with Plato – has rendered the modern deeply uneasy in the world. To a large extent, our treatment of the arts betrays the symptoms of a deep-seated moral predicament as the result of which we know how to behave neither toward each other nor toward the world. Aesthetic factors bulk large in the argument because they form the most prominent symptom of the general disorder. A fourth thesis – and this is more than a supporting thesis since it returns us to the heart of the matter – is that an account of relationality that gives due weight to both one and many, to both particular and universal, to both otherness and relation, is to be derived from the one place where they can satisfactorily be based, a conception of God who is both one and three, whose being consists in a relationality that derives from the otherness-in-relation of Father, Son and Spirit.

My overall concern is to aid a process of healing the fragmentation which is so much a feature of our world. There are, in the modern world, proper limits to how such an enterprise might be attempted. The will of Canon Bampton directs that the lectures he endowed should serve 'to confirm and establish the Christian faith, and to confute all heretics and schismatics'. The Christian faith is best defended, I believe, on the joint bases of a confidence in its truth and an openness to the reception of criticism and truth from whatever quarter. That has not always been the manner of things, and it makes the task of contemporary defence more difficult than it might be. That is another of the ways in which theology has at once to learn from and to qualify the dogmas of modernity.

I have argued here for the relevance of what I have called trinitarian transcendentals for the overcoming of some of the characteristic unease of the modern condition. Drawing on Coleridge's notion of the *idea*, and his belief that the Trinity is the idea of ideas, I have argued that trinitarian conceptuality enables us to think of our world, in a way made impossible by the traditional choice between Heraclitus and Parmenides, as both, and in different respects, one and many, but also one and many in relation. In this way, I have hoped to contribute both to modern thought and to what is now called the renaissance of trinitarian theology in our times. Of course, trinitarian theology only has point if God is indeed triune, and there is still much to be debated there. But theology is a practical, not a merely theoretical, discipline: it aims at wisdom, in the broad sense of light for the human path.[4] Our theological enterprises must therefore be judged at least in part by their fruit, and my hope

---

[4] See Daniel W. Hardy, 'Rationality, the Sciences and Theology', *Keeping the Faith. Essays to Mark the Centenary of* Lux Mundi, edited by Geoffrey Wainwright (London: SPCK, 1989), pp. 274–309; and Nicholas Maxwell, *From Knowledge to Wisdom. A Revolution in the Aims and Methods of Science* (Oxford: Blackwell, 1984).

is in this work to have directed a little light on to the dark paths that we moderns must tread in the years that lie ahead, and to have suggested that the paths are not as lonely as fashionable doctrines often make them. For are we not in a double sense beings in communion?

CHAPTER I

From Heraclitus to Havel. The problem of the one and the many in modern life and thought

I THE IDEA OF MODERNITY

There are those who speak almost as though human nature has changed in the modern era, so that some quite new kind of human being has emerged. That is quite wrong. Despite what is sometimes asserted, there is a common human nature, at least in the sense that certain patterns of human social behaviour are virtually invariant, recurring wherever there is human life. We can read letters between members of families from all kinds of times and places, and know what they are about because we ourselves have the same kind of worries and concerns. The same is true of the patterns of thought and culture which form the context of our social being. Some Greek plays speak more truly to our condition than do some modern ones, while Juvenal's satires on the mores of ancient Rome could easily be adapted to speak directly of modern ways. And yet, all eras are also different. Like the unhappy families of Tolstoy's famous saying, all cultures also express in quite different ways the being of the fallen human creatures who make them up. And that brings me to the question which will be at the centre of this book, the distinctive character of the modern world, or modernity as it is sometimes called.

My aim is to make a theological assessment of our era. I shall look at the world which we all share, believer and unbeliever alike, through a focus provided by the doctrine of the God made known in Christ and the Spirit, and in a process of identification and elucidation shall hope to illumine where we stand now, so laying the basis for an approach to a Christian theology appropriate to the time. But before I can do that, I face an immense difficulty, which is the definition of the subject. What do we mean when we use the word *modern* and its cognates? At a superficial level, it is quite easy to point to what we mean, as in a sentence such as 'Liverpool Street is the most modern station in Europe.' It is to do with science, technology and modern economic arrangements. But at other levels, the matter becomes more complex, because modernity is not a monolithic phenomenon, but a range of practices and attitudes, to the past, for example, as well as of ideologies not all of which are consistent with one another. The complexity is shown by the fact that from one point of view, we could take the French Revolution as a typical expression of the modern quest for freedom and progress, yet France was in certain respects modernizing more quickly before the Revolution than during its course.[1] From one point of view, the Revolution was predicated on freedom, while as a paradigm for repression and the absence of freedom it put into the shade the behaviour of the *ancien régime* that it sought to replace.[2] It might also be said of the Russian Revolution that, dedicated to the aims of freedom and modernization in conscious rejection of feudal bondage, it achieved neither. And when we come to the fashion to speak of *post*modernity, confusion is piled upon confusion. There is therefore no single idea of modernity so much as a family of dogmas and practices, among which I would include post-modernity, because, as I hope will become apparent, it belongs with them, and might better be called late modernity. Within and between them all there is a common direction, mood perhaps, and it is that which I shall seek.

What is widely agreed – and as I develop my analysis, I shall

---

[1] Simon Schama, *Citizens. A Chronicle of the French Revolution* (London: Penguin Books, 1989), pp. 184–5: 'What [most historians] usually have in mind is a world in which capital replaces custom as the arbiter of social values, where professionals rather than amateurs run institutions of law and government, and where commerce and industry rather than land lead economic growth. In virtually all these respects, though, the great period of change was not the Revolution but the late eighteenth century.'

[2] 'If one had to look for one indisputable story of transformation in the French Revolution, it would be the creation of the juridical entity of the citizen. But no sooner had this hypothetically free person been invented than his liberties were circumscribed by the police power of the state.' Schama, *Citizens*, p. 858.

draw on many writings which approach the problem from different perspectives – is that the modern condition presents our civilization with grievous intellectual and moral problems. Let me give one example which illustrates the approach I shall take. In his book on the philosophical problems of modernity, Robert Pippin alludes to the fact that from Swift to Nietzsche there have been those who have prophesied the outcome of modern developments: 'modernity promised us a culture of unintimidated, curious, rational, self-reliant individuals, and it produced ... a herd society, a race of anxious, timid, conformist "sheep", and a culture of utter banality'.[3] Behind the charge is a view that the pressures of modernity are pressures toward homogeneity. We might instance the consumer culture, with its imposing of social uniformity in the name of choice – a Coca Cola advertisement in every village throughout the world. As the quotation suggests, modernity is the realm of paradoxes: an era which has sought freedom, and bred totalitarianism; which has taught us our insignificance in the vastness of the universe, and yet sought to play god with that same universe; which has sought to control the world, and yet let loose forces that may destroy the earth.

2 MODERNITY AS DISENGAGEMENT

In the first four chapters, then, I shall hope to develop a theological account of the modern world, beginning, like some revivalist preacher, with the bad news, but so presented that the positive contribution will follow naturally in due time. In this first chapter, I shall set the scene by painting with very broad brush strokes, and present the thesis by the adumbration of a number of themes. The first theme is that modern thought and practice presents us with what Charles Taylor has called 'disengagement'. 'Descartes' ethic, just as much as his epistemology, calls for disengagement from world and body and the assumption of an instrumental stance towards them. It is of the

---

[3] Robert B. Pippin, *Modernism as a Philosophical Problem* (Oxford: Blackwell, 1990), p. 22.

essence of reason ... that it push us to disengage.'[4] What is meant by that? Disengagement means standing apart from each other and the world and treating the other as external, as mere object. The key is in the word *instrumental*: we use the other as an instrument, as the mere means for realizing our will, and not as in some way integral to our being. It has its heart in the technocratic attitude: the view that the world is there to do with exactly as we choose. Its other side – and I give an extreme view – is that we do not seek in the world for what is true and good and beautiful, but create our truth and values for ourselves.

The outcome of this instrumental stance will concern us in more detail later. But at this stage there are three things to be said about it. The first is that, like other modern attitudes, it is not entirely new. There is, in that sense, nothing new under the sun. It has its anticipations in the thought of some of the Sophists, those Greek philosophers who also sought to disengage culture from nature.[5] They were the opponents against whom Plato wrote his *Republic*, which was, in the sense of the word I am using, an *engaged* philosophy.[6] It was designed to show that human life is good life when it conforms itself to the way things truly are, when it takes shape in the world as it truly is. The thesis of this book is that modern disengagement has engendered alienation, and that a renewed thinking and expression of how we belong in the world, of the human habitation of reality, is an urgent requirement. Until modern times, and indeed during some of its phases,[7] social order was nearly always understood to

---

[4] Charles Taylor, *Sources of the Self. The Making of the Modern Identity* (Cambridge: Cambridge University Press, 1989), p. 155.

[5] Although it is characteristically modern to divorce social and political institutions from their cosmic context, it is significant that that development, too, was anticipated in the sophistic critics of Presocratic philosophy, whose discussions about the relation of *physis* and *nomos* anticipate much early modern debate. W. K. C. Guthrie, *The Sophists* (Cambridge: Cambridge University Press, 1971), chapter 4.

[6] Taylor, *Sources of the Self*, p. 148, brings out the contrast with Descartes: 'the insight is not into an order of the good; rather it is into something which entails the emptiness of all ancient conceptions of such order: the utter separation of mind from a mechanistic universe of matter which is most emphatically not a medium of thought or meaning, which is expressively dead'.

[7] Stephen Toulmin, *Cosmopolis. The Hidden Agenda of Modernity* (New York: Free Press, 1990), chapter 3, argues that much early modern thought suffers from too close an engagement with a particular universal philosophy, that of mechanism.

be rooted in some way in an insight into what we can call metaphysical order, the order of being as a whole. It is this that Descartes and his successors have destroyed, and with it the symbiosis of social and universal order.

The second observation is that we shall not understand our place in the world unless we face up to the way in which we are internally related to the rest of the world. Without a philosophy of engagement we are lost. Samuel Taylor Coleridge, that most comprehensive of Anglican minds and the presiding genius of this book, long ago realized that this was the case, and that Plato has here much to teach us. 'Plato...perceived...that the knowledge of man by himself was not practicable without the knowledge of other things, or rather that man was that being in whom it pleased God that the consciousness of others' existence should abide, and that therefore without natural philosophy and without the sciences which led to the knowledge of objects without us, man himself would not be man.'[8] A major debt owed to Plato, accordingly, is to be found in his focusing of certain central questions. The first is that of the relation of cosmology, thought about the nature of the universe, to social theory. Plato in effect shows us – although I put his point in modern terms – that pure philosophical or metaphysical specu-lation, a demythologizing of the gods in the name of pure rationality, is the beginning of disengagement.[9] Underlying the anthropomorphism of the Greek gods, however irrational and morally unacceptable, there lay a quite proper concern for a universe which made some sense of the human moral condition. Although there are exceptions, it appears that for the most part the Presocratics and their sceptical successors, in losing the anthropomorphic, also lost the personal. Ethos was lost to environment, and so person and world were torn apart. It is similar to what in our day is called scientism, which limits all claims for knowledge to the narrowly scientific, and thus abstracts knowledge of things from the human context in which

---

[8] *The Philosophical Lectures of Samuel Taylor Coleridge*, edited by Kathleen Coburn (London: Pilot Press, 1949), p. 176. I owe this reference to Michael Harrison.

[9] In his context, that means the demythologization achieved by Presocratic and Sophist alike.

that knowledge is shaped.[10] Giving attention to the environment in abstraction from its inhabitants leads to a world empty of personal meaning.

The greatness of Plato – and this is our second debt – is also to be found in the fact that he, apparently building on Socrates' beginnings, sought to join together that which his philosophical predecessors had put asunder. Human living is good, appropriate to the way things really are, when it conforms itself to the source of all being, the form of the good. Plato's achievement was to introduce a concern which has always been at the heart of Christian theology, the concern for what has come to be called salvation: with *salus*, right human being. For him, cosmology, an interest in the way things are, cannot be separated from the question of human living. Although there are, as I have already suggested, grave flaws – and we shall, in the next chapter, examine the weakness in his treatment of individuality – Plato's programme stands as a monument to the human concern to see life whole and to see it in context.

The third observation to be made about the modern programme of disengagement is that it happens in relation to the God of Christendom. The distinctive shape of modernity's disengagement from the world is derived from its rebellion against Christian theology. In that sense, there is something new under the sun. Modern disengagement is disengagement from the God of Christendom. How that can be understood will emerge as I outline my second main theme.

3 THE ONE AND THE MANY

The theme of the one and the many is that which gives the chapter its subtitle, and it also serves to introduce one of the sub-themes of the lectures. It is that certain questions about the universe and the human situation within it have been recurrent,

---

[10] In a passage which I shall cite in the next chapter, Václav Havel has indicated another modern dimension of the problem, the arbitrary disruption of the order of things that leads to the pollution that threatens human life. Václav Havel, *Open Letters. Selected Prose, 1965–1990*, selected and edited by Paul Wilson (London: Faber and Faber, 1991), pp. 249–50.

if not universal, throughout Western culture, and not only there. The questions do not, of course, arise in quite the same form in different eras, for they also belong in and take part of their shape from a particular historical context. But, as I shall hope to show, they are the same kind of question arising in different but recognizably similar forms over the last three millennia. Universal questions arise in particular forms, and if we are to understand the modern era and address ourselves to its distinctive problems we shall first require some inkling of its wider context. We shall begin in this chapter by giving our attention to one such characteristic object of enquiry, and one also of continuing central relevance. That will lead into the related questions that will form the subject matter of the three following chapters in this first, mainly analytic, part of the book.

The question of the one and the many takes us to the very beginnings of philosophy and theology. The contribution it makes to the argument is most clearly set forth in the famous disagreement between Heraclitus and Parmenides. Our information about the teaching of these two founts of Western philosophy is fragmentary and often obscure,[11] but it is as representative figures that they are of interest to us. Associated with the former is the view that everything is flux, and that war is the universal creative and ruling force, reality being suffused by forces pulling in both ways at once, so that the basic fact in the natural world is strife. Although there is for this philosopher a world order and not a radical pluralism, Guthrie points out that for Heraclitus the fire that animates all things, the *logos* of the universe, is not a permanent substratum that remains the same in all its modifications, as it was for Aristotle. That would introduce rest and stability. On the contrary, Heraclitus is the philosopher of plurality and motion: the many are prior to the one, and in such a way that there is to be found in nature no

---

[11] We must remember Stephen Clark's warning: 'We may well doubt whether we can have any clear or helpful grasp of Heracleitos' reasonings. The fragments from which we work have passed through many hands ... Barnes has commented that "Heracleitos attracts exegetes as empty jampots wasps; and each new wasp discerns traces of his own favourite flavour".' *God's World and the Great Awakening. Limits and Renewals* 3 (Oxford: Clarendon Press, 1991), p. 62.

stability.[12] Parmenides represents the opposite pole of thought. For him, the real is the totally unchanging, for so reason teaches, contradicting the appearances presented to the senses. Reality is timelessly and uniformly what it is, so that Parmenides is the philosopher of the One *par excellence*. The many do not really exist, except it be as functions of the One.

These two early philosophers present to later thought what are often considered to be exhaustive possibilities for an approach to the question of the one and the many. In variations between the two can be seen to lie one of the continuities linking the thought of every age since their time, so that the dialectic of the one and the many has provided the framework for most subsequent thinking about many of the basic topics of thought. In general, Greek philosophical thought, for reasons that Coleridge among others has explored, always tended in the direction of monism.[13] Although ours appears to be an era in which by contrast Heraclitean themes predominate, I shall argue to the contrary that, certainly in our time, the two tend to present a coincidence of opposites: that without the mediation of a third factor they tend to collapse the one into the other. Indeed, it is the false assumptions that the ancients and the moderns share which it is the purpose of this book to expose. But for the moment we shall remain within their framework, and use the expression of alternatives by Heraclitus and Parmenides as a heuristic device for studying the relation of antiquity and modernity, and so the character of modernity itself.

Why is the question of the one and the many important? One reason is that it focuses two of the central questions with which we shall be concerned. The first is the cosmological question of the unity and plurality of the universe. In what sense is our universe a unity, in what sense a plurality? The second is the matter of human society: in what manner is, or should be, a

---

[12] 'There was law in the universe, but it was not a law of permanence, only a law of change ... ' W. K. C. Guthrie, *A History of Greek Philosophy, Volume 1, The Earlier Presocratics and the Pythagoreans* (Cambridge: Cambridge University Press, 1971), pp. 435–69 (p. 461).

[13] Samuel Taylor Coleridge, 'On the Prometheus of Aeschylus', *The Complete Works of Samuel Taylor Coleridge*, edited by W. G. T. Shedd (New York: Harper and Brothers, 1853), volume 4, pp. 344–65.

human society a unity or totality; and in what sense a set of more or less loosely connected individuals? ('There is no society, only individuals and their families.') That the second, social question, is of immense significance is clear from the history of recent centuries. The Cold War was in part fought over the question of whether a collectivist or individualist vision of society is the right one: of whether the one or the many should have predominance. The collapse of communist totalitarianism in parts of the world may appear to have made the question redundant ('the end of history'), but, as I shall hope to show, that is far from being the case.

But is the first question, about the unity and plurality of the world, in any way relevant to an approach to the second? Are the two questions about the relation of the one and the many, the cosmological and the social, related? That takes us to the very heart of the matter of the nature of the modern world, and indeed of its difference from antiquity. In general, it was held in the ancient world that knowledge of the universe contained the key to human society. H. Schmid, in a seminal paper, has argued that one element that the creation myths of the ancient world have in common is a concern to root social order – justice – in the way things have been made by God or the gods. In that respect, the Old Testament is no different from other contemporary religious writings.[14] Similarly, Hugh Lloyd Jones has argued that from the earliest times to the Greek dramatists, including the supposed sceptic Euripides, there is a common belief in the justice of Zeus, a cosmic order that works itself out in the events narrated in Greek literature.[15] By contrast, it is generally held in the modern world that there is no link between cosmic and social order.[16] Indeed, one could define modernity as the era in which the human race has achieved, or attempted

[14] H. Schmid, 'Creation, Righteousness and Salvation: "Creation Theology" as the Broad Horizon of Biblical Theology', *Creation in the Old Testament*, edited by B. W. Anderson (Philadelphia: Fortress Press, 1984), pp. 102–17.

[15] Hugh Lloyd Jones, *The Justice of Zeus* (London: University of California Press, 1971).

[16] This is particularly true of secular thought. In the writings of religious thinkers such as Teilhard de Chardin and Whitehead clear links between the two realms are drawn. That may be one of the reasons both for their appeal and for their often scornful rejection.

to achieve, an autonomy from the environment which consists in freedom from any form of natural determination.[17] That is, after all, part of the meaning of disengagement. One of the marks of some modern secular – especially existentialist – thought is a deep pessimism deriving from the belief that the universe is an empty and hostile place, or whose scientifically perceived meaning is seen as an irrelevance to human living.[18]

Before we move to the third main theme of the chapter, there is a historical observation to be made. As we have seen, in response to the disengagement of the Sophists, Plato attempted to produce an engaged philosophy. A recent book on John Calvin has argued that much of the shape of his theology can be attributed to anxiety: the anxiety that derived from living in an age when all seemed Heraclitean flux.[19] Very much the same might be said of Plato, whose context was the decline of Athens and the apparent moral nihilism of those sceptical and sometimes cynical Sophists who had succeeded the Presocratics. Plato's philosophical interests were universal, but there is a sense in which the moral and social dimensions of his philosophy have some claim to be for him the prior. His ontology, after all, is an ontology of the good, and is concerned to provide an undergirding for a moral and political programme. Plato's enterprise is a theology, in the broad sense of the word. It is an attempt to make unitary systematic sense of the world, and to place human life within it. He develops the Presocratic critique of the Homeric gods, and produces a theology of goodness and

---

[17] 'We could say that rationality is no longer defined substantively, in terms of the order of being, but rather procedurally, in terms of the standards by which we construct orders in science and life.' Taylor, *Sources of the Self*, p. 156.

[18] This is particularly marked in the writings of some scientists, for example Jacques Monod, whose thought has clear affinities both with that of Sartre and that of another Frenchman, Descartes. See *Chance and Necessity. An Essay on the Natural Philosophy of Modern Biology* , translated by A. Wainhouse (London: Collins, 1972). But it is noticeable also that scientists in a different tradition can make similar points, holding together, surely paradoxically, an affirmation of the rationality of things and their ultimate meaninglessness. See Steven Weinberg, *The First Three Minutes. A Modern View of the Origin of the Universe* (London: Flamingo, 2nd edition 1983), pp. 148–9 (cited below, pp. 97–8). The springs of this paradox will concern us throughout the book, for they have to do with the fragmentation of modern culture, and in particular its divorce of science and ethics.

[19] William J. Bouwsma, *John Calvin. A Sixteenth Century Portrait* (New York and Oxford: Oxford University Press, 1989), chapter 2, 'Calvin's anxiety'.

unity with which to replace it. There is no doubt that, given the choice between the Heraclitean and the Parmenidean, he chose the latter. He chose, that is to say, unity rather than plurality. At times like his and ours, of real or threatened social disintegration, there is always a temptation to seek unity and stability above all, and that is one reason why totalitarianism is a constant threat in modern times. That is also why, however much it may be overstated, Popper's critique of Plato has some elements of truth.[20] There is in that philosopher's social and political thought a strong tendency to totalitarianism, not in the modern sense, but in the sense of a preference of the one to the many, of unity to diversity. As a statement in the *Laws* has it, 'all partial generation is for the sake of the whole in order that for the life of the whole blissful existence may be secured. For it [the whole] is not brought into being for your sake, but you [the particular] are for its sake.'[21] There are without doubt parallels between Plato's educational programme and that attempted in totalitarian political régimes. On the other hand we must concede to him the complete justifiability of his concern for unity. Is not some concern for unity at the heart of both a quest for rationality and a desire for the peaceful ordering of human relations in society? Can there, however – and this is the crucial question – be a unity that also respects plurality or, in human terms, individuality and freedom? Coleridge spent his life wrestling with that question. His observation in a letter of April 1818 summarizes the position: 'Make yourself thoroughly, intuitively, master of the exceeding difficulties of admitting a one Ground of the Universe (which, however, *must* be admitted) and yet finding *room* for any thing else.'[22]

[20] Karl Popper, *The Open Society and its Enemies*, *Volume 1, Plato* (London: Routledge, 4th edition 1962).

[21] *Laws* x. 903 c-d, cited by J. D. Zizioulas, 'On Being a Person. Towards an Ontology of Personhood', *Persons, Divine and Human. King's College Essays in Theological Anthropology*, edited by Christoph Schwoebel and Colin Gunton (Edinburgh: T. & T. Clark, 1992), p. 36, note 3.

[22] *The Collected Letters of Samuel Taylor Coleridge*, edited by E. L. Griggs (Oxford: Clarendon Press, 1959), volume 4, p. 849.

4 THE CONCEPT OF GOD

The third main theme with which we must engage if we are to understand the roots of modernity arises directly out of that of the one and the many. It is the idea of God, and with it we reach a topic with many facets. The first is that from the beginning of Western thought the concept of God, or its equivalent, has served to provide a focus for the unity of the world. Here we return to the thought of the Presocratic philosophers, with whom there can be held to begin those two enterprises which now coexist in so uneasy a relationship, science and theology. To attribute to them the beginnings of science is not, perhaps, a claim that many will dispute, though their science is different, perhaps in kind, from that enterprise we now call science. But the beginnings of theology? Is there none in those Old Testament documents parts of which at least come from well before the time of the Presocratics? Yes, but that is not quite the point. There is theology in the Bible, of a kind, so that we may speak of the distinctive theology of a Jeremiah or of the writer of the book of Genesis. But that it is distinctively different from that enterprise which followed the completion of the books of the Bible is shown by the fact that it has always been difficult to be clear about the relations between theology as a human intellectual enterprise and the books on which it generally claims to base itself. The Bible is full of theology, but it is not theology in the sense that later came to be understood, of a systematic attempt to formulate the rationality and truth of Christianity as a unity.

To be sure, the Presocratics were not theologians in that sense either, for reasons that require little pointing. Their theology is different, perhaps in kind, from Christian theology, just as their science was different from what we today call science. But they are theologians in so far as their programme – and it must be remembered that there are great variations between them – was to make some kind of systematic sense of their universe. Even though they did not always use the idea of the divine, the early Greek philosophers were theologians by virtue of the fact that they sought a principle which would make sense of reality as a whole. The enterprise was systematically theological in both a negative and a positive sense. Negatively, they helped to undermine the pluralistic theology of the traditional gods. In so far as theirs was a rational and systematic enterprise, it struck at the intellectual adequacy of ascribing the state of the world to a chaotic plurality of warring agencies. The personal deities of the Greek pantheon were rejected as immoral and irrational, as in a sense they were. The Presocratics were thus, as we have already seen in another context, the first demythologizers.[23]

Positively, the Presocratics were concerned to seek the reason for the overall unity of the way that the world was. For them the concept of the divine had a rational and moral function: it provided the basis for both thought and behaviour. It made sense of the world as a unity and of the human place within that world. Augustine and the great mediaeval thinkers maintained that tradition. 'God' enables the human mind to understand something of the way things belong together in space and time. The Presocratics were not all explicitly theological, of course, in the sense that they employed the word 'God' as that with which to express this unity. But that is not the chief point, which is that one of the main functions of that word (and its substitutes in philosophical discussion) is rational, for it expresses that which makes overall sense of being.

It is here that a direct link can be traced between the Presocratic enterprise and the thought of the greatest philosopher of the Enlightenment. The idea of God, said Kant, is an idea without a flaw, for it enables us to think about the totality of things. 'Thus, while for the merely speculative employment of reason the supreme being remains a mere *ideal*, it is yet *an ideal without a flaw*, a concept which completes and crowns *the whole of human knowledge*.'[24] Kant here writes in continuity with Thomas

---

[23] It is worth noting that in this respect Plato shared in the Presocratics' critique of mythological theology, although, certainly in *The Republic*, his criteria of theological adequacy were more strongly ethical than speculative and cosmological. His quarrel with the Homeric deities was as much that they undermined morality as that they were in a narrower sense irrational. But the effect of the critique was the same. Plato, *Republic*, 377ff.

[24] Immanuel Kant, *Critique of Pure Reason*, translated by Norman Kemp Smith (London: Macmillan, 1933), p. 531, cf. pp. 493, 497, 538. The italics are in the original.

Aquinas and many other Western theologians. Where he differed from both Aquinas and the more speculative of the Presocratics was in his agnosticism about the content of the idea of God. In continuity with the Enlightenment programme of disengagement, he reduced the idea of God from being constitutive to being merely regulative: merely 'as if'.[25] The concern, however, is a shared one: to express by the idea the unity of things, their belonging together in space and time as a meaningful whole.

And that brings us to the second facet of the discussion of the idea of God. There are varying ways in which God may be conceived to constitute or to undergird the unity of things. That is why Heraclitus was of interest to Coleridge. As we have seen, he was aware of the dangers of a concept of a unitary being which, by swallowing everything else into itself, left room for nothing else. Heraclitus' concept of the dynamic Logos or Reason served Coleridge as a model for a God who was not simply an unchanging principle of order, but in some way also allowed for, gave space to, the being of the other. This book is a quest for such a deity, for a conception of God who is a principle not of blank unity but of variety, richness and complexity. But why is it necessary? That brings me to the third facet of the modern discussion of the idea of God.

Coleridge's fondness for Heraclitus, philosopher of the many, serves to introduce the point that for the most part the Western theological tradition has preferred Parmenides to Heraclitus in its search for a focus of unity. The God of most Western philosophy is single, simple and unchanging. And that is the problem. It has often been claimed recently that there is a link between certain conceptions of God and absolutist types of political institutions, in that an absolute or unitary deity provides support for absolutist forms of political order. The one to whom exception has been taken was, to be sure, conceived in different ways. But two features can be discerned: the one God

---

[25] It is noteworthy that Kant is not always as agnostic in practice as in theory: 'there must be one sole supreme will ... omnipotent ... omniscient ... omnipresent ... eternal ... ', *Critique of Pure Reason*, pp. 641–2.

and the single ruler supposedly made in his image.[26] The association between a deficient theology and the suppression of the many by the one comes to focus in the view of some theologians, Erik Peterson and Jürgen Moltmann, for example, that a link can be made between a strong stress on the unity of God and a corresponding one on the unity of society.[27] Peterson's concern is of interest because it arose out of the development of authoritarian political institutions in Germany this century between the wars. But of even greater historical interest is the view of one of the first full atheists of the modern era, Naigeon, who is recorded by Michael Buckley as holding 'that of all religious convictions the deism preached by Voltaire and swallowed whole by the Revolution disclosed itself to be the most savage and the most intolerant'. An immense stress on the single God of deism – ironically, a theology derived by means of a criticism of trinitarian Christian theology – came to be associated with the most repressive behaviour of all.[28] But the point is the same: unitary deity, whether theist or deist, is commonly seen to be at the root of totalitarian or repressive forms of social order.

There is much to be said for the thesis, because there is little doubt that the form Western theology took, particularly with its strong Neoplatonist colouring, did encourage, or at least did not discourage, the connection. Rightly or wrongly, a deity whose

---

[26] It is often pointed out that Eusebius of Caesarea provided ideological underpinning for Roman absolutism by his correlation of one God and one emperor, though it must also be remembered that his view was by no means unanimous among early theorists of the relation of Christianity and Rome. See Robert Markus, *Saeculum: History and Society in the Theology of St Augustine* (Cambridge: Cambridge University Press, revised edition 1988).

[27] Erik Peterson, *Der Monotheismus als politisches Problem. Ein Beitrag für Geschichte der politischen Theologie in Imperium Romanum* (Leipzig: J.Hegner, 1935); Jürgen Moltmann, *The Trinity and the Kingdom of God*, translated by Margaret Kohl (London: SCM Press, 1981).

[28] Michael Buckley, *At the Origins of Modern Atheism* (New Haven and London: Yale University Press), p. 323. This is interestingly of a piece with Hume's view that polytheism is morally preferable to monotheism because of its greater tendency to toleration, and raises the interesting question, one very much at the heart of the matter of modernity, of the relation between types of theology and modes of toleration. If we bear in mind, however, the fact that ancient Rome was religiously tolerant – 'pluralistic' – within certain limits, and yet politically authoritarian and intolerant, we shall be saved from accepting simplistic versions of Hume's thesis.

oneness is stressed is commonly associated with totalitarian or repressive forms of social order.[29] There was something wrong and oppressive about the form Christian institutions took in what Paul Johnson called the 'idea of a total Christian society' which 'necessarily included the idea of a compulsory society'.[30] Parmenides did require supplementation by Heraclitus, and in Christendom rarely received it. Thus according to an influential stream of modern thought, pre-modern political institutions, and particularly those from which the modern world was seeking to escape, represented a Parmenidean subordination of the many to the one. It is in this sense that much modern social and political thought can be understood as the revolt of the many against the one. The outcome for the argument of this chapter is that modernity can be seen in some of its aspects, especially the political, as the assertion of elements of Heraclitus against the Parmenidean past.

But the outcome in modern thought has been more radical, because many progressive and influential minds have come to associate any belief in God at all with the suppression of the rights of the many. Coleridge's fear that the one might leave no room for the many became in the minds of many a settled hostility to theology of any kind. Important here, for many reasons but especially because of its association with the development of Marxism, is the thesis of Feuerbach, that the worship of God takes place necessarily at the expense of human individuality and freedom. The elevation of God necessarily diminishes the worshipper. 'To enrich God, man must become poor; that God may be all, man must be nothing.'[31] A more subtle version of the critique of theology had already taken place in the moral thought of Immanuel Kant, whose theory of autonomy precluded obeisance to any God other than the one realized in free and individual moral reason: it falls to *all* of the

---

[29] That the matter is not straightforward has been shown by David Nicholls, *Deity and Domination. Images of God and the State in the Nineteenth and Twentieth Centuries* (London and New York: Routledge, 1989).

[30] Paul Johnson, *A History of Christianity* (London: Penguin Books, 1978), p. 115.

[31] Ludwig Feuerbach, *The Essence of Christianity*, translated by George Eliot (New York: Harper and Brothers, 1957), p. 26.

many to dare, individually, to use their own intelligence. Anything else is heteronomous, and a denial of our humanity. The critique of theology became more radical as time went by, and its outcome was the belief that human freedom required the destruction of the ecclesiastical institutions that were the cause of the disease. The problem was, to be sure, conceived in different ways in different societies. But the point for our purposes is that much modern social and political thought can be understood as the revolt of the many against the one, and at the same time that of humanity against divinity. The conclusion was drawn with savage intensity by Nietzsche, as is well known, and it is that the one must be denied in order that the many should be free. In that light, one of the marks of modernity that we are seeking is that it represents the assertion of Heraclitus against the Parmenidean past, the rebellion of the many against the repressive one.

I shall go into no further detail here in view of the fact that the matter has become so much of a commonplace that the point appears to require little elaboration. So much is it a common feature of modern thought that monism is an easily available stick with which to beat an opponent, so that Barth can accuse Schleiermacher of a monotheistic denial of freedom,[32] only himself to be later accused of monistic, if not 'fascist' tendencies.[33] Here we appear to reach an absolute discontinuity between the main direction of antiquity, at least of the Parmenidean Christian antiquity against which the Enlightenment rebelled, and that of the modern affirmation of the many. But that would be to understand the matter according to modernity's own image of itself, which precisely here requires radical questioning. The nature of the question will become clear when we have seen something of what happens when the modern world makes its choice for Heraclitus against the Parmenidean past.

[32] Karl Barth, *Church Dogmatics*, translation edited by G. W. Bromiley and T. F. Torrance (Edinburgh: T. & T. Clark, 1957), volume 2/2, pp.552–3.
[33] F. W. Graf, 'Die Freiheit der Entsprechung zu Gott. Bemerkungen zum theozentrischen Ansatz der Anthropologie Karl Barths', in *Die Realisierung der Freiheit*, ed. T. Rentdorff (Gütersloh: Gerd Mohn, 1975), pp. 76–118.

5 MODERNITY AS THE DISPLACEMENT
OF GOD

The reference to Nietzsche brings us to the fourth main theme of the chapter. It is what I shall call displacement. Modernity is the era which has displaced God as the focus for the unity and meaning of being. What do I mean by that? Chiefly that the functions attributed to God have not been abolished, but shifted – relocated, as they say today. The crucial shift appears to have taken place in the late mediaeval period, and particularly in the thought of William of Ockham.[34] According to Hans Blumenberg, the positing by Ockham of the real existence solely of particulars and the accompanying denial of the reality of universals laid the way for the effective redundancy of the doctrine of creation.[35] We shall pursue this theme in later chapters, but here will simply state the thesis: God was no longer needed to account for the coherence and meaning of the world, so that the seat of rationality and meaning became not the world, but the human reason and will, which thus *displace* God or the world. When the unifying will of God becomes redundant, or is rejected for a variety of moral, rational and scientific reasons, the focus of the unity of things becomes the unifying rational mind. The importance of Nietzsche is that he realized that far from being a neutral development, the wiping clean of the horizon is of comprehensive intellectual, moral and social significance. Nothing is left untouched. As he himself proclaimed, there is a price to pay, and I shall argue in the

[34] That in its turn can be said to have its roots in Augustine's theology of history. The strongly voluntarist content of much modern political theory, influenced as it often is by Ockhamist and other nominalist mediaeval thought, is in some ways the fruit of the Augustinian tradition. Although Augustine has little of what we call political theory, the secularizing tendency of his view of church and state, in which he is to be contrasted with mediaeval Aristotelianism, did contribute to modern developments. According to Augustine, 'Society became intrinsically "secular" in the sense that it is not as such committed to any particular ultimate loyalty ... .Politically organised life was itself a consequence of the Fall ... In contrast with this sense of the precariousness of human order ... the Aristotelian tradition in Christian political thought saw human social order as part of an overarching cosmic order.' Markus, *Saeculum*, pp. 173–4.

[35] Hans Blumenberg, *The Legitimacy of the Modern Age*, translated by R. M. Wallace (Cambridge, MA, and London: MIT Press, 1983), Part 2, chapter 3.

fourth chapter that it is the fragmentation of human experience, and ultimately the destruction of our humanity, for the world unified only by us ceases to be any kind of shared context for human society. But the chief point to be made here is that the displacement of God does not and has not given freedom and dignity to the many, but has subjected us to new and often unrecognized forms of slavery. It will be the task of the remainder of this chapter to outline how this has come to be. The substantiation of some of the details will be the task of the next three chapters.

The point to be made in conclusion of this one is that it is only on the face of the matter that modernity has achieved a realization of the rights and freedom of the many over against the absolutist claims of the one. In some ways that is an obvious claim to make, and can be illustrated quite simply, at least if we look beyond the bounds of the liberal West. In ecclesiastical organization, for example, the Church of Rome became during the first centuries of the modern era for the most part more authoritarian, more impatient of national diversity than in earlier times. It is now widely recognized that the universal Western church of mediaeval times coexisted with a wide range of national diversity. If politically the Reformation, certainly as represented by England, took the form of the assertion of the rights of the many – nations – at the expense of the one Christendom, the ecclesiastical outcome has been the attempted imposition of a form of unity more rigid than that of preceding times.[36] Similarly, it scarcely requires pointing out that in more recent times there have arisen absolutist forms of the state which have derived their unifying power from the military, technical

---

[36] Stephen Toulmin, for example, has suggested that the ecclesiastical authoritarianism is a *function* of modernity, not its denial. Copernicus, nearly a century before Galileo, was able to exercise a freedom of thought denied to his successor, while the intellectual openness of mediaeval culture is now increasingly being appreciated. *Cosmopolis*, pp. 77–8. The suppression of free enquiry is very much a modern phenomenon, and Paul Johnson interestingly cites an observation from Beethoven's *Conversation Book*, that 'Before the French Revolution there was great freedom of thought and political action. The Revolution made both the government and the nobility suspicious of the common people, and this has led by degrees to the present policy of repression.' *The Birth of the Modern. World Society 1815–1830* (London: Weidenfeld and Nicolson, 1991), p. 115.

and bureaucratic advances of modernity. The French and Russian Revolutions provide plentiful evidence that the many have often been worse served politically by the absolutist drive of modernity than by – say – the sometimes enlightened despotism of a feudal society.[37] Parmenides wins hands down.

What then of the liberal and individualist versions of modern culture? Do not they, by their explicit affirmation of the rights of the many, provide the legitimation of the freedom and particularity of the person? Is not democracy one of the jewels in the crown of the modern age? Yes indeed, but without denying that, it must also be realized that some of the evidence points in the opposite direction. There is evidence that Parmenides is obtaining a good run for his money here, too. The much vaunted pluralism of modern secular cultures conceals an underlying tendency to deny plurality and individuality. Modern individualism breeds homogeneity. Support for such a thesis is to be found in a number of places, but an early reading of the signs of the times was offered by Kierkegaard, who protested in the name of individuality against what he saw to be the levelling tendencies of the modern age:

> For levelling really to take place, a phantom must first be raised, the spirit of levelling, a monstrous abstraction, an all-encompassing something that is nothing, a mirage – and this phantom is *the public* ... Only when there is no strong communal life to give substance to the concretion will the press create this abstraction 'the public', made up of unsubstantial individuals who are never united or never can be united in the simultaneity of any situation or organization and yet are claimed to be a whole.[38]

Kierkegaard's analysis reveals, I believe, the logic of the matter, which is that in the absence of an adequate way of accounting for and realizing socially the relations of the many to each other

[37] Barth's analysis of the Enlightenment as a whole as the 'Age of Absolutism' is one of the possible theological analyses of the monistic tendencies of modernity. Karl Barth, *Protestant Theology in the Nineteenth Century: Its Background and History*, translated by B. Cozens and J. Bowden (London: SCM Press, 1972), pp. 36–7.

[38] Søren Kierkegaard, *Two Ages. The Age of Revolution and the Present Age. A Literary Review, Kierkegaard's Writings*, volume 14, edited and translated by H. V. and E. H. Hong (Princeton: Princeton University Press, 1978), pp. 90–1.

– almost a definition of individualism – what I would call a false universal (the public, or 'the people' – or history or the market) rushes in to fill the vacuum.

The reason is somewhat as follows. When God is displaced as the focus of the unity of things, the function he performs does not disappear, but is exercised by some other source of unity – some other universal. The universal is false because it does not encompass the realities of human relations and of our placing in the world, and so operates deceptively or oppressively. If we wish to look beyond the apparently conservative polemic of Kierkegaard, we shall find remarkably similar analyses in more liberal and radical sources, for example, the young and still progressive Wordsworth, and J. S. Mill, who, in *On Liberty*, also spoke of modern pressures for homogeneity, observing that the Chinese:

> have succeeded beyond all hope in what English anthropologists are so industriously working at – in making a people all alike, all governing their thoughts and conduct by the same maxims and rules ... The modern *régime* of public opinion is, in an unorganized form, what the Chinese educational and political systems are in an organized ...[39]

He similarly comments that 'It is individuality that we war against; we should think we had done wonders if we had made ourselves all alike ... '[40]

The prophecies of these varied modern thinkers have been substantiated recently by a number of historical trends which serve to accentuate the one over against the many, in social systems which render the many subordinate or instrumental to the one. In individualism, quite contrary to appearances, there is to be found at work a tendency to suppress the other, who is

---

[39] J. S. Mill, *On Liberty and Other Essays*, edited by John Gray (Oxford: Oxford University Press, 1991), p. 80. It is the kind of observation that is made in a remarkably wide range of modern sources. See also a remark of the not yet conservative Wordsworth, that 'a multitude of causes unknown to former times are now acting with a combined force to blunt the discriminating powers of the mind, and unfitting it for all voluntary exertion to reduce it to a state of almost savage torpor'. Stephen Gill, *William Wordsworth. A Life* (Oxford: Oxford University Press, 1990), p. 189.

[40] Mill, *On Liberty*, p. 79. Here it is worth remarking that there is a distinction to be made between individuality and individualism.

made the mere means to an end, or reduced to an impediment.[41] Individualism is a non-relational creed, because it teaches that I do not need my neighbour in order to be myself. The logical outcome of one form of non-relational individualism is shown in Barth's critique of Nietzsche, one of the most clear-sighted exponents of modernity: 'the prophet of... humanity without the fellow-man':

> The new thing in Nietzsche was the man of 'azure isolation,' six thousand feet above time and man; the man to whom a fellow-creature drinking at the same well is quite dreadful and insufferable; the man who is utterly inaccessible to others, having no friends and despising women; the man who is at home only with eagles and strong winds;... the man beyond good and evil, who can only exist as a consuming fire.[42]

This individualism can be described as being monist in tendency, because it encourages the development of a doctrine or system in which the other is or becomes subordinate or instrumental to the I or the individual: the monism, we might say, of the finite individual. An order in which a Hitler or a Stalin treats all others as instrumental to his will is one such obvious form, but similar points could be made of the form taken by some more democratic orders.

There are, however, more subtle and insidious forms of monism threatening modern democracies, as has been shown by Václav Havel's recent reflections on the weaknesses of the Western societies he is being urged to imitate. The East, he says, holds up to the West a 'convex mirror of the inevitable consequences of rationalism, a grotesquely magnified image of its own deep tendencies...'[43] The mirror enables the West to see that it shares in what is essentially the same crisis. It lives under the illusion that its system of consumption in some way reflects the order of the universe, whereas in practice it is simply another ideology. Like that of the East, its order is built upon lies. It is therefore in the grip of a false universal: 'the irrational

---

[41] '[C]ollectivism is but a corollary of individualism, a belief that the social whole is ultimately nothing more than a collection of individuals'. David Nicholls, *Deity and Domination*, p. 32.

[42] Karl Barth, *Church Dogmatics*, volume 3/2, pp. 232, 240.

[43] Havel, *Open Letters*, p. 260.

momentum of anonymous, impersonal, and inhuman power – the power of ideologies, systems, apparat, bureaucracy, artificial languages and political slogans'.[44] And, borrowing the expression of a colleague, he writes of 'the eschatology of the impersonal'.[45]

We come, then, to a first paradox of modernity, and it is the first of many that we shall meet. It is that its own drive has often been toward forms of political repression far worse than most things perpetrated in despised Christendom. At one level, it is easy to make the point that it is better to be ruled in the name of a unitarily conceived deity, however Parmenidean, who at least reminded rulers of their limits, than by titanic rulers or states convinced, or attempting to convince themselves, of their own divinity. But to remain there is to ignore the elements of truth in the modern protest, and indeed to appear to advocate a reactionary return to old forms of oppression. The distinctive feature of the modern condition is rather to be found elsewhere. It is not that it represents an assertion of the rights of the many over the one, though that has been attempted. The feature which arises out of the discussion of this first chapter, and it will be supplemented in later ones, is rather that the assertion of the rights of the many has paradoxically, dialectically perhaps, achieved the opposite, the subversion of the many by new and in some cases demonic versions of the one. The logic of this is that when the one is displaced by the many, the displacement happens in two ways: either the many become an aggregate of ones, each attempting to dominate the world, the outcome being those régimes now labelled fascist, in which the strongest survives and dominates; or the many become homogenized, contrary to their true being, into the mass (Kierkegaard's 'public'). 'The trend today is in the direction of mathematical equality ...'[46]

It might be said that the latter is the real danger because it is more insidious: it is the flat unity of homogeneity. In the imposition of a unitary and homogeneous public culture, disseminated now throughout the world by the spread of

[44] Ibid., p. 267.   [45] Ibid., p. 260.   [46] Kierkegaard, *Two Ages*, p. 85.

Western technology and communications, is to be found one of the central features of modernity's distinctive way of achieving the priority of the one over the many. Homogeneity derives from the creation of an undifferentiated social or other reality. (Thus David Harvey speaks of the 'sham individualism' of fashion.[47]) It is not therefore the priority of the many that distinguishes modernity from other cultures, but the shape the priority of the one takes in practice. Thus both the ancient and modern eras, in so far as they can be distinguished in the way often attempted, share in a tendency to elevate the one over the many: to enslave the many to the heteronomous rule of the one. The pathos of the modern condition is that, after rejecting what it rightly sees to be the oppressive forms of unity deriving from the past, it has itself succumbed to various false universals that replicate or even exacerbate the bondage from which it had hoped to free itself. The truth is that many characteristic modern forms of life succumb in different ways to the false universals whose root we shall seek in the next section.

6 THE PATHOS OF THE MODERN CONDITION

The heart of the paradox of the modern condition is that a quest for the freedom of the many has eventuated in new forms of slavery to the one. How is this related to the displacement of God? The outlines of an answer will emerge if we review something of what has happened with the modern quest for autonomy over against the 'heteronomy' of engaged forms of philosophy. As we have seen, one of the roots of modern developments was the belief that human liberation was to be found in disengagement from any external grounding of life, whether in God or some metaphysical philosophy such as Platonism. We have also seen, however, that modernity has its own distinctive forms of servitude, indeed of heteronomy. Modern ideology tends to obscure the truth, which is that here ancient and modern show many signs of continuity, for there is

---

[47] David Harvey, *The Condition of Postmodernity. An Enquiry into the Origins of Cultural Change* (Oxford: Blackwell, 1989), p. 26.

a heteronomy in modernity, a form of servitude, whether the master take the form of history, materialistically or idealistically conceived, or the market. None of these differ essentially from those things from which modern dogma affected to free us. 'In modern times levelling is reflection's correlative to fate in antiquity.'[48]

The only superficially paradoxical outcome is that the attempted liberation from cosmic and theological heteronomy has resulted in the emergence of new forms of cosmic heteronomy, for the fragmentation of experience which is the outcome of modern displacement is alienating and heteronomous, not liberating. It is as though our relatedness to the rest of the universe, expelled through the front door, returns insidiously and unnoticed through the back. Displaced from its proper context, the one reasserts itself as a worse, because impersonal and often unrecognized, medium of control. Thus Nietzsche's recourse to the doctrine of eternal recurrence to save the significance of human moral action in an otherwise irrelevant universe may have been a device to save human moral autonomy, but in view of the fact that recurrence is behind as well as before, it can ultimately serve only as a new cosmic determinism. Similarly, more recent times show that surrogate divinities are conjured into being to take the place of the one that was rejected: for example, evolutionism and other forms of scientism such as sociobiology[49] and psychological behaviourism; or reference could be made again to modern faith in history or the market – 'this consoling replacement for the divinity'[50]

---

[48] Kierkegaard, *Two Ages*, p. 84.

[49] 'Molecular biology is now a religion, and molecular biologists are its prophets ... In the words of a popular bard of the legend, genes "have created us body and mind." ... How is it that a mere molecule can have both the power of self-reproduction and self-action, being the cause of itself and the cause of all other things? ... The problem with (the) story is that although it is correct in its detailed molecular description, it is wrong in what it claims to explain. First, DNA is not self-reproducing, second, it makes nothing, and third, organisms are not determined by it. DNA is a dead molecule, among the most nonreactive, chemically inert molecules in the living world.' R. C. Lewontin, 'The Dream of the Human Genome', *New York Review of Books* XXXIX (28 May, 1992), 31–40 (31–3).

[50] Fredric Jameson, *Postmodernism, or the Cultural Logic of Late Capitalism* (London and New York: Verso, 1991), p. 273. One could, of course, respond with a *tu quoque* about Marxist faith in the creativity of impersonal history.

– and the popularity of astrology. When God is no longer the one who holds things together, demons rush in to fill his place. An impersonal one replaces the despised one of traditional theism, and the slavery is greater than before. Ironical is the fact, pointed out by Leszek Kolakowski, that one of the historical origins of Marxist thought is to be found in mediaeval monism.[51] There is no concept of history without a cosmological price to be paid.

Much the same can be said of the response to some modern developments in theology, which, by conniving in the displacement of deity, has to a large extent been unaware of the theological and human cost. The significant feature of the displacement in theology is a shift in the spatial metaphors in terms of which God's relation to the world is understood. There has been a move from seeing God as 'outside' to locating him 'within' the world, a shift, that is, from a theology of transcendence to the various theologies of immanence which have become so much the fashion. It is arguable that such a move is based on a mistaking of the real enemy, which is not, as is supposed, a God conceived in terms of transcendence, or, better expressed, of otherness, to the world. In so far as theologians have accepted modernity's analysis of the problem, they have uncritically abandoned the solution to the problem bequeathed by antiquity. Theologies of transcendence allow for human independence and freedom by leaving a space between the divine and the human. Although there were elements of theological immanence in the thought of the Greeks, what Plato and early Christian theology share in general is a conception of some kind of 'space' between the divine and the world. As I hope to show in the final chapter, a distinction between Platonic and trinitarian forms of transcendence is of prime importance in a solution of the problem of the one and the many. But in so far as immanence is the matter under discussion, it is the source of the problem, not its solution. By opting for a theology of immanence – and that is the theological legacy of Kant, Schleiermacher and Hegel alike – modern theology opted for

---

[51] Leszek Kolakowski, *Main Currents of Marxism, Volume 1, The Founders*, translated by P. S. Falla (Oxford: Oxford University Press, 1978), pp. 23–39.

slavery by virtue of the fact that an immanent one is more subversive of the being of the many than a transcendent deity. It is not transcendence that is the enemy, but forms of the one that fail to give due space to the many. This is something that both Anselm and Barth realized in their different ways.[52] The modern world is wrong in so far as it conceives of otherness as necessarily heteronomous, believing that a God standing over against us in judgement and grace is an offence to independence and freedom. Regarding otherness as a threat is only a short step away from the individualistic belief that our neighbour meets us only as one to be feared or dominated. But that is precisely modernity's error, and on both counts, because it generates by reflex, by the workings of its own inner logic, a repetition of that which it sought to escape. The modern servitude of the immanent is a mark of our alienation from that which makes us what we are. That is the form that displacement takes, and depends upon the mistake of failing to recognize the fact that freedom requires otherness. Immanent forces, even more than the supposedly heteronomous deity of the tradition, deprive us of the very otherness without which we are not what we should be.

7 CONCLUSION

One thesis of this book is that central dimensions of the thought and practice of antiquity and modernity share a common failure in conceiving and practising relationality.[53] The many can find their true being and be understood only as they are related to each other and to the One, but the main streams of neither antiquity nor modernity have been able to conceive the patterns of relation adequately. But that focuses the question raised by our discussion of the one and the many. In what way

---

[52] See Anselm *Cur Deus Homo* I.v and Karl Barth, *Church Dogmatics*, volume 3/3, p. 87: 'It is only the heathen gods who envy man. The true God, who is unconditionally the Lord, allows him to be the thing for which He created him.'

[53] By relationality I do not mean what is sometimes taught, that things can be known only in so far as they are related to us, but rather the realistic belief that particulars, of whatever kind, can be understood only in terms of their relatedness to each other and the whole.

are we, or should we be, related to that which is other than ourselves? Which forms of relatedness are heteronomous, because they offend against the law of our being, and which tend toward a true autonomy? These questions will give shape to the remainder of this study.

At the close of this chapter, however, the conclusion to be drawn from our preliminary engagement with the question as it is focused by the categories of Heraclitus and Parmenides is that displacement is the chief symptom of the pathos of modernity. Rightly rejecting monist forms of belief, the modern world has simply displaced them into immanence, where they are more monistic, more heteronomous in their outworking. Our age is a matter of extremes, however, and we must not remain blind to the ways in which it has served the many well. Its chief beneficiaries are for the most part better fed, housed, educated and provided with medical care. The paradox is that in this century the same culture has also consigned more of the many to death by warfare and other modern means of mass destruction. My contention is that the distinctive failures of our era derive from its failure of due relatedness to God, the one, the focus of the unity of all things. That is the pathos of modernity. In both the failed experiments of modern totalitarian régimes and the insidious homogeneity of consumer culture there is a tendency to submerge the many in the one. Where the true one is displaced, false and alienating gods rush in to fill the vacancy.

The chief way to understand theologically the displacement that has taken place is with that which is the burden of R. J. Neuhaus' *The Naked Public Square*.[54] When God is expelled from the public square, he argues, from public discourse and thought about the development of political institutions, the outcome is not freedom, but a form of displacement that can only be called demonic. The room swept clear of one devil is replaced by seven far worse. We might say: the transcendent and apparently oppressive single deity is swept away only to be replaced by the demonic alternatives we have met. In place of the deity conceived personally, albeit inadequately so – and that is where

[54]   Richard John Neuhaus, *The Naked Public Square* (Grand Rapids: Eerdmans, 1984).

modernity is right to question – there appear immanent impersonal forces which mercilessly, like all idols, devour their devotees. It is significant that many modern thinkers, from Hobbes to Hegel, have tended to characterize the state as a deity, and that perhaps symbolizes the modern problem. An immanent deity, because it leaves no space between persons and between persons and world, is the most heteronomous of all. In that sense, modern godless forms of unitary order are worse than those of a mediaeval society in which the ruler tends to be less than absolute because he is seen to be subordinate to the deity.

What I am urging is not conservative reaction against the development of modernity. The unity of God has been stressed at the expense of his triunity, and to that extent the modern critique must be understood as a recalling of theology to its own trinitarian roots.[55] I have used Heraclitus and Havel as the two names on the title of this chapter not only because they represent the beginning and end of the intellectual development I wish to review, but because they are also important in their own right. Heraclitus affirms the importance of movement, plurality and variety at the very centre of life on earth. Any focus of unity which fails to allow for them is inadequate. In that sense, Heraclitus remains the patron of the modern affirmation of the many against the smothering charms of the one. But the way he has been affirmed has led the way for an insidious return of the oppressive one. The real threat in the modern condition is the relentless pressure for human homogeneity exerted by the success of Western technology and communications. It is the merit of Václav Havel, the new philosopher king as is sometimes said, to have realized this. His even-handedness about the drawbacks of the two leading social philosophies of the modern era points us to the outcome of modern disengagement and the displacement of God. At the close I repeat the quotation from Robert Pippin: 'modernity promised us a culture of unintimidated, curious, rational, self-reliant individuals, and it produced

---

[55] By contrast, the pathos of some Christian reactionaries – some of those, for example, chronicled with apparent approval in Maurice Cowling, *Religion and Public Doctrine in Modern England* (Cambridge: Cambridge University Press, 1980) – is that their protestations of the rights of eternity over time may appear to be merely reactionary invocations of the one at the expense of the many.

... a herd society, a race of anxious, timid, conformist "sheep", and a culture of utter banality'.[56] In the next chapter we turn our attention to the sheep, and to some of the pressures, ancient and modern alike, that work to make us all the same. After all, in a rather less disparaging sense of the word *sheep*, they are the ones for whom the great shepherd came to lay down his life.

---

[56] Above, note 3.

CHAPTER 2

The disappearing other. The problem of the particular in modern life and thought.

I THE LOSS OF THE PARTICULAR IN MODERN LIFE AND THOUGHT

In the first chapter, two concepts, disengagement and displacement, were used to identify the main shape of modernity. It was argued that by disengaging human life from its worldly context, and by doing so in the context of the God of Christendom, modernity achieved a displacement of the divine. The outcome was indicated by using Heraclitus and Parmenides as figures representing philosophies of the many and of the one. The Western theological tradition, I argued, was strongly Parmenidean in much of its thrust, so that modernity has rebelled against God, the one, in the name of the many. But the outcome has been quite contrary to expectation. In many respects, modernity's rebellion has achieved the opposite of that which it set out to do. Various secular forms of divine order represent in many ways a worse slavery to the one than anything that past theologies once imposed. I ended by referring to Václav Havel's even-handed criticism of the modern ideologies of East and West. According to him, the consumer culture of the West is a mirror image of the repressiveness of the East, so that the danger for us is of a homogeneity – the herd culture – imposed by the very forces that the modern world has let loose. The room swept bare and garnished has been invaded by the deities of immanence, so that for every advance achieved in the modern world there appears to be a destructive and demonic counterpart. Another important thesis of the chapter was that the two eras, antiquity and modernity, in so far as they can be distinguished, are in certain respects more in continuity than sometimes appears. Neither has adequately held in tension the concerns of the one and the many, of unity and diversity, of social cohesion and individual independence.

In the discussion of social order we were very near to one question that requires separate discussion. It is the reality and status of those who make up the many: the particulars. The matter came to the surface in the citation of Kierkegaard, whose life work was the assertion in face of the forces of homogeneity of a form of individuality that resisted their onset. The problem for the Kierkegaardian approach, however, as is shown in part by the rank individualism and irrationalism of some of those existentialists who apparently take their direction from him, is that the affirmation of the individual, of the distributed one, easily collapses into its dialectical opposite, especially when the relational character of human being is ignored. Without a means of maintaining the rights of both one and many they become two sides of a single disorder, for individualism so easily metamorphoses into the collectivism which is its *alter ego*.

In this chapter, accordingly, we turn to the many and to an examination of the status of individuality and particularity, for there is plentiful evidence that, because the modern world is able to do justice neither to the one nor to the many, it is also uneasy with those people and things which make up the manyness of reality. As we have seen, this is very much the case with the theory and practice of social reality. But just as I suggested that social realities should be conceived in relation to their broader cosmic context, so here I shall begin with the difficulty which modern scientific thought has sometimes had in dealing with particular, as distinct from universal or idealized, realities. The temptation of the scientist is shown by a quotation from a recent study of scientific theory:

the searchers for a unified Theory of Everything have focussed upon finding the all-encompassing laws of Nature to the exclusion of all else. At root, this prejudice has grown from an implicit subservience to the Platonic emphasis upon timeless universals as more important in the nature of things than the world of particulars that we observe and experience.[1]

The inherent Platonic or Parmenidean prejudice suspected by John Barrow is not a recent one, but is characteristic of much of the modern era. The much quoted saying of Laplace about the aims of science provides an earlier instance. An intelligence which knew at one moment of time:

all the forces by which nature is animated and the respective positions of all the entities which compose it, ... would embrace in the same formula the movements of the largest bodies in the universe and those of the lightest atom: nothing would be uncertain for it, and the future, like the past, would be present to its eyes.

According to this still highly influential ideal, the generalizing influence smooths away all distinctiveness and particularity. Michael Polanyi, to whom I owe the quotation, describes this as a 'decisive sleight of hand by which he [Laplace] substitutes a knowledge of all experience for a knowledge of all atomic data'.[2] Believing that the spell of the delusion remains with us to this day, Polanyi hoped to demonstrate that the basis of knowledge is a form of particularity: not the particularity of a disembodied empiricism, but that of an embodied mind in particular and determinate relations with the world. The personal capacity for pattern recognition and classification serves for him as a paradigm case for the form this experience takes.[3]

A disregard of particularity which derives from Platonic influences is found in other places in modern culture, and according to Stanley Jaki an ulterior theological motive similar to that of Laplace is often to be found at work. Particularity is an offence to certain kinds of scientific mind as it is to certain kinds of political theorist. It tends to be untidy, but also to raise questions about the nature of things that some would prefer to

---

[1] John D. Barrow, *Theories of Everything. The Quest for Ultimate Explanation* (Oxford: Clarendon Press, 1991), p. 30.
[2] Michael Polanyi, *Personal Knowledge. Towards a Post-Critical Philosophy*, (London: Routledge, 2nd edition 1962), pp. 139–41.   [3] Ibid, pp. 348–9.

leave unasked. Yet, Jaki claims, modern science is predicated upon particularity and specificity, in such a way as to render nonsensical the widespread view that the universe as we now understand it can derive from a fundamental homogeneity. Jaki cites Eddington's saying that 'undifferentiated sameness and nothingness cannot be distinguished philosophically. The realities of physics are unhomogeneities, happenings, change.'[4] In practice, science operates with particulars, sets of entities and events abstracted from the whole and mapped in their relations to each other and to their context.[5] Yet almost everywhere there operates a strong Platonist drive to turn particularities into abstractions, variety into homogeneity.[6]

Similar considerations apply in many discussions of human being in the world, where it is again all too easy to subordinate particularity to generalizing theories. It should be recognized that the question of particular persons is conceptually the same kind of question as that about the cosmos. As the reference to Stanley Jaki suggests, homogeneity is the spectre at the whole banquet of modernity, not merely in some of its courses. Here a distinction must be drawn between the notion of particularity, which is the locus of distinctiveness and variety – where the many truly are many, for everything is what it is and not another thing – and that of the individualism which only appears to do justice to particularity. The distinction is essential both for our understanding of what it is to be a human person and for the way we treat each other. The paradox of individualism is that it often reveals a genuine and powerful concern for the particular which in practice achieves the opposite, and the anti-particularist logic of individualism has

---

[4] S. L. Jaki, *God and the Cosmologists* (Edinburgh: Scottish Academic Press, 1989), p. 37.

[5] John Ziman, *Reliable Knowledge. An Exploration of the Grounds for Belief in Science* (Cambridge: Cambridge University Press, 1978).

[6] In his attack on the 'myth of simplicity', Mario Bunge argues that 'A definitely undesirable rationale sustaining the cult of simplicity is of a metaphysical nature: namely, the wish to attain the ultimate atoms of experience and/or reality ... This drive, which feeds metaphysical fundamentalism, is dangerous because it leads to postulating the final simplicity of some form of experience or some kind of substance, thereby barring any inquiry into their structure.' Mario Bunge, *The Myth of Simplicity. Problems of Scientific Philosophy* (Englewood Cliffs, NJ: Prentice Hall, 1963), pp. 86–7.

been pointed out recently by a number of writers. The general point is made by Stanley Hauerwas in criticism of John Rawls' egalitarian philosophy. His:

book stands as a testimony to the moral limits of the liberal tradition ... The 'justice' that results from the bargaining game is but the guarantee that my liberty to consume will be fairly limited within the overall distributive shares ... Missing entirely from Rawls' position is any suggestion that a theory of justice is ultimately dependent on a view of the good; or that justice is as much a category for individuals as for societies ... In an effort to rid liberalism of a social system built on envy, Rawls has to resort to the extraordinary device of making all desires equal before the bar of justice. As a result, he represents the supreme liberal irony: individualism, in an effort to secure societal cooperation and justice, must deny individual differences.[7]

To Hauerwas' testimony I add that of Alistair McFadyen, who traces the link between individualism and social homo-geneity to Kantian ethical theory. The logic of this, he argues, generates a suppression of the individual, or more accurately of personal particularity. The weakness – and it is precisely the same weakness that we discerned in the discussion of the one and the many – is to be found in an inadequate conception of relationality, that is, of how we are each distinctive and different by virtue of and not in despite of the fact that we are related to each other. The following three sentences together make the point:

In the fiction of the ontological priority and independence of the individual from relations, each may be considered as merely the bearer of the rational characteristics and universal dispositions which constitute universal individuality: an abstract form of individuality with no significant individual content ...

Because individualism may not acknowledge essential differences in individual identities as essential, they can have no ethical significance ...

In ethical individualism anything really particular is considered pathological.[8]

[7] Stanley Hauerwas, *A Community of Character . Toward a Constructive Christian Social Ethic* (Notre Dame and London: University of Notre Dame Press, 1981), pp. 82–3.

[8] Alistair I. McFadyen, *The Call to Personhood. A Christian Theory of the Individual in Social Relationships* (Cambridge: Cambridge University Press, 1990), pp. 183, 184 and 185.

That is the problem. If you are real and important not as you particularly are, with your own distinctive strengths and weaknesses, bodily shape and genetic pattern, family history and structure, loves and sorrows, but as the bearer of some general characteristics, what makes you distinctively you becomes irrelevant.

Here, then, is a further characteristic of the modern condition: its homogenizing abolition of particularity. In the next section, I move to a consideration of its roots as well as its conceptual continuities with antiquity, and shall begin with a treatment of personal particularity as one key to the matter. Before that, however, one important point must be made. The fact that similar conceptual disorder is revealed in both dimensions of culture, the scientific and the social, indicates that we are impinging on one of the central topics of theology, the doctrine of creation. The fact that we are here concerned with the very character of reality in all its dimensions will become increasingly evident as the argument proceeds. But now, in view of the fact that Plato has already been identified as one source of the suppression of particularity, it is to his treatment of the particular that I now turn.

2 PLATO

In this second section of the chapter I shall try to enrich the discussion of the historical roots of modernity begun in the first chapter by taking soundings in the history of ideas. I begin by repeating two points. The first is that it was in response to the Sophists' philosophies of disengagement that Plato embarked on the engaged philosophy represented in *The Republic*. In this chapter, I shall trace an opposing theme: how in his thought there are also to be found the roots of modern disengagement. The second point was that it was in the philosophy of the late mediaeval William of Ockham that we find one watershed of Western intellectual history. It was partly as the result of his thought that there developed a belief in the redundancy of the doctrine of creation and the displacement of the source of rationality from God or the universe to the human mind. In this chapter, I shall try to say something of how that came to be. As I do so, I shall hope to bear in mind the point that emerged in my introductory remarks: that we abolish or ignore particularity and distinctiveness in so far as we reduce the richness and complexity of things to the mere sharing of common characteristics. My opponent in all this is the Parmenidean drive of modern rationalism, which too easily forces diversity into uniformity and homogeneity.

It is in the ancient world and Plato as its representative that we shall find the root of the modern inability to do justice to particularity. The Platonic political programme emerged at a time, like ours, of loss of confidence in social, religious and political institutions. Such are the times of temptation to authoritarian political systems, and such, too, may well come to be the temptation of ours. No such sense of crisis pervaded the works of Homer and the earlier two of the great Athenian tragedians, and it is probably no accident that rather different concepts of human being in the world are to be found in them. For all the anthropomorphism of Homer's deities, there is in the poems an interaction between the divine and the human, a communication between personal particulars, which cannot take place in relation to the form of the good. Again, despite all the operation in their background of impersonal fate, there is room within the Greek tragedies for determinative human action and passion. Particulars, concrete and material human actions and passions, are the stuff of things in a way that they cannot be in the theoretical polity of Plato.

By Plato's time, however, the theology of the Greeks had collapsed under its own inadequacies, to be replaced at the forefront of thought by the great tradition of philosophy. One of the weaknesses of the Platonic philosophy, and it is a weakness shared by most of its successors, is its difficulty in giving full reality to material particulars, or individual things. The reasons can be found in all aspects of Plato's thought, but we shall begin with his anthropology, for the concern of this chapter and the rest of the book is with the placing of human life and culture in its worldly context. The relevance of the approach will be seen in the fact that it is little exaggeration to say that the main direction of ancient anthropology, including that of the Western Christian tradition, found its beginning in two of Plato's dialogues, the *Phaedo* and the *Symposium*.

The achievement of those classical dialogues is that they mapped out the two central dimensions of human being in the world. The *Symposium* contains a discussion of the shape that relations between human beings should take; the *Phaedo* brings to the light of day the question of the human relation to the physical world. The popular use of the word *platonic* to describe non-physical love points us to the fact that the notion of the person as essentially a soul has consequences for our understanding of the relation of persons. The *Symposium*, with its systematic downgrading of bodily sexuality and of sexual distinctions – with some of which Augustine and other Christian thinkers unfortunately colluded[9] – reveals an evasion of what I believe to be the fact that the whole person, body, mind and spirit, and not merely a part, is definitive of human being. Underlying the evasion is the well-known Platonic teaching that the essential person is to be found in its non-bodily dimensions. The true person is the soul, so that the material body comes to be understood as that which *divides* one human being from another rather than *relates* them to each other. The general implications for an understanding of the human are as follows. If I am a piece of soul or mind-stuff incarcerated in matter, my materiality is what effectively debars me from relation with you, except only by word or reason. Accordingly, what we have in common is our possession of timeless soul-stuff, so that our relatedness is effectively limited to the rational; or at the very least that is elevated at the expense of the bodily, which becomes only secondary.

The shape of the problem is as follows. Human beings are particularized and identified by their bodies, because they are the chief means by which we are able to distinguish one person from another. But if we are essentially souls, a number of unfortunate implications follow. The first is that there is a major

---

[9] See Derrick Sherwin Bailey, *The Man-Woman Relation in Christian Thought* (London: Longman, 1959).

breach between appearance and reality. I am not or may not be what I appear to be, and this in the radical sense that my particular being is not in essential relation to my embodied being. It follows from this, and the conclusion was drawn by Plato,[10] that reincarnation is a possibility.[11] The second implication is that we do not really have our being in relations of mutual constitutiveness with each other across the whole range of our relations, bodily and mental or verbal. And so we are not in this discussion only concerned with the theory of how we *recognize* particularity. It is a matter of our being also, for on the Platonic view our particular reality is not shaped by all aspects of our relatedness to each other, merely by the inward or narrowly rational dimensions of our being. Just as we found with Kant's and Rawls' concept of the individual, so here the person is pared down to abstract qualities supposedly held in common. Our personal distinctiveness, our human particularity and individuality, so manifest both from what appears and from our bodily constitution, become irrelevant to who and what we truly are.[12] What is lost, in sum, is a recognition of the otherness-in-relation in which alone can particularity be truly preserved.

The outcome is also an essentially rationalist conception of human being according to which we are related to each other more really by our minds than by any other aspect of our personal being. Rationalism, in the light of the discussion in the first chapter, involves a tendency to premature unification: the reduction of the many to the one that in political terms spells totalitarianism. In the terms of this chapter, it means a tendency to conceive the rational capacities of the human being at the

---

[10] Plato, *Timaeus*, 41d-e, cf *Phaedo*, 249b, *Republic*, 618a. I owe these references to John D. Zizioulas, 'On Being a Person', p. 36, note 4.

[11] That the point is by no means irrelevant to modern thought is shown by the reported increase in belief in reincarnation in the West. Twenty-five per cent of Californians, it is said, believe that they are extra-terrestrial walk-ins. I owe this illustration to my colleague Peter Clarke.

[12] The widespread assumption that we are unaffected or unconstituted in our essential being by sexual relations, taking shape as it does in a view of the person as an essentially unchanging individual who goes round seeking 'relationships' is the modern equivalent – inversion perhaps – of the *Symposium*'s quest for a purely spiritual sexuality. In contrast, the Bible everywhere witnesses to the constitutive character of what we are to each other across the whole range of our relationships.

expense of other dimensions of being, especially the aesthetic and material. We truly are when we think, but not when we love or make music. And that leads us to the second dimension of Hellenistic philosophy's problematic legacy, the rationalizing of the human relation to the rest of the world. The teaching of the *Phaedo* is that because the real person is the immaterial soul, engagement with materiality should be reduced to a minimum, particularly because the pleasures of sense rivet the body to the soul, and so prevent that progressive separation of the two that is the aim and end of philosophy.[13]

Here we are able to make an important connection. The doctrine that matter is dubiously real was one of the reasons for Plato's well-known suspicion of art, well illustrated by the expulsion of the poets from his ideal state.[14] The significance of the arts for us is that they mark an important aspect of what we make of the particular things in our world. It is what we make of this piece of clay, that succession of tones, that makes all the difference. Change one note of a piece of music, and you have a different piece. The results of human craft or art are particular: the outcome of engagement with the material world in all its brute particularity and intractability. The downgrading of art is thus one of the results of Plato's disqualification of the particular from being the bearer of truth. As a result, and that is something to be explored in a later chapter, the Western world has, despite Aristotle's defence of the aesthetic, never recovered from what we can call the fragmentation of culture. It is difficult enough on any account to understand how science is related to morality, morality to art, and so on. Unless we find a way of coming to terms with the material world in all its particularity, the difficulty is magnified. That is the point of the first main thesis for this chapter, that the modern discomfort with particularity, whose outlines I traced in the first section, has its roots in the Platonic – and ultimately Parmenidean – suspicion of the world of matter, plurality and becoming. But it also enables the repetition of a point made at the end of Section 1, that this is a matter of the doctrine of creation: of the

---

[13] Plato, *Phaedo*, 83b5-e3.   [14] Plato, *Republic*, 597ff.

conception of the nature of things and of human culture that our theology makes possible. The question for the next section will be whether Platonizing elements have expelled from the Western mind features of the theology of creation which enable particularity to be truly conceived.

3 THE WEST'S DOUBLE MIND

The argument so far is that elements of continuity between ancient and modern thought and culture are to be seen in the fact that both eras, in so far as the examples I have chosen are representative, tend to suppress particularity by deriving the essential being of things or people from their possession of identical or common properties. Their otherness-in-relation is not constitutive of their real being, which is rather seen to lie in a universal whose tendency is to render them homogeneous. In a later chapter, I shall trace the common problem to a defective conception of substance, but in this section am chiefly concerned to isolate the distinctive character of modernity by a brief evocation of some of the central areas where it arose out of antiquity. A beginning can be made by saying that, for all its faults in threatening the fragmentation of human culture and in failing to establish an adequate ontology of particulars, the work of Plato and his successors did at least succeed in providing a framework for their integration in an overall vision of being and life: an orientation to the good within which human life could take shape. That the vision came to be seen as an oppressive rather than a liberating one does not detract from the fact that it provided something without which life is fragmented and diminished.

But how did it come to appear so problematic? Here I develop the point made at the end of the two previous sections about the doctrine of creation, adding that Christian theology, although it had every opportunity to develop a theology of creation in which the rights of the particular were given due place, made the major mistake of entering into the wrong kind of compromise with Platonism. But it is a complicated tale. At the heart of it is the fact that there was to be found in the mediaeval era, out of whose dissolution modernity arose, the unstable presence together of alternative and, as the outcome shows, incompatible frameworks. It will aid in an understanding of what happened if we distinguish between the anthropological and theological dimensions of what developed. Anthropologically, the Platonic framework for the understanding of the human being remained relatively unchanged, as is shown by the fact that the theology of the image of God in man almost universally held it to consist in reason. What we find accordingly is an institutionalizing or sedimenting of the rationalist view of the person that derived from Plato. Alongside it there developed an ever-increasing stress on the inward dimensions of human being.[15] During the process, there took place what can be called a substantializing of the divine image, a tendency to conceive it to consist in the possession of certain fixed characteristics, characteristics moreover that tend to preclude relationality[16] – just as we saw Plato's view to preclude relationality – because they abstract a part and make it the whole.[17]

---

[15] See Charles Taylor, *Sources of the Self*, chapter 7, 'In Interiore Homine', on the development of conceptions of inwardness in Augustine.

[16] To be sure, and as a result of Augustine's trinitarian thought, there are relational elements in the concept of the person, but it is chiefly a vertical relationality. The relation to God is rightly held to be constitutive of human being, but the relation to other persons is ontologically irrelevant rather than, as it ought to be, consequent upon, albeit to that extent secondary to, the primary relation, that to God. According to this tradition of thought, I really am when I am related to God, not quite really so when I am related to other human beings and the earth.

[17] Aquinas is a case in point, although he is in many respects developing a starting point to be found in Augustine. The influence of Boethius' definition of the person as *naturae rationabilis individua substantia* was also crucial, as I have argued in *The Promise of Trinitarian Theology* (Edinburgh: T. & T. Clark, 1991), chapter 5. In Aquinas there is a Platonizing or rationalizing of the doctrine of the image of God, whose perhaps most telling symptom is to be found in his discussion of the way in which women can be said to share the divine image. Like Augustine, Aquinas is sceptical about suggestions that the image belongs to the body as well as to the mind, interpreting Genesis 1's 'male and female' as referring to the fact that the image is common to both sexes, as being principally realized in intelligent nature (*Summa Theologiae* 1a 93. 4). The substantive point is made later, that 'not even in the rational creature will you find God's image except with reference to mind' (93. 6). Notice that the three characteristics of the image he cites from John of Damascus, 'his capacity for understanding and for making free decisions, and his mastery of himself' (approvingly though not as part of his primary exposition, 93. 5), are essentially moral and intellectual qualities possessed individually: they are not constituted in

The unstable, and ultimately disruptive, element in all this is the concept of the will, already central in Augustine's view of the person, and coming into its full effect with William of Ockham. It is Christian theology's distinctive but ambiguous contribution to the mixture. As can be seen from a simple distinction, the will is a morally ambivalent faculty. It can serve either to give reality and freedom to others, or to deprive them. Thus I can will your being and freedom, by allowing you to be yourself and to share in making me what I am; or by the exercise of my will I can attempt to make you the mere instrument of my desires or plans. In Kantian language, I can will you as an end in yourself, or as a mere means to my end. In the language of this chapter, I can will you to be particularly what you are, by enabling you to be yourself; or I can deprive you of particularity by subsuming your being within mine.[18] It is very much the same in the case of our relations with the rest of the world, which can also be the object of a merely exploitative human will. The orientation of the will is essential in any understanding of what it is to be a person and to be a personal agent in the world. It is its misplacing that is at the heart of the problem of particularity.

Light is thrown on what has happened if we introduce the second and theological dimension of our discussion. At the appropriate stage in the development of this and of the two subsequent chapters, I plan to introduce a contrast between different ways of interpreting the first chapter of Genesis. On the one side will be the anti-gnostic theology of creation of Irenaeus of Lyons. I do not wish to idealize Irenaeus, but to use his insights to reveal certain indispensable resources available in the doctrine of creation for the development of our theme of human life in the world. On the other side of the contrast is the way in which the doctrine of creation developed subtly but

structures of human relationality. The double mind of the West is well illustrated by Calvin, in different dimensions of whose anthropology is to be found both a Platonic dualism of the person and the view that the whole person, spiritual and material, is the locus of the image of God. Significantly, Calvin is least Platonist in this regard when he is thinking in the light of the resurrection, *Institutes*, III. 25. 8.

[18] It is, of course, because modernity has suspected, with some justification, that its being is subsumed into that of God that it has rebelled against theology.

crucially differently in the thought of Augustine. My contention is that the difference became magnified by later thinkers in such a way that distinctive features of modern culture emerged out of the finally incompatible mixture that Augustine produced. The heart of the instability is to be found in the interpretation of the biblical creation story with the aid of elements of Platonic philosophy.

The first consideration in support of my claim is as follows. Through its development of a concept of the will of God Christian theology contributed the basis of a theology of particularity which represented an advance on the conceptions inherited from Greece. According to the theology of Irenaeus, the will of God is essentially a particularizing will, a will giving rise to the existence and directedness to perfection of the world and the beings within it. The basis for this conception of the will of God as directed to the other is to be found in Irenaeus' christology and pneumatology. The contribution of the former is clear. To base a theology on the particularity of a human life is to render inseparable divine will and created particular, and at the same time to emphasize the centrality of embodiment in matter, in complete contrast to a Platonizing abstraction of the two. As will be argued in Chapter 7, the pneumatological dimensions of a theology of particularity are even more decisive, for one of the distinctive modes of action of God the Spirit is to render particular. The point for our purpose here, however, is that Irenaeus' triune God is one who creates by his will a particular world to which particularity is integral.

The obscuring of particularity begins in Augustine's theology of creation, where the christological element plays little substantive role, and the pneumatological even less. The result is that the way is laid open for a conception of creation as the outcome of arbitrary will, and though there is a christologically formed directedness to the other in Augustine,[19] it is less

---

[19] In *Confessions*, 12. 7, Augustine argues – and it is an argument that is crucially important for the doctrine of creation – that 'You created heaven and earth but you did not make them of your own substance. If you had done so, they would have been equal to your only-begotten Son ... ' Translated by R. S. Pine-Coffin (Harmondsworth: Penguin Books, 1961), p. 284. It is noteworthy that although the argument

determinative than in Irenaeus. *The root of the modern disarray is accordingly to be located in the divorce of the willing of creation from the historical economy of salvation.* According to Michael Buckley, the development of a non-christological and non-pneumatological account of the relation of God and the world was crucial in the development of modern atheism, and indeed provides a recurring refrain in his account.[20] But there is a case for arguing that what Buckley roots chiefly in the mediaeval tradition of natural theology can be traced far further back in the Western theological tradition. On an Irenaean account, what holds the creation together – its *inscape*, to use the expression of G. M. Hopkins to which I shall return in the seventh and corresponding chapter of the book – are the Son and the Spirit, by whom the world is held in continuing relation to God the Father. After Augustine that function comes, increasingly, to be performed by the universals, which are traditionally conceived to be a timeless conceptual structure informing otherwise shapeless matter. Augustine's interpretation of Genesis 1 in terms of a creation of forms, eternal archetypes, turns that celebration of particularity and variety into something dangerously like its subversion, because the replacing of christology by Platonic universals generates a very different conception of the

---

is christological in form, it is not incarnational. In the matter of particularity, it is the latter which is essential.

[20] Buckley, *Origins*, pp. 33, 55, 64–7, 350–69. Two citations will make the point. 'In the absence of a rich and comprehensive Christology and a Pneumatology of religious experience Christianity entered into the defense of the existence of the Christian god without appeal to anything Christian' (p. 67); and 'The origin of atheism in the intellectual culture of the West lies … with the self-alienation of religion itself' (p. 363). It is for reasons such as this – and others will be given in later chapters – that I find Buckley's thesis more convincing than that of John Milbank in *Theology and Social Theory. Beyond Secular Reason* (Oxford: Blackwell, 1990). He attributes the development of the problematic aspects of modernity – which he centres on secularism – to nominalism and the Reformation. It seems to me, however, that such a thesis makes modern conditions develop out of earlier culture more rapidly than is plausible, while his defence of the essentially non-trinitarian ontology of creation in Augustine and Pseudo-Dionysius fails to take account of Buckley's central point. The thesis of this book is that the roots of the problematic aspects of modernity lie far further in the past than that, so that Milbank himself runs the risk of making modernity emerge too suddenly out of the past. This is not to deny the many perceptive observations Milbank makes in the course of his critique of modern secularism; rather, it is to contend that in this respect Augustine is more of the question than the answer.

relation of universal and particular. Not the particularizing will
of God, but general conceptual forms come into the centre.[21]

It is often pointed out that it was the instability of the
mediaeval synthesis of Christian faith and philosophical reason
that underlay the collapse of the ancient tradition which was
engendered by nominalism and its modern successors. Here we
find another purchase on the nature of the instability, for side by
side in the tradition there compete the conception of a
christological and pneumatological mediation of the creation,
and a conception centring on a structure of timeless forms. The
one establishes a world of particulars, the other always threatens
its reality by concentrating attention on that which is not
particular.[22] As we have already seen,[23] the process comes to a
head on the threshold of modernity, with William of Ockham.
It may appear paradoxical to charge the philosopher of the
particular with the abolition of particularity, but paradox is
very much the mark of the world we are in, for the modernity
with which we are concerned is the product and the realm of
paradox. The problem is that sketched in the previous chapter,
though transposed into the key of this one. Ockham abolishes
particularity by asserting the existence only of particulars while
simultaneously denying that there are real relations between
them. Ockhamism is thus a doctrine of the Platonic abstract

---

[21] See Augustine, *Confessions*, 12. 9, for the distinction between the creation of 'some
kind of intellectual creature' before the creation of the material world. Here
Augustine is, as in some other respects, a follower of Origen, another Platonizer of the
process of divine creation. The long-term effects of this, for example in the way in
which theology so clumsily responded to the theory of evolution in the nineteenth
century, can hardly be exaggerated, for the tradition was saddled with the view that
creation involved the production of timeless forms – precisely what Darwinism
rejected. It can also surely be no accident that theologies in the West from Scotus
Erigena through Spinoza to modern theologies influenced by Hegel frequently
reveal a drive to pantheism. The heart of pantheism is to be found in the abolition
of particularity because the world and everything in it becomes reduced to a logical
implication of the being of God: the many *reduced* to the one. The chief weapons
against pantheism are christology and pneumatology.

[22] It is noteworthy that although for Aquinas, the greatest exponent of the synthesis of
the two worlds, the reality of particulars is central, they tend to be of interest chiefly
as a ladder to eternity and not in their own right as particulars. Later thinkers would
not be able to hold together the two contrary drives, and it is then scarcely surprising
either that a major medieval debate centred on the reality of universals, or that the
synthesis finally collapsed under the weight of its own structural weaknesses.

[23] See above, Chapter 1, p. 28.

particular deprived of the support of the forms, which at least had the merit of conceiving a form of relatedness between things. What is generated is an intellectual vacuum, and whatever may be the truth about nature, there is little doubt that thought abhors a vacuum.

The nature of the vacuum and its outcome is well illustrated by Hans Blumenberg's account of the successors of Ockham in the modern world. According to him, Ockhamism renders God redundant:

> the denial of universals directly excludes the possibility that God's restriction of himself to his *potentia ordinata* [ordered, or ordained, power] in nature too could become comprehensible for the benefit of man and his reason. Divine spirit and human spirit, creative and cognitive principles, operate as though without taking each other into account.[24]

Referring to the correspondence between Leibniz and Clarke, Blumenberg suggests that 'Theological absolutism denied man any insight into the rationality of the Creation'. Attributing creation merely to the will of God invites the use of Ockham's razor, which 'helps [man] to reduce nature forcibly to an order *imputed* to it by man'. Thus the theological voluntarism and absolutism of the late Middle Ages generates a rejection of God and the transfer of his powers to man. In Blumenberg's words, 'Theological absolutism has its own indispensable atheism and anthropotheism'.[25] Despite – or rather, because of – the differences of their interests, the convergence between Blumenberg and Buckley is remarkable. One sees the root of the matter to be in theological voluntarism; the other in the loss of christology and pneumatology in the way God is understood. As we have seen, both are aspects of the same process.

The outcome of ancient Christianity's ambivalent theology of creation is thus to be seen writ large in the transition between William of Ockham and the leading exponents of modern cosmology. In Ockham, we can say in summary, there are three features whose combination proved to be explosive. First is the reassertion of the priority of particulars, or rather the view that

---

[24] Blumenberg, *Legitimacy*, pp. 153–4.   [25] Ibid., pp. 149, 179.

only particulars exist. Second is the denial of the way of relating them that had been inherited from Plato and Aristotle. Third is the non-christological and non-pneumatological – that is to say, arbitrary and ambiguous – concept of the will that had developed in both anthropology and theology. If there are no universals, then only the will of God is able hold things together. But it is a divine will of a very distinctive kind. The link between the particulars of our experience is made by a God essentially conceived after the image of the individual rational will so prominent in theological anthropology after Augustine. It is so applied to God that it makes the world appear to be simply the arbitrary product of the divine will, abstractly conceived and essentially unknown.

The scene is thus set for a contest of wills: between the God who appears to impart particularity only to that which is a function of his will, and therefore to deprive of true particularity; and the human will which appears to achieve independence only in the kind of arbitrary self assertion which appears to be the mark of divinity. The ingredients of the development are a God unitarily conceived, and largely in terms of will; the divorce of creation and redemption in the concept of the divine action – as Blumenberg shows, a recurrence of certain features of gnostic thought;[26] and a world whose shape is attributed largely to the (essentially unknown) predestining will of God. There can accordingly be seen to take place a kind of reflex process which takes the form of a human filling of the vacuum left by the irrelevance of the unknown God: a process of self-assertion, in which responsibility for the ordering of the world – personal and non-personal alike – is transferred to the human from the divine will. Buckley sees the outcome to be personified in the thought of Malebranche, in which 'the inner contradictions of the tradition he so carefully developed have reached a crisis. Either god engulfs consciousness by this dominant presence or the divine existence cannot be asserted.'[27] As we shall see in more detail in later chapters, the image of God as reason, or reason allied to will, becomes the

---

[26] This claim will be examined in the next chapter .
[27] Buckley, *Origins*, p. 353.

locus of a rebellion against the very God in whose image it understood itself.

In sum, then, there develop side by side a Platonized concept of the image of God and a Platonizing interpretation of the doctrine of creation. Their joint outcome for the modern world's conception of particularity is as follows. The abolition of the world of the forms, and of the deity which succeeded them as the metaphysical framework for thought in the mediaeval era, effected a radicalization of the Platonic anthropology. The particular person, whose calling according to Plato was to escape the chains of embodiedness to live in the eternal world of the forms, came to be seen as freed from all constraints of external reality – alone in an empty world or disengaged from a meaningless one – and so displaces God by taking on the attributes of divinity. To be human is not now to be chiefly a mind but an essentially rational and at least potentially divine will: or rather, as it so often turns out in practice, a multiplicity of wills competing one with another for dominance.[28] The Platonic cutting off of the mind from its material environment was a recipe for disaster. The additional ingredient of Christian theological voluntarism has radicalized the mixture into something explosive.

What, in the light of all this, is to be said about the relation of the ancient and modern eras? We have already met, in the opening section, cases which suggest that, on first appearances at least, many modern theories of particularity are like Plato's in making the basis of individuation a shared identical or general property rather than concrete relationality. That is not to say that they are the only modern attempts to conceive particularity, but that prima facie at least there is a continuity with antiquity at a crucial point: in the failure to give adequate

---

[28] Kenneth Hamilton points in this connection to the expression of George Grant, 'the triumph of the will': 'the moral foundations of western culture given by the Christian vision of life have crumbled before organised selfishness. Any vocal group is ready to *demand* what it considers its rights and tell the government what it *must* do. The will is no longer thought of as the ability to choose – and, it is hoped, choose wisely. It is regarded as the means to power.' 'Doctrine and the Christian Life: Reflections on Kingdom and Triumph of the Will', *Theological Digest* 5 no. 2 (July 1990), 14–17 (15).

conceptual and actual weight to the material particular. We saw that part of the cause of the failure was Platonic rationalism, and that the Platonic view is with us still in deep-seated assumptions of our culture is shown, for example, by the widespread belief that if a computer could be made to think, it would be a kind of person, as if relationality and especially love were not also essentials of our being.[29]

Here we light upon a surprising and illuminating feature of the modern condition. To all appearances, the heart of the difference between the ancient and the modern can be put by saying that whereas the ancient mind tended to spiritualize the human, by seeing the person as essentially a soul or mind, the modern has tended to react by placing an immense emphasis on human embodiedness. Evidence for the materialist emphasis in modern culture does not need to be marshalled. At many levels there has indeed developed a tendency, in large part in reaction against supposed ancient spiritualizing, not only to stress the material determinants of our being but sometimes to turn them into the whole, for example in Marxist anthropology, sociobiology or many of the assumptions underlying the consumer society. As with many such simplifications, however, although there is some truth in the claim that here the modern is very different from the ancient, there is to be found a greater measure of continuity than meets the eye. It has been pointed out, for example, that some representatives of early modernity show a contempt for the material the equal of anything found in antiquity,[30] while the ecological crisis derives from precisely

---

[29] The tendency achieves a kind of *reductio ad absurdum* – or, from another point of view, apotheosis – in the final chapter of J. D. Barrow and F. J. Tipler, *The Anthropic Cosmological Principle* (Oxford: Clarendon Press, 1986): 'though our species is doomed, our civilization and indeed the values we care about may not be. We emphasized ... that from the behavioural point of view intelligent *machines* can be regarded as people. These machines may be our ultimate heirs, our ultimate descendants, because under certain circumstances they could survive for ever the extreme conditions near the Final State' (p. 615). In one brief passage we thus meet two typical tendencies of the modern age: the depersonalization of values and the evasion of death. For a different approach, see Roger Penrose, *The Emperor's New Mind. Concerning Computers, Minds and the Laws of Physics* (London: Vintage, 1990).

[30] See Buckley, *Origins*, p. 355, for another telling illustration: 'both Malebranche and Clarke linked their glorification of god to the denigration of matter .... The time was soon to come when this despised matter would wreak a terrible vengeance on both

that: the belief that the human will may impose what shape it wishes upon the material world. Much modern technology shows a clear contempt for nature of the kind portrayed in Václav Havel's reminiscence:

> As a boy... I used to walk to school in a nearby village along a cart track through the fields and, on the way, see on the horizon a huge smokestack of some hurriedly built factory, in all likelihood in the service of war. It spewed out dense smoke and scattered it across the sky. Each time I saw it, I had an intense sense of something profoundly wrong, of humans soiling the heavens... It seemed to me that... humans are guilty of something, that they destroy something important, arbitrarily disrupting the natural order of things and that such things cannot go unpunished.[31]

We are not in every way so different from our predecessors. Rather, the distinctively modern contempt for matter takes shape in the light of the displacement of God that I traced in the previous chapter and have again displayed here.

4 PARTICULARITY IN PRACTICE I: FREEDOM

To explore the matter further, and to expose the distinctive features of modernity's treatment of particularity, I propose to develop two case studies, corresponding to the two focuses of this chapter: who we are as particular persons, and what the world is with which we engage as we eat and drink to remain alive, pursue science and make music. Together, they will suggest that the modern is no more at home in the world, perhaps less so, than many a representative of eras apparently bound to the cosmos. For the former, I could well discuss the fate of the concept of the person in recent times, but for a

theologians and their god. Christology, with its doctrine of the Incarnation, would have read matter religiously in a very different manner.' Blumenberg, *Legitimacy*, p. 77, makes a similar point: 'The early centuries of the modern age exhibit a "spirituality," or at least an aversion to the world, that is strained, often convulsive, and that sometimes – in appearance – puts everything medieval in the shade.' Why it is only 'in appearance' is not explained.

[31] Havel, *Open Letters*, pp. 249–50. Similarly, it is not difficult to realize that the Cartesian theory of the self is the Platonic transposed into a modern key, and its dissolution in recent theories of the loss of the self almost entirely parasitic upon it.

number of reasons am taking instead the concept of freedom. Chief among them is that it combines well with a discussion of particularity. Our human freedom is in large measure what we make of our particularity: it is what you and I do, or would do, as distinctly ourselves, and not as someone else. To place the discussion in context, a beginning should be made with the expression of a firm preference for modern libertarian conceptions of individual freedom over against those that mark the authoritarian dimensions of modernity. Their strength is the recognition of the centrality of particularity, along with their view that the person who is required to submerge his or her particularity in a mass society of any kind is thus far deprived of it. For all the danger of instability, institutionalized selfishness and their being transmuted into their opposites, modern liberal systems of government are in general more suited for the formation of true particularity than perhaps any others known to history. While probing the weaknesses of modernity, we should be delighted to affirm its blessings.[32] The problems of the modern concepts of freedom are best approached through Sir Isaiah Berlin's *Two Concepts of Liberty*.

The points of interest in this classic discussion are manifold. First, it shows clearly the competing concepts of freedom which are in currency in the modern world. We might say that they correspond to the pluralistic and monistic sides of modernity, respectively. The former is what he calls the negative concept: 'I am normally said to be free to the degree to which no human being interferes with my activity. Political liberty in this sense is simply the area within which a man can do what he wants.' '[L]iberty in this sense means liberty *from* ... ' The latter and positive sense 'derives from the wish on the part of the individual

[32] There are reasons for holding that the coherence of liberal societies depends in part on the continuation of teaching and practices that contradict aspects of the theory of modern society. For example it is true, especially in the United States of America, that Christian assumptions, often contradicting the reigning liberal ideology, are more determinative for the lives of many people and therefore of the structure of their societies than 'official' secular ideology allows. The influence of Christian belief on the recent revolutions in Eastern Europe is also becoming increasingly evident. Some of the factors were spelled out by David Martin in his 1991 Maurice Lectures at King's College, London.

to be his own master.' In general, it refers to the idea of freedom as the realizing of one's true being or nature. The second strength of Berlin's discussion is its recognition of the short-comings of both concepts on their own, especially of the ease with which the positive concept, notably in its modern rationalist form, so easily transmogrifies into its opposite. Rationalist forms of liberalism, for example that of Kant, lead to despotism. '[T]he rationalist argument, with its assumption of the single true solution, has led from an ethical doctrine of individual responsibility and individual self-perfection, to an authoritarian state obedient to the directives of an élite of Platonic guardians.'[33]

Third, Berlin realizes that notions of freedom are correlative with doctrines about the nature of human being. Speaking of negative freedom, and asking, as must necessarily be asked of such a conception, 'What then must the minimum be?', he replies:

That which a man cannot give up without offending against the essence of his human nature. What is this essence? What are the standards which it entails? This has been, and perhaps always will be, a matter of infinite debate.

Fourth, Berlin realises that the preference for freedom of the negative kind or freedom from interference – for the many over the one, as the title of his last section puts it – is linked with the fallibility and imperfection both of human beings and of the world. More positively, he sees that it derives from the fact that there is a plurality of goods, not some single purpose in life that can be rationalistically discovered and imposed.[34]

Fifth, and here we reach the core of the problem of modern individualism, he argues that there can be no finally satisfactory individualist account of freedom. We are social beings in a deeper sense even than that signalled by the fact that 'everything that I do affects, and is affected by, what others do'.[35] He is, however, unable to give a convincing account of what follows

---

[33] Isaiah Berlin, *Two Concepts of Liberty. An Inaugural Lecture delivered before the University of Oxford on 31 October 1958* (Oxford: Clarendon Press, 1985), pp. 7, 11, 16, 37.
[34] Ibid., pp. 11 (cf. 19, 55), 56, 54.   [35] Ibid., pp. 39–40.

from the social nature of human reality for a conception of freedom, because he cannot strengthen the argument for individual freedom with considerations drawn from the social nature of human reality. If we are, as he says, what we are both materially and in other ways by virtue of our interrelatedness, the inadequacies of the preferred negative, and essentially individualist, account, come into greater prominence. Is freedom no more than my not being prevented from doing what I want? It is here that arises the irresistible desire for some ontological account of freedom, for an account tied to what I am and not simply what I want. But, as Berlin has himself shown, the ontological account in its modern form leads inexorably to unfreedom. It appears, then, that the modern accounts of freedom collapse under the weight of their own inadequacies. Their chief requirement seems to be the benefits of positive freedom gained by the application of the methods of the negative. It is rather like expecting the unregulated market to achieve moral ends automatically.

Here again modern doctrine appears to be dogged by inherent paradox, and the reason to lie in the truths underlying respectively the negative and positive accounts, that freedom is both something exercised and something received. If both are to be present together, there must be a relational content, according to which freedom becomes a function of unnecessitated reciprocity, something we confer – or, more often perhaps, fail to confer – on each other by the manner of our bearing to one another. Despite – because of – Berlin's brilliant discussion, therefore, it remains in general true that the modern individualistic concept of freedom tends to separate the person from other people, rather than simply distinguishing them from each other in relation. That is to say, it is essentially and irremediably non-relational. Its *alter ego*, the collectivist conception, recognizes the necessity of relationality, but believes that it can be imposed. Both fail to incorporate the other into their conception of what it is to be a free person.

As we have seen in the discussion of the doctrine of the image of God, the Christian tradition itself tended to take an individualist direction, locating human particularity in the possession of a soul or some qualification of inwardness. It maintained one dimension of human relationality, the vertical, but not the other, the horizontal. To be was to be in internal relation to God, but not, essentially, to the neighbour or the world. So it is with modern doctrines of the human. The thought that our freedom comes to us from God is not inconceivable for the modern mind; the thought that it also comes from each other, as a function of our relationality, almost is. The measure of the continuity of past and present, ancient and modern, is to be found in the fact that freedom is almost invariably freedom *from* the other: to 'realize' or 'fulfil' ourselves, to 'do our own thing' is to be human, not to find our being in reciprocal relatedness with our neighbour. Neither era can handle particularity without falling victim either to the Scylla of fragmentation or the Charybdis of social monism.

By contrast, the difference between the eras is to be found in the same pattern of displacement that was the lesson of the previous section, and, indeed, the conclusion of the first chapter. The worst aspects of modernity result when that structure collapses under its own inadequacies. God, believed to be redundant or malevolent, is displaced, so that the individual becomes self-grounded – that is, not truly grounded at all – and so unrelated to the overall truth of things. The heart of Kant's view, that in different ways underlies both individualist and collectivist accounts of freedom, is to be found in the requirement that the moral agent in effect replace God as a self-contained source of moral freedom. To take his programme seriously is to replace God with a plurality of finite wills each aspiring to divinity. The demonic aspects of this have revealed themselves in recent history, although it is fortunate that here too in practice inherited wisdom is not entirely rejected. There is something about the modern demand that life and choice be continually created out of nothing that is in practice so absurd that it is honoured in the breach as well as in the fulfilment. The permanent practice, which it in effect involves, of human creation out of nothing just is beyond human capacity, because it represents a falsification of our being as finite. In contrast to this, a trinitarian doctrine of divine creation which was in continuity with that of Irenaeus would hold that we are beings who exist, under God, only in mutually constitutive relations with each other and with the world of which we are a part. It will be the aim of the seventh, and corresponding chapter, to explore some of the ways in which that may be understood. In the next section of this chapter, we continue with a further exploration of modern difficulties with particularity.

5 PARTICULARITY IN PRACTICE 2: THE AESTHETIC

The realm of the arts also provides an excellent illustration of the unstable way in which the modern world does not seem to know where it stands in reality, staggering as it does unsteadily between one position and its opposite, as in the case of the one and the many. The general problem of aesthetic meaning will concern us in Chapter 4. Here I am concerned with the characteristically modern difficulty of making sense of the relation between subjective making and shaping by the artist, and reception by the public, on the one hand, and the objective reality of the piece of material reality that is produced or experienced on the other. If you make a pot or paint a picture, what is your contribution, and what that of the world you shape? What should art be or do? Does or should it reflect the values of current society, or should it be the bearer of distinctive aesthetic meaning? Does art have a redemptive or consolatory function, or should it disturb and enrage? Can and should it reflect an underlying universal order?

The problem of the relation of objective and subjective meaning in aesthetics is an exact parallel to the problem of the one and the many that we met previously. Not only do the two, as they are conceived and practised in the modern world, oscillate unstably between each other, but the conceptual and practical disorder derives from a similar absence of a mediating concept. Just as in the former case there was nothing intermediate between the one and the many to hold them in relation, so here there is no adequate relating of subject and object, with the result that we appear to be forced to choose –

counterintuitively – between object and subject. That is not to say that modernity is in no ways better able than Plato to give adequate treatment to the particularity that is of the essence of a work of art. Rather, it is that there are characteristically modern intellectual forces which generate an incapacity to understand the relation between subjective action and experience, on the one hand, and the objective reality of the piece of material reality that is produced or experienced on the other.[36]

Although there are many modern theories of aesthetics, the chief matter at issue is between broadly subjectivist and objectivist views. The former approach is perhaps best represented by the conclusion to Pater's well-known study of the Renaissance, which, significantly, is headed by an allusion to Heraclitus' doctrine that everything is in flux. 'For art comes to you proposing frankly to give nothing but the highest quality to your moments as they pass, and simply for those moments' sake.'[37] That emphasis on the subject, depriving as it does the particular artefact of substantial objective significance, can be seen on the one hand to derive from the Platonist suspicion of materiality we have already met in another context, but also on the other from a ceding to the sciences of all claims for objective truth. If only science tells us the truth, what remains to art?[38] A doctrine of the meaninglessness of material particulars combines with scientism to deprive the artistic object of its inherent meaning and substantiality.

The latter, critically objectivist, approach, is represented not only by Peter Fuller, who, though not a Christian believer,

[36] Here I am employing a broad conception of material, to include things heard. In that sense, as Victor Zuckerkandl has demonstrated in his remarkable books on the philosophy of music, music is something that is materially *there*. His argument is an excellent refutation of the vulgar, but all too frequent, error of supposing that things heard are somehow less real than things seen or felt. Victor Zuckerkandl, *Sound and Symbol. Music and the External World*, translated by Willard R. Trask (Princeton: Princeton University Press, 1969); and *Man the Musician. Sound and Symbol Volume 2*, translated by Norman Guterman (Princeton: Princeton University Press, 1973).

[37] Walter Pater, *The Renaissance. Studies in Art and Poetry*, edited and introduced by Adam Phillips (Oxford: Oxford University Press, 1986), p. 153.

[38] For a forthright attack on the scientism of much popular belief, see Mary Midgley, 'Strange Contest: Science versus Religion', *The Gospel and Contemporary Culture*, edited by Hugh Montefiore (London: Mowbrays, 1992), pp. 40–57.

rightly saw that the matter is at root a theological one, but also by a surprising number of modern writers, particularly anti-modernist and anti-idealist ones. The chief point to be made here is that the debate is often conducted in terms of mutual incomprehension and abuse because of an inability to conceive adequately the relationship of particular artist, as agent, and particular items of material reality as those which are being used, shaped or transformed (and each of the three verbs supposes a different conception of the relation of human artist to his or her material).[39] It is of a piece with other observations to the effect that modern culture shows many signs of having lost the capacity by which, or the common language in which, to decide questions of meaning, especially in art and ethics.[40]

A recent edition of *The Independent* gives an instance of the problem of particularity as it affects aesthetics, and it concerns the way in which we may conceive that a building fits into its setting. (That, of course, is one of the chief ways in which the problem of particularity reveals itself in architecture.) Two comments in separate articles highlight the problem. The first comes from an appreciation of the work of Frank Lloyd Wright by one of his pupils. Terry Farrell commented that Wright 'was not a modernist. He never had any truck with mainstream international modernism ... The new internationalism, which prescribed essentially the same building for any site in any place, was diametrically opposed to everything Wright stood for in terms of carefully adjusting buildings to their setting.'[41] It is noteworthy, he continued, that this did not prevent Wright from eclectically using the techniques of modernism when it suited him. Whatever the truth of that particular observation, it makes a similar point to the one I have made elsewhere, that there are trends in modernity that would have the effect of imposing a homogeneity of culture, largely through the universal imposition of Western technology. That contrasts with a concern, voiced again recently by the Prince of Wales, of suiting

[39] '*Modern Painters* is shit, SHIT, moral shit ... .Peter Fuller was FAKE as well.' Peter Jenkins, interview with Norman Rosenthal, *The Independent*, 8 June 1991. Compare Fuller's remarks on Gilbert and George and others, *Theoria*, pp. 3–4, 213.

[40] See the books discussed in Chapter 4, Section 1, below.

[41] *The Independent*, 8 June 1991.

buildings to their environment; that is, of treating them as particulars. Modernism as an ideology is Parmenidean. The whole point of a stress on the particular is to liberate from the pressures of homogenizing ideology, modernist or other. Wright's resistance to the 'package' of modernism is here seen as the basis of his ability to deal with particulars.

The second comment is also interesting, for it concerns the way in which both modernism and postmodernism are different forms of one modern and procrustean ideology. It comes from a review by Ziauddin Sardar of Fredric Jameson's *Postmodernism*. 'Whereas modernism tried to come to terms with the "other" by excluding it, postmodernism simply seeks to render it irrelevant. The underlying fear of it continues unabated.'[42] Both forms of modern culture are unable to deal happily with the particular in its relation to other particulars. Postmodernism shares modernism's fundamental disorientation as the Heraclitus to its Parmenides, but neither can do justice to both unity and multiplicity. Peter Fuller identified the Heraclitean character of postmodern judgements:

> Postmodernism knows no commitments: it takes up what one of its leading exponents, Charles Jenks, once called a 'situational position', in which 'no code is inherently better than any other'. The west front of Wells Cathedral, the Parthenon pediment, the plastic and neon signs of Caesar's palace, Las Vegas, even the hidden intricacies of a Mies van der Rohe curtain wall: all are equally 'interesting'.[43]

What is new in postmodernism[44] is the loss of the commitment to objective truth, one of the positive concerns of the Enlightenment, along with the Parmenidean drive it gave to modernism's formalism. It is no accident that it is Marxist writers such as Jameson and David Harvey who are particularly acute in noting the continuities between modernism and postmodernism. Both have observed that underlying the Hera-

---

[42] I have cited the review rather than the book because that was what I first read, and because I did not find in Fredric Jameson's *Postmodernism* so luminous an expression of the claim. What does come out very clearly in the book under review is the link between art and consumption; between, as Jameson puts it in one place (pp. 353-4), the media and the market.   [43] Fuller, *Theoria*, p. 213.

[44] Or at least in some forms of postmodernism, for it would appear that some of its exponents deny that they are subjectivist.

clitean drive of postmodernism is an ethic of consumption. 'The odd thing about postmodern cultural production is how much sheer profit-seeking is determinant in the first instance.'[45] Harvey's appeal to Marx's theory of the fetishism of money puts a finger on the central point. Marx had the eye of an Old Testament prophet for idolatry, however disastrous may have been his prescription for its cure. He saw that one of the roots of modern alienation is the failure of relation to the material world that is symbolized by money-fetishism. That may be part of the reason why the pressure to homogeneity – to the suppression of the other, we might say – is very much the same in both modernism and postmodernism, and for similar reasons.

One further remark must be made. The points about Wright and from Fuller enable us to confirm the important observation that modernism and modern life in general are not coterminous. There are moderns who happily refuse to accept 'package deal' doctrines and opinions, to use an expression of Lord David Cecil's. But their very refusal throws into relief the general tendency of modernity's doctrines and practices, which is the suppression of otherness and so of particularity. The fact that every thing is what it is and not another thing entails the otherness of everything to everything else. That does not mean an absolute otherness, but the kind that involves the affirmation of the belief that people and things are what they distinctively are by virtue of their relations to other people and things: what I would call constitutive relatedness. It is that which so much modern dogma prevents us from realizing. Thus it is that the failure of Plato to give due place to particularity in his vision of things is replicated both in modernism's suppression of the particular through the universal and in postmodernism's homogenizing tendency to attribute to all particulars essentially the same value.

[45] Harvey, *The Condition of Postmodernity*, p. 336.

6 A PATTERN OF DISPLACEMENT

We come to the same kind of conclusion as in the previous chapter. The problem is one of displacement, of the displacement of the other, transcendent, deity into human subjectivity, and the consequent denial by human subjectivity of the necessity of respect for the other. The other becomes the person or thing from which one must escape or over which one must rule if one is to be human.[46] The terms within which Václav Havel diagnoses the modern human predicament are here of interest:

> I believe that with the loss of God, man has lost a kind of absolute and universal system of coordinates, to which he could always relate everything, chiefly himself. His world and his personality gradually began to break up into separate, incoherent fragments corresponding to different, relative, coordinates ... [47]

The term 'coordinates' is the crucial one here, for it implies a system in which particulars are truly related to one another, and yet in such a way that 'space' remains between them. We need coordinates if we are to know who we are and what our world is – a perspective from which to view and assess our various interests and actions. If there is no space between God and the world; or, rather, no God to give things space in which to be, we lose the space between one another and between ourselves and the world of particulars without which we are not truly what we are.

In the matter of aesthetics, and of human agency towards the world in general, we come face to face with the *theological* matter of the relation of God the maker and human making. The loss in recent times of the distinction between making and creating has led to the gross overuse of the latter concept in connection with human activity. The price, however, has to be paid, for once the distinction is lost between the divine act of creation out

---

[46] A speaker at a recent General Assembly of the United Reformed Church observed that the houses retired ministers were able to afford often did not allow spouses sufficient space to escape from one another. The fact that this was not put more positively is a symptom of the conceptual malaise with which we are here concerned.

[47] Havel, *Open Letters*, pp. 94–5.

of nothing and human *poiesis* on its basis, lost too is the set of coordinates which enables us to discover an appropriate stance towards the world. What eventuates is a repetition of the human self-divinization according to the argument of *The Naked Public Square* that we met at the end of the argument of the previous chapter. The exclusion of God opens the way for the admission of the demonic. When we behave towards the world as though we were God, we misconstrue and misuse in thought and action its characteristic particularity and otherness.[48]

It is significant, too, that the displacement of the concept of creation out of nothing from God to man has been observed to operate also in the sphere of social relations. Here we come to the heart of the discontinuity between ancient and modern brought about by the displacement of God. Plato, remarks Blumenberg,

had pursued ... the principle of preceding the theory of the state by a theory of the cosmos. Hobbes emphasizes – in contrast to Plato – the differentiation within the analogy ... Political reason ... does indeed come upon natural law as a preexisting circumstance, but this pregiven nature is for it nothing but the antinomy whose solution is its task, the chaos from which its creation springs. The function of philosophy, accordingly, is no longer to be the theory of the world or of the Ideas, no longer to administer a treasure imparted to man along with his existence, but rather to imitate the Creation (*imitare creationem*), to renew the original creative situation in the face of unformed matter.[49]

There lies the heart of the displacement, which is also the heart of the problem of the moral – rather than technological – irrelevance of so much of our science. When any human activity becomes the realm of pure will, of a putative creation out of

---

[48] As I have already suggested, it may be that one long-term cause of our plight is to be found in Augustine's Platonizing interpretations of the Genesis story. The understanding of the act of creation as the making of the eternal forms in the light of which particular beings were later shaped led to immense and unnecessary difficulties when theology had to encounter nineteenth-century theories of evolution. So it is here. It is more helpful both in that context and ours to consider the narrative of creation as concerned with the creation of particular beings, with giving them space to be themselves, and so 'very good'. The same kind of point is made by Adam's naming of the animals, which should not be seen in the light of modern ideologies of technocratic domination but as acts of entering into particular relations with natural things, of a giving of space within the proper dominion over the rest of nature that is the human calling.   [49] Blumenberg, *Legitimacy*, pp. 219–20.

nothing, the problems of particularity and freedom are exacerbated, not solved.

That the era of naive reconstructionist politics – the view of the politician as the *creator ex nihilo* – has apparently come to an end is from this point of view a relief.[50] But a continuing threat is to be found in the naked public square – and the naked laboratory. What devils may rush in to fill the empty space? The development of a theology of human and created – and fallen – particularity is one of the urgent tasks of our time. But before it can be attempted, further analysis of modern thought and institutions is required. In the next chapter, I shall examine the distinctively modern dimensions of the problem of living in time and space, and focus on one strange paradox. Why is it that a world dedicated to the pursuit of leisure and of machines that save labour is chiefly marked by its levels of rush, frenetic busyness and stress? But, as in the previous chapter, I would end on a positive note. The matter of particularity is, I believe, the matter of enabling the things and people of which our world consists, each in their own way, to serve as vehicles of the praise of God. It is through Christ and the Spirit, who bring us and our world, perfected, to the Father, that people and things can come to be that which they are particularly called to be. To show something of that is the ultimate purpose of this book.

---

[50] In *The Persistence of Faith. Religion, Morality and Society in a Secular Age* (London: Weidenfeld and Nicolson, 1991), p. 11, Jonathan Sacks has rightly called into question 'a tenacious modern fallacy: the omnipotence of politics ... Roughly speaking, this amounts to the view that the political system is the only significant vehicle of change in societies as secular as our own. Crime, addiction, education, environmental exploitation, even rates of marriage and divorce, are to be controlled, if at all, by government legislation.' It is to be hoped that we are freed from the view that in politics is to be found salvation, though how near it still is to the surface of much liberation and feminist theology is a question that must be asked.

CHAPTER 3

A plea for the present. The problem of relatedness in modern life and thought

I MODERNITY'S THIS-WORLDLINESS

In the second chapter, discussion centred on the modern treatment of particulars: what makes things and people particularly and distinctively what they are. I argued that modernism and postmodernism alike work for the destruction of particularity and for homogeneity, the former in subordinating the particular to rigid and universal patterns of thought and behaviour, the latter failing to make any links between things at all, and so treating everything as of equal value. At the centre once again was the theme of displacement. God is displaced from the centre of things, and just as in the first chapter he was seen to be displaced into impersonal forces, so here he is displaced into human subjectivity, with the consequent loss of coordinates charted by Václav Havel. Not God but the human will becomes the creator of value. In this third chapter we move from the problem of particularity to the corresponding question of how particular things and persons are understood to be related to one another. It will be similar in form to the second chapter, moving from an indication of some symptoms, through a brief account of some ancient and modern sources of the malaise, to two related theological analyses of the underlying problems.

One way of speaking of the modern condition is to say that, in reaction to the supposed other-worldliness of pre-modern, and especially mediaeval, culture, the modern world has affirmed in a unique and far-reaching way the priority for both being and life of time over eternity, space over infinity. We live in a this-worldly culture. Our time and space and not some distant heaven is the important reality. The affirmation has a number of aspects. One is that to be modern is to be conscious of history, of the passing of time, in a way that much pre-modern civilization was not. It is often claimed that the mediaeval world had little or no sense of history, so that Mary and Joseph would be portrayed in paintings as though they were peasants from the next village.[1]

A second aspect of modernity's this-worldliness is the repudiation of tradition which is associated with the programme of the Enlightenment and of more recent modernism to affirm the importance of the present by throwing off the dead hand of the past. The past, particularly the relatively recent past, is widely seen as oppressive and stifling for freedom of thought, enquiry and artistic endeavour. A third and related illustration would be to say that modernity is the era when a belief in fate – or, and the difference is immense, a belief in providence – gives way to a belief in the efficacy of human agency and will to determine the direction of events in time. No longer does transcendent reality dictate the form of human being in the world, but human willing. Fourth is science, in many ways the most characteristic and certainly the most successful feature of modern Western culture. In science, attention is given not to formal patterns underlying the order of space and time, as was characteristic of both ancient and mediaeval philosophical enquiry, but to configurations inherent within the structures presented to experience. Modern science studies the world of space and time, not some reality beyond them, and arose when a logical quest for timeless patterns gave way to a mathematical, hypothetical and experimental approach to the contingent rationality of space and time, as was charted by Michael Foster in his justly celebrated and frequently reprinted article.[2]

---

[1] Though would one say that the ancient Greeks and Hebrews lacked historical consciousness? Perhaps in the modern sense, but despite that there is a sense here, as in the discussion of the topics of the first two chapters, that modernity's ideology of ancient backwardness is largely coloured by a particular interpretation of mediaeval culture.

[2] Michael Foster, 'The Christian Doctrine of Creation and the Rise of Modern Natural Science', *Mind* 43 (1934), 446–68; reprinted in *Science and Religious Belief*.

All of those attempted evocations of the spirit of modernity involve oversimplification. But they make the point that must now be further probed if we are to seek the distinctiveness of modernity in this third area of human culture, and to explore the nature and outcome of the this-worldliness of the age. Although in this chapter I shall be concerned almost exclusively with time, because it is the main factor by which the many may be conceived to be bonded historically, I shall begin with allusion to space and time together because they form the parameters of this world and are to be contrasted with the supposed timelessness and unlimitedness of the world beyond. Immediately, a striking feature comes to light. One of the achievements of twentieth-century thought is the conceptual integration, especially as a result of the work of Albert Einstein, of the realms of time and space. As we shall see, they had been given surprisingly dubious status in the Newtonian world. Even in Einstein there is a Spinozistic drive to timelessness, yet as a result of his work not only were the two thought together, but they were thought of as real, as belonging to the constitution of the universe. In that respect, twentieth-century physics represents the intellectual fulfilment of the modern quest to take this world with full seriousness.

The paradox of modernity, however, is that however successful the understanding of time and space, the modern is less at home in the actual time and space of daily living than peoples less touched by the changes that have been listed. This point was suggested some years ago by a comment by Fritz Schumacher in *Small is Beautiful* that, 'the pressure and strain of living is very much less in, say, Burma, than it is in the United States, in spite of the fact that the amount of labour saving machinery used in the former country is only a minute fraction of the amount used in the latter.'[3] The paradox is that there is to be found more genuine leisure in 'undeveloped' societies than in those dedicated to the creation of leisure. It may be a

   A Selection of Recent Historical Studies, edited by C. A. Russell (London: Open University, 1973), pp. 294–315.

[3] E. F. Schumacher, *Small is Beautiful. A Study of Economics as if People Mattered* (London: Sphere Books, 1974), p. 48.

price we are willing to pay; but its origin and character are none the less worth probing.

An analysis of the situation is offered by Robert Banks in *The Tyranny of Time*, one of whose chief claims is that a culture dedicated to the creation of leisure has produced the precise opposite. 'According to one survey, almost four out of every five people in societies like our own feel continuously or regularly rushed for time.'[4] While different groups and people are differently affected, being under pressure by time is in general a clear mark of the developed West, attributable to 'regulation by the clock and our corresponding pace of life ... '[5] Banks' analysis is convincing, and points to a salient feature of modern life. Whatever the integration of space and time in science, in modern life there is at once cultural stagnation and febrile change, a restless movement from place to place, experience to experience, revealing little evidence of a serene dwelling in the body and on the good earth.

The theological analysis is interestingly parallel to David Harvey's Marxist identification of what he calls the 'time-space compression' that is so much a mark of modern consumer societies:

I mean to signal by that term processes that so revolutionize the objective qualities of space and time that we are forced to alter, sometimes in quite radical ways, how we represent the world to ourselves. I use the word 'compression' because a strong case can be made that the history of capitalism has been characterized by speed-up in the pace of life, while so overcoming spatial barriers that the world sometimes seems to collapse inwards upon us.[6]

I would, on the whole, not wish to attribute the development to capitalism, but rather to see capitalism as one of a number of features of the form of modern action in the world responsible for the syndrome Harvey has identified. The general point is

---

[4] Robert Banks, *The Tyranny of Time* (Exeter: Paternoster Press, 1983), p. 18. If one looks at the more brutal and inhumane instances of modern architecture, one could add that in many ways we are no less alienated from space. [5] Ibid., p. 25

[6] Harvey, *The Condition of Postmodernity*, p. 240. See also Marshall Berman, *All that is Solid Melts into Air. The Experience of Modernity* (New York: Verso, 1983. 1st edition 1982).

that whatever the theoretical and practical successes of our culture, and they are immense, they are bought at a price which is also very great. Once again, the possibilities for both good and evil are magnified under modern conditions. What underlies so strange a situation? As in previous chapters, we shall find paradoxes that have their roots in antiquity. I shall concentrate on the temporal dimensions of the matter, both because they are are at the heart of the problem – which may, in fact, lie in large measure in a spatializing of time – and because they raise the most pressing theological questions, some of which will be treated in Chapter 6.

In view of the range of possible ways of identifying the shape of the topic, some simplification and choice of direction will be involved. One choice will be made at the outset, and it is that we are not here concerned to pay chief attention to the concept – or rather concepts – of time developed in the modern world. Conceptual matters will concern us all the time, but the focus will be more practical and existential, for it is becoming clear that whatever we know about time, we are not in the modern world very good at using it. By looking at the way we live in the world, I shall hope to complement the themes of the previous chapter. There, it will be recalled, I said something about the failure of the modern world to treat particulars adequately. Here the interest shifts to the matter of relationality: of how the universe is bonded together, and how we indwell and so participate in that relationality. To an understanding of that the concepts of space and time are central, for they focus the relatedness of things and our place within the network they form. That is to say, they enable us to consider how we and our world belong together.

My approach will be to take up once again the four dimensions of modern this-worldliness outlined above, and consider in their interrelations history, tradition, human agency and science. And the first point to make is that the modern affirmation of the importance and centrality of time emerged by the denial of certain doctrines that were believed to be characteristic of antiquity. Among them was the belief that time was not fully real, or, if it was real, was so only as a route to eternity. As always, we must beware of simplifications of antiquity. Greek historiography, that of Herodotus for example, may have hoped to learn timeless truths from its enquiries, but it none the less looked for them within the structures of things happening in time. Similarly, things happening in and over time were of the essence for the dramatist. Greek drama shares with some of the Hebrew authors the belief that the fathers have eaten sour grapes and the children's teeth are set on edge. What is to be seen in the tragedies is a pattern of events following a remorseless temporal logic generation after generation, from the events of the Trojan War through the murder of Agamemnon, its avenging, and on into the next generation. The logic of eternity – the justice of Zeus – embraces that of time, not denying it, but shaping and controlling it.

Despite all this, it must be observed that there is a marked measure of pessimism in the way in which things are seen to work themselves out. While it is now thought wrong to make absolute distinctions between Hebrew and Greek consciousness of time, there are elements of contrast. One suggestion is that the difference of atmosphere has something to do with the fact that while Hebrew memory centres on a delivery from slavery, Greek consciousness is marked by a series of historical disasters.[7] Whatever the truth of that, it is noticeable that once the philosophers begin their work, the full reality of time and that which has its being in time is frequently called into question. This is most marked in Parmenides' absolute denial of the reality of change, but emerges also in Plato's description of time as the moving image of eternity.[8] From that time on, despite exceptions, the drive of the ancient intellect is to find reality beyond the temporal, in the timeless forms which either underlie or overlie the unreliable world of change and decay. Whatever the precise meaning of the teaching that time is the moving image of eternity, it is not meant to resound to the ontological glory of time. Put theologically, the truth seems to be that for the representative Greek mind time was not the realm in which

---

[7] So Robert Jenson, *The Triune Identity. God According to the Gospel* (Philadelphia: Fortress Press, 1982), pp. 57–8.   [8] Plato, *Timaeus*, 37d5.

to find redemption. For the most part, Greek thought cannot easily distinguish between temporality and fallenness; just as ours, in so far as it is still marked by a belief in progress, tends to equate temporal process and redemption. For the heirs of Greek philosophy, salvation, if any, is to be found by escape from time, classically in Aristotle's recommendation of the contemplative life of the philosopher as the highest form of existence.[9] Here, surely, there is an absolute divide between ancient and modern, at least so far as antiquity is represented by its Hellenic strand?

2 CHRISTIANITY'S FALSE ETERNITY

Christian theology, too, has for much of its history been somewhat ambivalent about the reality and value of time, and here we come to the second variation of the contrast between some early and some later theological accounts of the status and nature of creation. Things began well, in so far as Irenaeus can be said to represent a beginning. What is to be found in that admirable theologian is an affirmation for christological and pneumatological reasons of the goodness of the created order. The central concept he uses for his christology is one which involves time. *Recapitulation* expressed not only what would now be called the narrative structure of the Christ-history, but of that history as it takes up into itself the whole of created reality. Irenaeus' pneumatology also has an orientation to time, for he shares the eschatological orientation of the New Testament in his view of the work of the Spirit. Eschatology for him is not oriented primarily to another world that is temporally and spatially discontinuous with this one, but to that eternity wherein lies the perfecting of the created order, a perfecting that continues to be shaped as recapitulation works itself out in the life of the church.

Of central importance is that in Irenaeus no major contrast is drawn between the perfection of the timeless eternal and the imperfection of the temporal. That would have been to concede too much to gnosticism. If the order of time is the order of

---

[9] Aristotle, *Ethics*, X. 7–8.

imperfection, it is not due to its ontological inferiority but for two reasons: first its fallenness, its falling away from its due directedness, and second, and far more important for our purposes, its specific ontology, as *created* and so as depending upon God for being as it is and for being what it is. That is to say, the being of the temporal order consists in its temporal nature. It is what it is only through the fact that it must be *perfected* in and through time, by the action of the creator of time. Like a piece of music, its peculiar perfection consists in the fact that it takes time to be what it is. *In that respect* it is not ontologically inferior to that which is eternal, but merely different. In the goodness of God who created it as it is and directs it to its end, it just is like that. Temporality, taking shape in time, is its ἀρετή, its particular virtue as *creation*.

In writing a positive estimation of temporality into his doctrine of creation, Irenaeus thought together man and nature, the human and the cosmic, in a way fraught with positive possibilities for an integrated approach to being in all its dimensions, intellectual, practical and aesthetic. But his successors were not so careful, and those who followed him, particularly those more open than he was to Platonic influences, often thought apart the human and the material in such a way as to tend to alienate culture from nature. Two early culprits are Origen and Augustine. Origen was less able than Irenaeus to encompass within his thought the goodness of the material order. While his is certainly not – not quite – the gnostic negation of the world against which Irenaeus fought, there are signs that he treats the temporal order as instrumental to human salvation – as a rather unfortunate pedagogic necessity – rather than as in some way itself also redeemable. Thus he argues that God creates the material world in order to find a place of correction for the fallen spirits, while the plurality he takes to be characteristic of the material order is a sign of its inferior way of being.[10] Further, his contemplating the possibility of a plurality of worlds effects an at least partial downgrading of the space and time of this particular universe.

---

[10] Origen, *On First Principles*, II. 9.

Similarly, although Augustine anticipates later scientific thought in toying in the *Confessions* – albeit briefly and in apparent contradiction of what he says elsewhere[11] – with a relational view of time, he can never fully distinguish the temporal from the fallen. The Manichee never quite disappears. Three features of Augustine's theory of time are heavy with threat for the future. The first is his philosophy of the disappearing present. As is well known, Augustine's analysis of his experience of time appears to deny reality to the present as the disappearing margin between past and future. The decisive step is the move inwards and away from drawing out the implications of his own teaching that time is created along with the world.[12] If, by contrast, we were to conceive time not in terms of our analysis of experience but of our experience *of things*, we should not, I believe, be so inclined to say with Augustine and after Plato that 'we cannot rightly say that time *is*, except by reason of its impending state of *not being*'.[13] One of the theses I should like to affirm – and one that is a possible implication of Augustine's view that time is created with the world – is that time is best understood by virtue of what takes place in it. It is the common failure of some ancient and of some modern thought to deny this.

The second feature of Augustine's treatment is his decisive move, in drawing out the consequences of the first feature, in the direction of a view that time is a projection – in his words, an extension – of the human mind.[14] Some of the implications of that were later to be drawn out by the greatest philosopher of modernity, and we shall meet Kant later. Before that, however, let us pause for a brief account of the third feature of Augustine's view of time, as it is incorporated in his theology of history, that

[11] Augustine, *Confessions*, XII. 8: 'For time is constituted by the changes which take place in things as a result of variations and alterations in their form … ' (Pine-Coffin, p. 286). Compare XI. 26 for Augustine's rehearsal of some of the problems inherent in a relational view.

[12] To characterize the move inwards as a mark of modernity is to give to Augustine some responsibility for the development of modernity.

[13] *Confessions*, XI. 14 (p. 264).

[14] Ibid., XI. 26: 'I begin to wonder whether it is an extension of the mind itself' (p. 274).

sphere where a major feature of our culture's concept of time comes clearly into the light of day. The question to him is this: how far does he conceive the order of time to be inherently and essentially the place of disorder rather than – say – of a fallenness whose redemption is the hope of the Christian gospel? As Robert Markus has shown in his classic study of Augustine's thought, the answer is not an easy one. One key to Augustine's view of the historical process is to be found in the eschatology that derives from his view of the completeness of what happened in Christ. After that, and before the end, 'No historical conditions can provide so much as a shadow of this fulfilment ... '[15] There is no realized eschatology for Augustine, or rather there is an eschatology realized only in the incarnation and at the end of time: accordingly, there is no anticipated eschatology. After the incarnation and before the end, all history is equally fallen. His mature view, says Markus interestingly, is of the essential homogeneity of history: 'since the coming of Christ, until the end of the world, all history is homogeneous ... '[16]

It is the occurrence of the word *homogeneity* that gives real pause for thought in connection with the theme of this book.[17] As that account shows, and as Dietrich Ritschl long ago argued,[18] underlying Augustine's eschatology is a particular christology, and christology has crucial bearing on the concept of time, for it concerns the place where God and the world are thought together.[19] Is God truly involved in temporality according to Augustine's doctrine of the incarnation? Ritschl thinks not, but if God is not, that is to say, if the incarnation is

[15] Markus, *Saeculum*, p. 166.
[16] Ibid., pp. 20f. That is tantamount to saying, or at least does not discourage the thought, that what happens in time is of necessity fallen. It is similar to the postmodern view that everything that happens is equally interesting (and therefore equally uninteresting).
[17] It is surely no accident that it has been a feature of all the aspects of modernity we have so far examined. Later in this chapter, my argument will be that it is where it is most like antiquity that the modern world falls into its characteristic tendency to homogenize.
[18] Dietrich Ritschl, *Memory and Hope. An Enquiry Concerning the Presence of Christ* (London: Collier-Macmillan, 1967).
[19] Indeed, *are* together: *tempus est forma in qua Deus cum mundo concurrit.*

for Augustine a timeless presence inserted into time rather than a genuinely economic action, there is written into Western thought the antinomy which has since the end of the Middle Ages been of much importance in the way things have turned out. In Chapter 2 I argued in support of the claim made by Michael Buckley in particular that much of the responsibility for the development of modernity against theology lies in the mediaeval tendency to conceive God apart from his temporal manifestation in the historical economy. At the root of Buckley's enquiry is a question:

The absence of any consideration of christology is so pervasive throughout serious discussion that it becomes taken for granted, yet it is so stunningly curious that it raises a fundamental issue of the modes of thought: How did the issue of Christianity vs. atheism become purely philosophical? To paraphrase Tertullian: How was it that the only arms to defend the temple were to be found in the Stoa?[20]

If I am here ascribing various ills to modernity's displacement of God, it should also be made plain that much of the responsibility for that displacement is to be attributed to unsatisfactory Christian theology, and particularly the theology of creation, so that modern theological scepticism can in part be understood as a call to Christianity to be true to its own lights. In this case, the insight we must maintain is the one already attributed to Irenaeus: that the economic divine involvement in the world of time and space has important implications for the way we shall regard our time and history, and therefore our modern times. It is the positive concern for living in time that Christianity submerged in a false eternalizing of the divine economy, and which modernity has attempted to appropriate apart from Christianity. That is both modernity's and Christianity's tragedy. I would here also allude again to Blumenberg's extended argument that late mediaeval theology bears many of the marks of gnosticism, and that modernity therefore can be held to represent a form of liberation from gnosticism. Gnosticism, in the sense of a denial of the goodness and meaningfulness of the world of time, is encouraged by a theology that is

---

[20] Buckley, *Origins*, p. 33, cf. pp. 47, 54–5, 67, etc.

pessimistic because it lacks christological and pneumatological determinants and thus divorces creation and redemption. We shall return to Blumenberg's thesis, only part of which I accept.

3 MODERNITY'S FALSE TEMPORALITY

When we consider the fourth and most characteristic feature of the modern world's this-worldliness, the development of natural science, we shall find complications, and above all the lineaments of our now familiar paradox. I have already alluded to Michael Foster's well-known article about the origins of modern science as the realization in culture of the Christian theological affirmation of the meaningfulness inherent within the created order. The point has been developed in more recent times by Professor T. F. Torrance and others: the rationality of science is, unlike that of the Greeks, a contingent rationality, being found as a function of the intrinsic relationality of space-time configurations and not in abstract formal concepts underlying space and time.[21] At least to that extent, the thesis that the Christian doctrine of creation had a positive hand in the development of one aspect of modern culture is plausible. But it is also becoming evident that other cultural and ideological forces shared in giving modern science the particular form that it took.

One significant cuckoo in the nest is the Platonizing contrast between appearance and reality, which made its chief impact in the development of Newton's concept of absolute space and time. According to the much cited scholium to his *Principia Mathematica*, there exists, underlying the space and time of our experience – relative space and time – absolute space and time. The significant feature of the concept is its effective relegation to secondary status of experienced space and time, for it encourages the belief that experienced space and time are in some way not fully real.[22] Because absolute time is not really

---

[21] T. F. Torrance, *Divine and Contingent Order* (Oxford: Oxford University Press, 1981).

[22] 'Here, then, on the one hand, time and space are considered absolutely in themselves without relation to anything external, as homogeneous and isotropic, undifferentiated and unchanging ... On the other hand, time and space are also considered in

temporal, time does not really belong to the inner being of things. Thus the science of temporal things is undergirded by an appeal to a timeless substratum, and in a different way time becomes but the moving image of eternity. One particular corollary cannot be stressed too strongly: for Newtonian science, time is spatialized, in the sense that it is conceived as reversible.[23] It therefore becomes irrelevant to the real being, as distinct from the appearance, of temporal reality. A similar and parallel process takes place in Kant, except that he makes the second rather than the third of Augustine's moves, to a form of projectionism. But the effect is much the same. According to Kant, too, time (and space) are not part of the being of things; they are only part of the being of things as perceived by the mind. Just as out of Newton comes a science of a timeless universe, from Kant emerges a theory that teaches that ideas of space and time are imposed upon the world, rather than intrinsic to it.[24] We experience time because it is, in Augustine's words, an extension of our minds. The outcome is a science that is fundamentally sceptical about the mind's knowledge of what is really there: a truly radical version of Plato's ontological divide between appearance and reality.

It was against this background that the great modern philosopher of time, G. W. F. Hegel, entered the lists. Hegel's interest for us is that he accepted what I have called the displacement theory – according to which one of the marks of modernity is the displacement of the unknown, late mediaeval deity into forms of immanence – and turned it to Christian theological use. All the Christian themes – Christ, the Trinity, time, history – are employed in the service of a new vision of

terms of different particular systems which arise within the universe…' T. F. Torrance, *Transformation and Convergence within the Frame of Knowledge. Explorations in the Interrelations of Scientific and Theological Enterprise* (Belfast: Christian Journals, 1984), p. 21.

[23] The late modern move away from a conception of time as reversible is one of the leading themes of Ilya Prigogine and Isabelle Stengers, *Order out of Chaos. Man's New Dialogue with Nature* (London: Fontana, 1985).

[24] 'It is, therefore…indubitably certain, that space and time, as the necessary conditions of all outer and inner experience, are merely subjective conditions of all our intuition, and that in relation to these conditions all objects are therefore mere appearances…' Kant, *Critique of Pure Reason*, p. 86.

things. Salvation takes place in time; time is the realm of divine action. Christologically, Hegel focused on the passion and death of Christ as a way of finding room for a theology of the death of God. That is to say, he accepted the displacement theory and turned it to theological advantage. In this way, the doctrine of the Trinity became a way of providing an interpretation of the meaning of time. The Christian concern for history as saving history was made a way of showing that time is the locus of salvation, the realm where saving divine reality takes shape. But it was very much an immanently conceived form of divine action. Time became the realm of divine self-realization *by means of* human cultural achievement.

That there is an unacceptable price to pay for all such forms of theological displacement is one of the theses being argued in this book. The price has been particularly high in this case because it has been exacted not only by Hegel but by those who rejected his metaphysical thesis while remaining within the framework in which he sought the meaning of things in time. The price demanded by Hegel himself is that required by all forms of explicit and implicit divinization of the finite. What appears to be designed to save the realm of time, and especially the Christian economy within it, concludes by abolishing it. Not only does the unique divinity of Christ become, as Kierkegaard pointed out, its opposite – a pagan ascription of divinity to all – but the movement of divine Spirit immanently within time has the effect of nullifying the original intent. Thus for Hegel the outcome is finally the same as that we have found with Newton and Kant. Something happens to bring about the relegation of time to unimportance, because it is the means of the realization of something that is not time. The theological root of the development is that for Hegel God is so displaced into time that time loses its own proper being. In effect he concedes this point in the obscure and fragmentary last section of the *Phenomenology of Spirit*, by suggesting that the realization of Spirit eventually renders time obsolete:

Spirit necessarily appears in time, and it appears in time, so long as it does not grasp its pure notion, i.e. so long as it does not annul time. Time is the pure self in external form ... not grasped and understood by the self... When this notion grasps itself, it supersedes its time character... Time therefore appears as spirit's destiny and necessity, where spirit is not yet complete within itself...[25]

By ascribing supratemporal significance to a merely immanent phenomenon, whether christologically defined or not, Hegel has finally deprived time of its significance as time. It is thus abolished. As I hope to show in a later chapter, the mistake is not the use of christology or of the concept of spirit, but the way in which they are construed by Hegel.

Two historical responses to Hegel show the price that has been paid. They both suggest that to make the process of time absolute – to lose the coordinate of transcendent eternity – is effectively also to lose the very time that is so important. The first is Marxism – Hegel inverted – which is in large part a historical determinism. It says that what happens is bound to happen, so that temporal process is closed. What happens in time is simply the outworking of fate, so that its truly temporal character is destroyed. Marxist historical determinism has undoubtedly proved an effective – if usually baneful – motor of human action, yet has destroyed the significance of time by directing it to a goal merely immanently prescribed. The second historical response to Hegel is to be found in historical relativism, which, in its modern form arises when the historical process is deprived of the rational thrust provided by Hegelian Spirit.[26] There are, to be sure, different forms of historical relativism, but they all tend to have the effect of suggesting the homogeneity of history. On the one hand, they suggest that all times and places are to be understood exhaustively in terms of their temporal context, with the result that no era or event can be distinguished from any other with respect to its significance. On the other, for example in the Troeltschian form, they tend to impose extraneous criteria of meaning – for example, criteria derived from deterministic Newtonian physics or other modern

[25] G. W. F. Hegel, *The Phenomenology of Mind*, translated by J. B. Baillie (London: George Allen and Unwin, 1949), p. 800. The word annul, *tilgt*, is a strong one. *G. W. F.Hegel's Werke, Band* 2, Berlin 1841, p. 584.

[26] Helmut Kuhn, 'Personal Knowledge and the Crisis of the Philosophical Tradition', *Intellect and Hope. Essays in the Thought of Michael Polanyi*, edited by T. A. Langford and W. H. Poteat (Durham, NC: Duke University Press, 1968), pp. 111–35 (p. 132).

dogma – on historical eras and so reduce all eras to homo-geneity. Despite all the complexities of Troeltsch's position,[27] the logic of the matter is similar to that of the other metaphysics of immanence that we have met. The lack of transcendent coordinates provided by a theology of God as other than the historical process encourages the generation, by reflex as it were, of homogenizing immanent criteria. Notable in this case is the 'principle of analogy' which has been used to undermine, in the name of historical method, the occurrence and in-telligibility of unique and miraculous historical events such as the resurrection.[28] Once again, as we saw in the last chapter, the loss of theology leads to a disorientation in the way coordinate realities are treated. Or rather, it is not so much the loss of theology that is the cause as its displacement into the patterns of judgement of the human mind. As we have found before, modernity in that way comes to replicate the intellectual vices attributed to antiquity, but in a displaced form: the homo-geneity of history effected from within, rather than from without.

4 THE DISPLACEMENT OF ESCHATOLOGY

What is the theological root of the problem? I have already used the notion of displacement, as in the preceding chapters. The unique feature of the situation as we view it in the light of an analysis of time is that we meet in it the displacement not only of the divine will, but of the divine Spirit also. In Chapter 2, in connection with Blumenberg's analysis of modernity, we saw that creation is displaced from divine to human agency. In this context, redemption as well as creation becomes a human achievement. In the case of time, the displacement takes interesting temporal form: it has to do with the way we come to regard the process of time. There results what can only be called a displaced eschatology. As previously we traced the way in

---

[27] Sarah Coakley, *Christ without Absolutes. A Study of the Christology of Ernst Troeltsch* (Oxford: Clarendon Press, 1988), chapter 1.

[28] The method is used to destructive effect in Van Harvey, *The Historian and the Believer. The Morality of Historical Knowledge and Christian Belief* (London: SCM Press, 1967).

which the concept of creation came to be called into question, so it is here with eschatology. Responsibility for the *end* of things as well as for their beginning is displaced from divine to human agency. It is at this point that there develops the characteristically modern stress upon the future as, we might say, the place where it all happens. The motifs of both displacement and immanence reappear:

> The transformation of progress into a faith encompassing the future requires not only that it should be a principle immanent in history – that is, that it *can* emerge from the reason that is operative in individual human actions – it also requires that this principle should *in fact* be active and continue to be so.[29]

It thus falls to the human agent not only to impose patterns of rationality on to recalcitrant nature, but to determine its future also.

One revealing symptom of the displacement of eschatology is to be found in the modern obsession with the future. The anxiety to bring the future about is the cause of the frantic rush that is one mark of the modern failure to live serenely in time. Projects and lives are not allowed to mature in their own time, but must be catapulted into the future with ever increasing desperation because, as is well known, the future never comes. To borrow a distinction from George Steiner, innovation replaces originality, with its rather different temporal connotations:

> Originality is antithetical to novelty. The etymology of the word alerts us. It tells of 'inception' and of 'instauration', of a return, in substance and in form, to beginnings.[30]

'The future', as it serves as a modern ideology, is another of the false abstractions that we have met elsewhere and that operate oppressively because they constrain life into false patterns of meaning. The placard on a building site bearing words such as: 'Sainsbury's: creating a new future' illustrates the point. What they mean is that someone is building yet another probably

---

[29] Blumenberg, *Legitimacy*, p. 49.
[30] George Steiner, *Real Presences. Is There Anything in What We Say?* (London: Faber and Faber, 1989), p. 27.

unnecessary supermarket. But the words are symptomatic of the great illusion of modernity that we create the future. That is rather different from the more modest desire to shape it by considered action in the present, for it generates an incapacity to live in the present, with what is given. The given disappears because it is grasped at.

As the result of the displacement, a number of things happen. The effective divinization of the agent brings about, as Robert Banks has pointed out, a parallel divinization of time. Describing the modern proliferation of clocks and other mechanical devices, he comments that, 'Having consciously shaped our desires in certain new directions, we become further shaped by the very mechanisms created to achieve those desires, and the mechanisms in turn create still further desires that we seek to satisfy ... Clock time has become tyrannical and all-pervasive. Our pattern of life is largely controlled by the clock and calendar.'[31] Thus does the personal come into demonic subordination to the impersonal or cosmic forces it has itself let loose: the Sorcerer's Apprentice with a vengeance.[32] Another parallel outcome is that substitute cosmic eschatologies rush in to fill the vacuum, as is illustrated by the speculations to be found in Barrow and Tipler's *The Anthropic Cosmological Principle*.[33]

There is a number of ways in which much modern theology colludes in the pursuit of an abstraction. It is not, of course, a straightforward collusion, but derives from a mistaking of what

[31] Banks, *The Tyranny of Time*, pp. 126–7.
[32] Karl Barth makes a similar point in speaking of the 'lordless powers of earth that lord it over us'. 'Why does it seem to be to even the most sensible women, if not an act of lese majesty, at least an impossibility to be old-fashioned? Who wants it this way? The particular industry that tirelessly makes money out of it and whose kings, we are told, reside especially in Paris? But who has made these people the kings?' *The Christian Life. Church Dogmatics Volume* 4, 4 *Lecture Fragments*, translated by G. W. Bromiley (Grand Rapids: Eerdmans, 1981), p. 229. There follow remarks to the same effect about the modern worship of 'what is called sport'.
[33] Barrow and Tipler, *The Anthropic Cosmological Principle*, chapter 10, and note the passage cited in Chapter 2 above, note 29. The debate about the anthropic principle replicates the two sides of the question of the modern world that I have been tracing. In some – the more objectivizing – constructions of the latter principle, the ancient doctrine of the interrelation of cosmology and anthropology reasserts itself; in others – the more subjective or idealist interpretations – we have echoes of the view that human rationality constitutes the rationality of things.

is required for the revision of traditional eschatology. The latter, as is often pointed out, tended to reduce eschatology to a pure future, unconnected to the present except as the end to which earthly life was directed. Despite the inadequacies of this conception, I do not believe that we should wholeheartedly adopt the modern disparagement of ancient other-worldliness and see in it only an evasion of the value of this life. It is not so in every respect. Orientation to a divinely promised future sets human life in context, and is by no means a disincentive to appropriate use of this world. (We should remember Luther's remark that if he knew that the end of the world was coming tomorrow, his response would be to plant a tree.) What mainstream mediaeval eschatology lacked was rather a sense of the interweaving of the times: of a way in which the divinely ordered destiny of life could, by the work of the Spirit, be anticipated in the present. According to such a view, the future destination of the world is, by grace, anticipated in the present. Indeed, in the teaching of Jesus the present is reconstituted – not *created* – by the breaking in from the future of the promised Kingdom of God. It is to do justice to the biblical notion of the openness of the times to one another that 'theologians of hope' have rightly attempted a shift in the temporal orientation of theology.

However, I do not believe that the revision of eschatology is satisfactorily achieved merely by a shift of temporal orientation, like that according to which Pannenberg wishes to accord priority to the future. His teaching that the world is created from the future is justified as an attempt to correct the felt inadequacy of those theologies, both ancient and modern, which, by weighting the being of things completely to the past appear to close them off from freedom and change. But his failure is to be found in his replicating the past weakness in a new form. It is significant, if ironical, that, as Timothy Bradshaw has argued, Pannenberg is weakest where he appears strongest, in eschatology. According to him, Pannenberg has no conception of what happens at the end of time,[34] so that the eternity

---

[34] Timothy Bradshaw, *Trinity and Ontology. A Comparative Study of the Theologies of Karl Barth and Wolfhart Pannenberg* (Edinburgh: Rutherford House, 1989), pp. 340–1.

of God appears finally to be dependent on the future of the world: a version of the displacement we have noticed in secular thought.[35] The problem seems to be that Nietzsche's concept of an open future – yet another time that is not defined by what takes place concretely in it – has replaced the notion of hope, which, certainly in its theological form, is directed to that which will take place in the future, not as the effects of arbitrary human willing, but as particular acts in fulfilment of divine promise.[36] As a mere abstraction, empty of actual or promised content, the future is a much overrated realm.

A more adequate account of the relation of God to time is to be found in maintaining the delicate balance between, on the one hand, creation and redemption and, on the other, divine action and human response. The breaking in of the future kingdom does require obedient and active human response. But, given human fallibility and fallenness, that can take shape only on the basis of the past divine creation and reconciliation by means of which is laid the foundation of present and future redemption. Once we take it that the end of human action is in some way to bring about the future without reference to the orientation provided by the coordinates of creation and reconciliation, the displacement that I have noted comes into play. Human fallibility and sin are, or tend to be, ignored, so that divine functions are almost inevitably transferred to the finite agent, with disastrous results.

In opposition to such a conception, I would argue that we require a reaffirmation of the centrality of the present for those whose createdness makes them creatures who know little of the past and even less of the future. In that respect the words of Ecclesiastes 3.11, like so many of his words, can come to us as gospel: 'he has put eternity into man's mind, yet so that he cannot find out what God has done from the beginning to the

---

[35] Ibid., p. 295. It must be emphasized that in his more recent work Pannenberg appears to be moving to a rather different position.

[36] 'Work without Hope draws nectar in a sieve / And Hope without an object cannot live.' Those lines, cited by Kathleen Coburn, are not the most profound of Coleridge's output, but make the point well enough. *In Pursuit of Coleridge* (London: The Bodley Head, 1977), p. 190.

end'. Human action is concerned first of all with the present, because that is where we are. That is not to deny any future directedness, for it would be a mistake to ignore the fact that human action is necessarily teleological. The point is rather to indicate firmly the limits of human agency. The anonymous graffito cited by John Barrow[37] that 'Time is God's way of keeping things from happening all at once' is a strangely telling way of reminding us that unlike God we do try to make things all happen at once. That is the point of an abstract desire to make the future happen. Rather, it is the present that must be understood as that which, through Christ and the Spirit, is given from the past and redirected to its true end by the one God, creator and redeemer. The breaking of the balance between past creation and present redemption exacts a price, and it is there that the colluding of theology with modernity's alienation is to be found. In the light of such a revised theology of the economy, I turn to an analysis of the distinctive character of modernity's alienation.

5 GNOSTICISM RENEWED

Earlier in this chapter I cited some writers who are of the opinion that the modern attitude to and use of time shows symptoms of the pathological: a neurotic rather than a free use of time. It is that latter concept which provides the greatest difficulty for one who would attempt to identify the distinct character of the malaise, if such it is, for the human use of time is bound up with freedom. We should welcome the modern age in so far as it has increased consciousness of the openness of time and the consequent broadening of possibilities. My question in this section concerns the way in which *in certain respects* freedom has been diminished rather than increased. It is not intended as a root and branch attack on all aspects of the modern concern for freedom, but rather to ask in which respects our way of doing things is self-defeating.

An approach can be made through observation of the

---

[37] Barrow, *Theories of Everything*, p. 44.

ambivalence of modernity to tradition. One widespread characteristic of modernity is its rejection of tradition in the name of freedom. We must remember the original context of the rejection: the early modern concern to free thought from what it believed with some justification to be its restriction by ecclesiastical obscurantism. While the theology of the Reformers was in practice marked by a dispute about the place and use of tradition rather than the rejection of it that is sometimes suggested,[38] later thought tends to lose all patience with the past, and, with Descartes, to attempt to begin all over again. It is as if the only way to be free is to begin with an absolutely clean sheet.

What, in general, is the matter at stake? The use of tradition concerns the way in which later generations of thinkers and agents shall receive that which their predecessors hand on to them in process of time. Although it is largely a word implying a passive stance, reception is a process involving both passive and active dimensions, at least in the sense that the grateful reception of a gift has implications for its responsible use and offering for reception to future agents. Tradition, that is to say, involves a personal relatedness to others in both past and future time. It involves recognition of the uniqueness and value of that which is given, but also of its incorporation into the – equally unique – present personal action. But it is also very much bound up with our concept of freedom. What is it to be free in relation to other people? To deny the salutary character of tradition is to say that we can only be ourselves by freeing ourselves *from* others – by suppressing the other – rather than being set free by them. Again, this is not a simple matter. Tradition mediates also fallibility and fallenness, and in order to make grateful use of the work of my teachers I must also come to decisions about what I shall take from them, and what reject. But if I come to believe that I have nothing to receive, I am denying something central to their humanity and mine.

---

[38] Although it is sometimes stated that the Reformers rejected tradition, it is rather the case that they rejected it as an independent source of truth. Their positive attitude to it as a relation to the past is to be seen in their use of the Fathers and Councils as authorities, although not absolute authorities.

It is very important for us to remember that in the most successful realm of modern culture, the natural sciences, there is a very strong sense of tradition, as Polanyi has demonstrated beyond dispute. As an illustration we can cite the generous avowals by Einstein of his debt to such as Newton, Faraday and Clerk Maxwell.[39] As Polanyi shows by reference to the social structures of the enterprise, science is not individualistic, whatever is sometimes said by some of its ideologues. On the contrary, its success in large part depends upon its organization as a range of interacting human communities with a strong sense of communal authority and tradition.[40] But that is not the widely believed modern account, which is that truth comes by the denial of the past, that is, by fundamentally sceptical reception of tradition, and it is that which appears to have made it difficult to receive the tradition gladly and yet critically. In so far as culture attempts to live by the ideology of beginning all over again – the permanent exercise of creation out of nothing – it falls into schools that appear to contradict each other's very basis. The outcome is a culture parts of which appear to be attempts to be free of history, while other parts fall into gross historicism: with, for example, some musicians seeking to free themselves completely from historic forms, while others slavishly reconstruct the exact manner of playing and instrumentation of the era in which the music was written. Side by side we find a restless and irrational thirst for novelty and the development of the museum and heritage culture.[41] It is this paradox which surely marks modernity uniquely, and it derives from a failure to understand what it is to live in time, which is neither to be free from time nor to be slavishly bound to it.

Below that level, however, there are more malevolent forces at work. I approach their identification with a return to

---

[39] Albert Einstein, *The World as I See It*, translated by Alan Harris (London: John Lane the Bodley Head, 1935), pp. 146–63.

[40] Polanyi, *Personal Knowledge*, chapter 7.

[41] Harvey, *The Condition of Postmodernity*, p. 303: 'The irony is that the tradition is now often preserved by being commodified and marketed as such ... At best, historical tradition is reorganized as a museum culture ... of how things once upon a time were made, sold, consumed, and integrated into a long-lost and often romanticized daily life ... '

Blumenberg's thesis that modernity represents a second over-coming of gnosticism. Over against the late mediaeval rupture of creation from salvation, he argues, the modern scientific enterprise represents the human imposing of rationality where it had been theologically denied during the period from Irenaeus to the Middle Ages.[42] The essence of his contention is that because culture is united subjectively, gnosticism is overcome. The outcome, I wish to argue, is, quite to the contrary, a renewed form of gnosticism, which enters to fill the vacuum left by theology. It is of the essence of, for example, the Manichaean form of gnosticism, that it regards the material world of space and time as fundamentally evil.[43] To this it dualistically contrasts the power of human freedom and rationality. Much modern ideology is touched with a Manichaean denial of the intrinsic goodness of the spatio-temporal order and a correlative overestimation of the possibilities of free human action in and towards it.

Characteristically modern forms of failure to come to terms with the limitations of existence in time are to be found in the work of some scientists. One feature is the alienation of science from the rest of culture, for example in failures to relate scientific discovery to ethics. A good example here is to be found in Jacques Monod's divorce of the logic of biological temporality from patterns of human living in the world. The world, he believes, is shown by his discoveries to be humanly meaningless; therefore one must make an ungrounded choice for one form of politics – in his case, socialist – rather than any other.[44] Similar is the much cited concluding judgement of Steven Weinberg's *The First Three Minutes* on the first moments of the evolution of the universe:

It is very hard to realize that this all is just a tiny part of an overwhelmingly hostile universe. It is even harder to realize that this present universe has evolved from an unspeakably unfamiliar early condition, and faces a future extinction of endless cold or intolerable

---

[42] Blumenberg, *Legitimacy*, Part 2, chapter 3.
[43] Peter Brown, *Augustine of Hippo. A Biography* (London: Faber and Faber, 1969), chapter 5. [44] Jacques Monod, *Chance and Necessity*, pp. 166–7.

heat. The more the universe seems comprehensible, the more it also seems pointless.[45]

Characteristically – that is, rather gnostically – Weinberg proceeds to offer the rational life, by which all this is given the grace of tragedy, as a way of elevating ourselves out of the mess.

However, what assumption underlies that pessimistic denial of the point of it all? It appears to be that because the universe is temporally limited, it is pointless. For all the mysterious rationality of its structures, it is fundamentally meaningless because it is destined to disappear. But must the universe be eternal if it is to have meaning? Modernity's robust affirmation of the present has declined into a loss of confidence that there is a logic of temporality: a meaning to be found within the structures of created temporality. But is a piece of music pointless because it has a last note, a life because it is bracketed by birth and death? The answer to that is: not necessarily. It depends upon what is understood of the possibility of salvation, of a final meaning, of recapitulation, indeed, of resurrection. But the fact that it remains an open question for culture does not detract from the basic point that it smacks of gnosticism to *equate* temporality and meaninglessness.

Manichaean denial of the goodness of the world is, without doubt, to be found in plenty in modern culture. Some modern art and music appears to be predicated upon it, and one or two examples will suffice. The first comes from a review of the Metropolis exhibition in Berlin:

Its ostensible theme is the speed, sex and violence available so freely in the cities of the West... The commentary informs us... that 'the present situation as outlined by Rosenthal suggests that reality is above all produced by man and not by nature.' Philosophers please note.

What, then, is the 'man-made reality' the Western world has to offer for those fleeing the gruesome rhetoric and grey homogeneity of the Marxist world at this, the very gateway between the two? What would a young worker from the East ... glean from a first face-to-face encounter with the envied culture of the West? The first object he would see on entering the ... exhibition would be a 35-foot-high

[45] Steven Weinberg, *The First Three Minutes. A Modern View of the Origin of the Universe* (London: Flamingo, 2nd edition 1983), pp. 148–9.

Disneyesque figure clad in ballet attire and clown's head twitching one hand and foot feebly in some faint parody of natural movement ... Does the figure's occasionally spasmodic jerk suggest more strongly the vitality of Western culture or a society of deepening decadence acting out its death throes?

I use this illustration partly because in the same symbolic city the reviewer visited another exhibition, of the works of Anselm Kiefer, which are, he says, concerned with the Holocaust, death and inhumanity. 'Unlike most of the artists of *Metropolis* he is a true poet; an archivist of his country's myth and history, he puts the colours of dust and death to the service of a redemptive vision.'[46]

There are, as we see from this, at least two modernities, the one gnostic, the other still able to envisage the possibilities of redemption. Without denying the presence of the latter – that would itself be a gnostic pessimism – I am concerned in this work with the nature and symptoms of those aspects of modernity which lead to the undermining of human values and the integrity of the creation. In this chapter, there is added to the picture sketched in the first two a third dimension. To the loss of the other, the theme of the second chapter, we add the loss of the present, lost to an abstraction and to a renewed gnosticism. Modern culture is marked by a pathological inability to live in the present, while at the same time, as in the consumer culture, it is unable to live anywhere but in the present. Both arms of the paradox alike derive from a gnostic denial of the goodness of the creation. The main distinctive feature of the modern gnosticism is that it is to be found in a characteristically post- (often anti-) Christian and demonic form. As we have found in earlier chapters, add to ancient gnostic and rationalist dogmas both the denial of God and the

---

[46] Giles Auty , 'Prosaic Pontificators', *The Spectator*, 27 April, 1991 34–5. Peter Fuller makes similar points about Gilbert and George and Francis Bacon. Of the former: 'In fact, their images cannot rise above their obsessive preoccupation with urban violence, lumpen philistinism, sexual products and organs, and personal depravity.' Similarly he speaks of 'the evil genius of Francis Bacon, who had abandoned a career as a designer of modernist furniture ... to paint images of irredeemably fallen men and women, living in a world in which Cimabue's *Crucifixion* was, according to Bacon, of no greater significance than an image of a worm crawling down a cross.' *Theoria*, pp. 3, 199.

Christian theological emphasis on the free and rational will, and there results an explosive mixture. As we are beginning to see, that which began in a modern reassertion of rationalism has led by a process with which we are now familiar to the denial that meaning and truth are there to be found in our universe.

And that leads us to the fourth problematic feature of the modern world. How is it that modernity, dedicated as it once was to the pursuit of truth, has given birth to a range of ideologies which deny truth's existence? That will be the concern of the final chapter of Part One. But, looking towards Part Two, I end this chapter by affirming my belief that Christianity's calling in the world remains that of offering the modern world a redemptive vision, centred on the life, death and resurrection of him through whom all things cohere, who by his incarnation shared our time in all its fallenness, so that with us it might come redeemed and perfected to its creator.

CHAPTER 4

The rootless will. The problem of meaning and truth in modern life and thought

I DISSENTING VOICES

In the previous chapters three aspects of a theology of modernity were traced, and there was an examination of the ways in which the modern world both arises out of the ancient and reduplicates, in its own distinctive ways, questionable features of antiquity's view of things. I argued that in both eras there are to be found grave deficiencies in the way in which the relation of the one and the many is conceived and practised, and that these in turn entail that the particularity of the many is in different ways endangered. The characteristic peril of the modern is to be found in the tendency to homogeneity, to the intellectual and social pressures by which the distinctive individuality of people and things is endangered. In Chapter 3, with particular reference to the concept of time, I examined one dimension of the way in which we conceive the relatedness of things, that is, the way in which the universe and its inhabitants are bound together. Here, too, there are symptoms of a lack of ease with living in the world, so that, paradoxically, the modern conquest of time has appeared to engender a new slavery, a tyranny of time, in which, once again, human and worldly integrity are brought into question. What makes modernity distinctive is its displacement of God. Modernity as an ideology arises not only out of antiquity, but also by means of an attempt in various ways to displace God as the transcendent focus of life in the world, that is, as the one who provides our being with its coordinates.

Part One comes to an end with an encounter with some of the

ways in which the question of meaning and truth is treated in modern culture. Here we discover another paradoxical feature of the intellectual firmament. Where some theologians are embracing with enthusiasm the postmodern denial of the possibility of objective meaning and truth, so sharing in the betrayal of what is best in modern culture, the angriest and often most authentically theological protests come from those outside the ranks of the official defenders of religion. The burden of the complaints of these writers concerns the deleterious effects upon culture, society and morality of the subjectivism, emotivism and relativism that are so prevalent in modern thought. By emotivism I mean the belief that judgements of value, whether moral or aesthetic, are to be understood as the expressions of the emotions of those making them rather than of the truth of being. Relativism is by no means so easy to define, in view of the variety of forms it can take. Some forms of relativism are compatible with a view that truth is in some way objective. The burden of the complaints of those who oppose particular modern versions is that radical forms of relativism undermine human culture in a way detrimental to, if not destructive of, human social living. These are the versions of relativism which hold that judgements of fact are so radically relative to the individuals or cultures which make them that there is in principle no way of deciding whether they are true in themselves, independently of the subjectivity of the makers of them. It is noteworthy that many recent books dealing with different aspects of modern culture have arisen from engagement with what their authors believe to be the consequences of modern relativism.

Wayne C. Booth's *Modern Dogma and the Rhetoric of Assent* arose out of a concern with the behaviour of the embattled parties in the American student unrest in the 1960s. What he believed to underlie the behaviour he met there was the death of the tradition of rhetoric as an institutionalized way of isolating questions in dispute and moving towards a solution. Two of Booth's observations concern us particularly. The first is that the death of rhetoric is the reason why much modern political dispute takes the form of aggressive confrontation rather than rational engagement: the demonstration rather than the *disputatio*. Given loss of confidence in argument, the noisy and potentially violent demonstration is all that remains. The second is that the death of the practice of rhetoric derives from a combination of the overvaluation of the success of scientific method and an undervaluation, if not complete relativization, of the methods of the humanities.[1] It will be evident how much this analysis has in common with Alasdair MacIntyre's more famous characterization of the breakdown of communication in disputes about moral questions. MacIntyre has argued that there is in the modern world a complete breakdown of a common language in which to argue and decide moral disputes. Listen, he says, to any argument about abortion or nuclear arms, and you will find that opponents speak past each other's shoulders because they lack a common language in which to communicate. The reason is to be found in emotivism.[2]

A diagnosis of American conditions similar to that of Booth's underlies Allan Bloom's much discussed *The Closing of the American Mind*. His concern is the more general one of the moral and intellectual health of American culture, which he believes to have been undermined by the almost axiomatic relativism of the educators. The problem is the cult of openness:

Openness used to be the virtue that permitted us to seek the good by using reason. It now means accepting everything and denying reason's power. The unrestrained and thoughtless pursuit of openness, without recognizing the inherent political, social or cultural problem of openness as the goal of nature, has rendered openness meaningless ... Openness to closedness is what we teach.[3]

Two of those analyses, however, are largely restricted to North America. By contrast, Alain Finkielkraut's thesis takes us into the effects of modern relativism on the cultures of nations.

---

[1] Wayne C. Booth, *Modern Dogma and the Rhetoric of Assent* (Chicago and London: University of Chicago Press, 1974), pp. 3–11 and chapter 3.

[2] Alasdair MacIntyre, *After Virtue. A Study in Moral Theory* (London: Duckworth, 1981), chapter 2.

[3] Allan Bloom, *The Closing of the American Mind. How Higher Education Has Failed Democracy and Impoverished the Souls of Today's Students* (London: Penguin Books, 1987), pp. 38–9.

In *The Undoing of Thought* he describes how the efforts of
Western nations to expiate through UNESCO the effects of an
earlier tendency to impose their culture on others led to a
doctrine of the equality of all cultures and the denial of all
universal values. But the expulsion of one devil leaves room for
the entry of a worse one, for lost is the notion of a common
humanity. 'Of the two European versions of what a nation is,
the Third World has massively opted for the worse one, and
done so with the active blessing of Western intellectuals.' 'They
seek to rehabilitate the foreigner; accordingly they deny the
existence of any common outlook among men.' Similarly, 'no
timeless or universalising critique must be allowed to disturb *the
cult of time-honoured prejudices.* In sum, the spirit of the herd must
prevail over all other spirits.' The outcome is the condoning of
new forms of racism, militarism and totalitarianism in the name
of cultural equality. Freedom was sought, but the outcome is its
subversion: 'Relativism was the product of the anti-colonial
struggle; but it ends up as a hymn to servitude.' The outcome
is not unlike that predicted by George Orwell: 'the annihilation
of the individual is called "liberty"'; and the word "culture"
serves as a humanist standard for the division of the human race
into collective, inaccessible and irreducible entities'.[4]

But, adds Finkielkraut, it is not simply a matter for the Third
World. The rot has set into ours also, and he has no difficulty in
tracing the source of the disorder to what he regards as the
nihilistic relativism of postmodernism. 'A pair of boots is as
good as Shakespeare.'[5] He links the disease, as do so many
modern commentators, with the schizophrenic bifurcation of
culture into the sciences and the humanities. He cites a report
from the Collège de France on the development of French
Education. 'A well-attuned education has to bring together the
universalism integral to scientific thinking and the relativism

---

[4] Alain Finkielkraut, *The Undoing of Thought*, translated by Dennis O'Keeffe (London:
Claridge Press, 1988), pp. 73, 65, 67, 105, 83. Italics are the author's. 'The spirit of
war peters out in a limp and moralising celebration of mutual understanding;
dialogue is invoked by a cult of national separateness which absolutely precludes it
...' (pp. 82–3).

[5] Ibid., p. 111. In the light of recent discussion, we might want to add, Frederick
Forsyth.

which characterizes the human sciences, sensitive as they are to the wide variety of ways of life, understanding and culture.' The disastrous nature of the development is summed up in the conclusion that 'We live in the age of *feelings*. Today there is no more truth or falsehood, no stereotype or innovation, no beauty or ugliness, but only an infinite array of pleasures, all different and all equal.'[6]

I need not claim agreement with all of these writers in every respect if I am to build with their assistance a critique of aspects of the modern treatment of meaning and truth. But they are firm evidence for a number of themes I wish to develop. The first is that by virtue of the fact that authors like them are prepared to dispute what they take to be the main directions of modernity, they are themselves exceptions to what they deplore. Implicit in their complaints about the development of certain modern dogmas is an affirmation of the importance of some form of objective and formulable truth which contradicts any claim that there is one irresistible tide of modernity. There is in point of fact a plurality in modern culture which is distinct from the homogenizing pluralism that they are exposing. As Finkielkraut in particular has shown, there is a pluralism that grows from the denial of truth. In contrast, the plurality – in the sense of a diversity of voices contending for truth – of modern culture as it actually exists is evidence against, not for, the postmodernist denial of objective meaning and truth. Because the authors I have cited believe in the importance of objective meaning and truth, they are prepared to contend rationally for their beliefs.

The second theme is that what can be called a pluralism of indifference, the death of the concept of objective truth, however understood, is destructive of human social living, not an aid to it.[7] Finkielkraut's argument in particular is evidence for a claim that much modern liberalism is selective in its tolerance, and indeed it can be argued, more strongly, that just as it has the insidiously totalitarian tendencies I mentioned in Chapter 1,

---

[6] Ibid., pp. 95, 116.
[7] The essence of that kind of pluralism has been well captured by Sacks, *The Persistence of Faith*, pp. 64–5, 88: 'The irony of pluralism is that it leads us to expect a growth of tolerance, while in fact it lays the ground for new forms of intolerance.'

so there is an inherent logic in modern relativism which generates an intolerance of any position which makes claims for truth. Radical relativism implies an imperious claim for its own truth which is viciously intolerant because it is undiscussable in the terms of the ideology in which it is propounded. Thus we come to what has long underlain the topics of this book, the epistemological dimension of the question of modernity. But, in the light of the foregoing chapters, it must be emphasized that interest is not focused on the problem of knowledge alone. It is knowledge in relation to culture and other created reality that focuses the question, which is essentially one of fragmentation, by which in this context I mean the breaking of Western culture into parts that scarcely communicate with one another.

2 PROTAGORAS TODAY

Alasdair MacIntyre has argued that modern emotivism derives from the failure of what he calls the Enlightenment project.[8] Underlying that development is another of the paradoxes of modernity, that a movement concerned to defend the priority and objectivity of truth against those who would subvert it for ecclesiastical or other purposes has its outcome in widespread doubt as to whether truth exists at all. Once again, however, the matter is by no means uncomplicated, and if we are to put our finger on the real character of the modern age, we must once again turn our attention to some of the ways in which modernity arises out of antiquity. A place to begin is the fact that relativism is not a modern doctrine, and that its classical form, like ours, arose out of the questioning of a theological system. It is widely agreed that the two poles of the thought of Protagoras, the first and greatest of the Sophists, were theological agnosticism, on the one hand, and epistemological and moral relativism on the other. The one led inexorably to the other, because by questioning the divine and so universal source of *nomos* or law it located its meaning in the legislating power of the human mind. 'All the direct sources agree on the general meaning of

---

[8] MacIntyre, *After Virtue*, chapters 4 and 5.

Protagoras's saying, namely that what appears to each individual is the only reality and therefore the real world differs
for each ... '[9]

That modern relativism is not in every way original or
distinctive will be evident from the continuity between the
cultural relativism so deplored by Finkielkraut and the heart of
Protagoras' position. It is yet more evidence of the way in
which certain fundamental – perhaps I could say transcendental – possibilities for thought were laid out by the Greek
mind once and for all.[10] More evidence still is provided by the
fact that certain forms of postmodernism can be understood as
republications of the doctrines of Heraclitus, in Protagorean
form, as is clear from one recent account of it. 'Postmodernity is
a flux of images and fictions', so that 'truth is human, socially
produced, historically developed, plural and changing.'[11] All is
flux, the difference being that the only *logos* underlying the
postmodernist world is that of a dissipated and fragmented
cultural pluralism.[12]

So much, briefly, for the continuity. What is the difference
between Protagorean relativism and the main features of that of
today? Two chief features are to be observed: its relation to
Christian theology, particularly in its mediaeval form, rather
than to a Greek pantheon; and its relation to science. The
relation of modern relativism to Christianity derives from the
ways in which modernity is understood as a conscious return to
values associated with Hellenism against those deriving from
what is known as the Judaeo-Christian heritage. Two related
features of this Hellenizing tendency require mention. The first
is a quest for certainty, modelled upon the apparent certainty of
mathematics. Plato's educational programme in *The Republic*

---

[9] W. K. C. Guthrie *The Sophists*, p. 171.
[10] Paradoxically, the community between Protagoras' formulation of relativism and
later forms of the doctrine are an argument against the relativist thesis. They suggest
a continuity between the thought of different eras that almost amounts to an
ontology of history.
[11] Don Cupitt, *Creation out of Nothing?* (London: SCM Press, 1990), p. 77.
[12] It is, however, as Finkielkraut shows, more of a unity in its general direction than it
would pretend: it has a universal *logos*, the logic of a closedness that pretends to be
open (Bloom) and it is totalitarian in its direction.

recommended for study especially those disciplines achieving, or thought likely to achieve, mathematical demonstrability.[13] The equivalent modern quest for certainty took form largely through the influence of Descartes, whose programme is in that respect precisely parallel to Plato's. The second feature of Greek thought is a tendency, which the Christian tradition has always, though only more or less successfully, resisted, to see in human rationality something inherently divine. It is the mind which in some way participates in the divine substance, so that it is in rational activity or contemplation that the human is most divine, a doctrine perhaps best illustrated by Aristotle's recommendation of contemplation as the highest of *ethical* values.[14] It is when those two features are combined that we find developing the characteristic features of the modern world with which the chapter opened.

The chief aspects of the modern version of this syndrome of certainty and divine rationality – and they can be seen to underlie the more ecologically disastrous aspects of the notion of science as domination – have been spelled out in Edward Craig's important *The Mind of God and the Works of Man*. What he finds to emerge in modern philosophy, beginning with Galileo and Descartes, is a tendency to suppose 'quantitative difference but qualitative identity'[15] between divine and human minds. That is to say, a version of the doctrine of the image of God in man operates often unconsciously in the philosophy of our era, as can be shown by the way in which it emerges in the thought of one twentieth-century writer who can claim to write in the tradition of Hume and yet produce a doctrine in direct contradiction of 'Hume's sceptical caution':

The way in which Schlick ... with such massive self-confidence conjures our potential omniscience into being is a show-piece of human self-deception ... Schlick's conclusion, 'in principle there are no limits to our knowledge', no very distant relative of the Image of God doctrine, is not so much Hume's teaching as his target.[16]

---

[13] Plato, *Republic*, 522–34.
[14] Aristotle *Ethics*, X. 7–8, and see above, Chapter 3, p. 80 n.9.
[15] Edward Craig, *The Mind of God and the Works of Man* (Oxford: Clarendon Press, 1987), p. 32.   [16] Ibid., pp. 129–30.

Craig proceeds to show that the Romantic era, with its production of its own variant of the image of God doctrine, was in this respect little different from the age of rationalism that preceded it.[17] With Hegel comes a development in which the image is understood in terms of action as well as of thought, so that 'the philosophical spotlight' is turned 'away from the divine mind and the knowledge of its works and on to *the works of man*'[18] – which are as such the works of God. Thus not only human thought, but also human action is held to be godlike.

Here we reach one of the roots of modern disarray, another of its paradoxes. The image of God doctrine as Craig shows it to have developed in the modern era represents, as many of its proponents intended it to represent, the reassertion of Hellenic values against the Judaeo-Christian. In so far, however, as the values institutionalized in science owe much of their origin to Christian theological inspiration, much of the self-understanding of modernity can be held to manifest a kind of intellectual schizophrenia. On the surface, and according to much of its own estimation, science is a quest for Cartesian certainty, essentially the free individual's quest for truth untrammelled by external authority or the bondage of tradition, a freedom won by a heroic struggle against ecclesiastical obscurantism.[19] Yet as a cultural enterprise, modern natural science originates in and belongs to the Christian West, as a number of studies have demonstrated beyond reasonable doubt.[20] It may be that there is room for doubt, as Amos Funkenstein has argued, whether science was *caused* by the Christian doctrine of creation, and he rightly warns against confusing 'after' with 'because'.[21] But it has been argued by numerous philosophers, theologians and historians that, for a number of reasons, there is a positive

---

[17] Ibid., e.g. pp. 157–8.   [18] Ibid., p. 174.

[19] That there has been a measure of ecclesiastical obscurantism and repression cannot be denied, but its having occurred only contributes to an obscuring of the fact that the ideology erected on its mythology is false, as we saw in the first chapter.

[20] Foster, 'The Christian Doctrine of Creation'; R. Hooykaas, *Religion and the Rise of Modern Science* (Edinburgh: Scottish Academic Press, 1972); Stanley Jaki, *Cosmos and Creator* (Edinburgh: Scottish Academic Press, 1980).

[21] Amos Funkenstein, *Theology and the Scientific Imagination from the Middle Ages to the Seventeenth Century* (Princeton: Princeton University Press, 1986), pp. 361–2.

relation between things that Christian theology has taught about the relation of God, the world and the human response to the world in the practice of science.[22]

So much then for the first of the distinctive features of the modern condition: science's rather schizophrenic relation to its theological past. Its bearing on the question of this chapter, the epistemological disorder charted in the first section, will be seen when we move to the second main feature of our time, the relation of modern relativism to science. There is a case for arguing that one of the causes of modern relativism in ethics and aesthetics, or more broadly in the humanities in general, is the apparent failure of these disciplines to deliver the certainty and universality supposedly characteristic of the sciences. The Platonic distinction between knowledge and opinion, according to which knowledge and opinion are different human faculties because they are respectively oriented to different types of object, takes a different form in the culture of modernity. Where Plato tended to distinguish between the certainty of philosophical knowledge and the uncertainty of the kind of information obtained by the senses, we tend to distinguish between science and everything else, and particularly, as we have already seen, between universal truths in science and relative uncertainties in the humanities. Science gives knowledge, everything else is relative and uncertain. This cultural distribution of cognitive respectability is, as an example given by Wayne Booth suggests, patently false: there are certainties in the humanities and manifest uncertainties in the sciences.[23] But it dies hard, and helps to account for the disorder chronicled in the opening section of the chapter.

But now we reach another intriguing feature of the modern

---

[22] It is worth recurring here to the sociological observation of science made in the previous chapter, that science is far from the enterprise extolled in the writings of the individualistic enlightened, but a communal one – Polanyi refers to structures of conviviality – with a strong sense of tradition. In that sense, its sociology is more like that of a church than of an association of unrelated individuals.

[23] 'I read in the morning paper ... that "rarely in history have theorists [in the physical sciences] questioned so fundamentally the percepts of their time" ... I am not surprised. But you could shock me into catatonia with the headline, "Majority of Experts at Annual MLA Convention Deny Irony in Austen's Works".' Booth, *Modern Dogma*, p. 120.

intellectual firmament. What has happened in the aftermath of the cognitive overvaluing of science is that, by a kind of reflex, some theorists have come to include science in the same boat as those repositories of unreliability and uncertainty, the humanities. Canons of cultural relativity are now being applied to the once immune sciences, some of whose philosophers are suggesting reasons to doubt the claims of the sciences to objective truth. Prominent among the relativizers of natural science are philosophers belonging in the American pragmatic tradition, notably Paul Feyerabend.[24] The interesting thing about them is that they, too, as Craig has argued, are the outcome of the image of God tradition that is so characteristic of modernity. It is noteworthy that in the philosophy of Richard Rorty are two features which come together in the development I am charting: an attack on 'epistemology' and its replacement with a form of pragmatism.[25] Rorty instantiates the movement charted by Craig from the image of God exercised in reason to that realized in action. He thus belongs in the very tradition he affects to repudiate.

And that is precisely where Craig's point becomes sharpest. Pragmatism too, the giving of priority to practice over truth and theory, derives from the same tendency to the divinization of the human that underlies the modern reassertion of Hellenism against the Judaeo-Christian tradition. It represents a shift of the image of God from divine knowledge to divine agency, and it is more dangerous still, for in it 'we are being said to be not so much like God as a replacement for God ... '; 'no longer a spectator, but a being that actively creates, or shapes, its own world'.[26] The outcome is that which we observed at the beginning of the chapter:

---

[24] Paul Feyerabend, *Against Method. Outline of an Anarchistic Theory of Knowledge* (London: Verso, 1978, 1st edition 1975). As it is argued, Feyerabend's is not a relativistic thesis, but such might be expected to be its outcome. The general point about the relativizing features of some modern philosophies is made pungently in Stephen Clark's recent attacks on non-realism. As he has remarked, he and I appear to be aiming at similar ends by rather different routes. See *God's World and the Great Awakening* and 'Orwell and the Anti-Realists', *Philosophy* 67 (1992), 141–54.

[25] Richard Rorty, *Philosophy and the Mirror of Nature* (Oxford: Blackwell, 1980).

[26] Craig, *The Mind of God*, pp. 284, 229.

Quite apart from the instability of the world which it might easily encourage [Craig is thinking of some forms of pluralism], it is psychologically unstable in itself. It is the philosophy of the confident man, or, as its opponents would very likely have it, the over-confident man. Should that confidence flag it offers no secure consolation. The image of the void, from being a symbol of the limitless liberty of the agent, becomes a menacing abyss waiting to engulf all his purposes and reduce him to a nullity.[27]

The abyss is glimpsed in Orwell's 1984: 'if both the past and the external world exist only in the mind, and if the mind itself is controllable – what then? ... what follows is the invincibility of the party'.[28] A modern but alienated version of Plato's rationalism thus lies behind the intellectual and cultural fragmentation of modernity. As the citation from Orwell reminds us, we are presented with the problematic of the first chapter in another form. Out of modern rationalism by a strange development there emerge both a Heraclitean flux and its *alter ego*, the totalitarian state that rushes in to fill the social and political vacuum. The modern Protagoras is not the friend of freedom and plurality that he appears to be.

3 THE FRAGMENTATION OF CULTURE

The difference between ancient and modern forms of relativism and scepticism can be approached with the help of George Steiner, according to whom there is something radically new in what has happened in modern times. Until about a century ago, he believes, even the most radical of sceptics remained committed to language, to a belief in intelligibility:

It is my belief that this contract is broken for the first time, in any thorough and consequent sense, in European, Central European and Russian culture and speculative consciousness during the decades from the 1870s to the 1930s. *It is this break of the covenant between word and world which constitutes one of the very few revolutions of spirit in Western history and which defines modernity itself.* [29]

---

[27] Ibid., p. 271.   [28] Ibid., p. 342.
[29] Steiner, *Real Presences*, p. 93. Italics are the author's.

Whether the modern breach between word and world, as there described, is different in kind from that which underlay the thought of Protagoras and was closed by the Platonic theory of forms, may be doubted. None the less, Steiner's thesis provides an introduction for an examination of what does uniquely characterize modern scepticism.

Without falling into excessive Hegelian schematization, I would like to suggest that the present situation has much to do with the development of certain patterns of thought. The history of thought shows how one emphasis in philosophy tends by a kind of reflex attempt at correction to give rise to trends that stress what is lacking in previous enterprises. It is a process of affirmation and negation, although because only parts of a thesis are negated while others continue as often unrecognized assumptions, the relation of earlier and later is complex, and always particular. Thus there is a complex dialectical pattern, which is illuminating for us as we seek to understand our own era, to be discerned in the movement of Greek thought from the Presocratics, through the Sophists, to Socrates and Plato. What the Presocratics and Sophists share is a rejection of what can be called the mythological character of Greek theology. Thereafter, the differences are great. Seeking a principle of unity for the multiplicity of phenomena, the philosophers produce speculative systems which are then rejected by their sophistic critics because they seem to be empty of practical usefulness, and to be mutually contradictory to boot.[30] The criticism of religion leads in different ways, in the Presocratics and the Sophists respectively, both to the flowering of speculative systems and to their radical critique.

Both the parallels and the differences between this process and the development of modern thought are instructive. The critique of what could be considered the mythological theology of the pre-modern era – hidden essences, Aristotelian and other teleology and the like – gave rise to an enterprise in which conceptuality developed in connection with the new sciences was regarded as the resource for new rational systems which it

[30] As in the movement from 'epistemology' to pragmatism, there is one here too from theory to practice.

was hoped would provide the key to the nature of being. That both the philosophies and the scientific systems were intended to be theologies as well as accounts of the mechanics of nature has become abundantly clear in the light of a number of magisterial recent studies. Particularly interesting is the way in which the approaches of Descartes and Newton, despite having much in common, fought for pre-eminence in the years after their begetters.[31] The manifest incapacity of these systems to deliver what they promised – a system of science that was also rationally and religiously satisfying and complete – soon found their sophists, notably perhaps Berkeley and Hume.

But perhaps the distinctive direction that modernity has taken in contrast to Greece is that in Immanuel Kant it found at once its leading Sophist and its Plato. To him is owed both a radical critique of the pretensions of reason, and its restoration on a new basis. It is in the direction that some leading modern thought has taken since Kant that is to be found the root of the postmodern disorder that so distresses the writers with whose concern the chapter began. Kant's sophistic function is to be seen in his criticism of the pretensions of the new rational theologians. Like the Sophists, he saw in the work of his predecessors a series of indecisive because undecidable contests. His response was to relegate the concept of God, which formerly had provided a basis for meaning and truth, to a realm of which there could be no knowledge.[32]

On the other hand, Kant's Platonizing function was to attempt to mediate between Newtonian metaphysics and Humean scepticism by a strong affirmation of the transcendental basis of all thought in the structures of the mind – a mind characterized by many of the attributes once held to be the prerogative of the deity. This is, of course, the point taken from Craig, that the human mind fills the space left empty by the displaced deity. *But it fills it in ways that differ significantly for the different spheres of human culture.* I believe that the cultural disarray that is so marked a feature of our times derives from our failure

---

[31] See especially Funkenstein, *Theology and the Scientific Imagination* and Buckley, *Origins*.

[32] That, to be sure, is an oversimplification of Kant's theology. But it is not a simplification of the way that it has been read by more sceptical successors.

to integrate or combine the different objects of human thought and activity: in brief, science, morals and art. I have in Chapter 2 suggested that the problem is anticipated in Plato's symbolic exclusion of the poets from the city, which elevated the philosophical and the ethical at the expense of the aesthetic. In Kant, a similar process of fragmentation takes place.

First, according to his understanding of science, the mind provided the framework of concepts by means of which the manifold reality presented to the senses was ordered. It did, to be sure, discover what was really there, but only what was presented there by the ordering function of the mind. Second, in his ethical thought the mind becomes more decisive still. Just as scientific reason provides the concepts, practical reason performs the function of God in deciding what is right and wrong. There is an objectivity about it, for practical reason's function is to discover the laws of behaviour. Yet what is discovered is the laws that godlike reason itself prescribes. There was indeed a place for God in the latter exercise of rationality, but it was not God as an other, but one realized *within* the structures of ethical rationality who was the source of moral wisdom.[33] Third: artistic judgements are even more subjective. They are judgements of feeling, and 'Feeling is something entirely personal ... It does not teach us anything at all ... '[34] That means that the realms of science, ethics and art are understood in radically different ways and that the very possibility of a universe of meaning, a world and experience making overall unified sense, is lost to view. Crucial here is the fact that science, ethics and art are activities whose relation to one another is rendered

[33] A passage, cited by L. W. Beck, from Kant's *Opus Postumum* perfectly illustrates and, indeed, substantiates, Craig's thesis. 'God is not a being outside me, but merely a thought in me. God is the morally practical reason legislating for itself. Therefore there is only one God in me, about me, above me.' Lewis White Beck, 'Kant's Theoretical and Practical Philosophy', *Studies in the Philosophy of Kant* (Indianapolis and New York: Bobbs Merrill, 1965), pp. 51–2.

[34] Quoted from Kant's *Religion within the Limits of Reason Alone* by Barth, *Protestant Theology in the Nineteenth Century*, p. 315. The essentially subjective character of aesthetic judgements according to Kant is made clear in the opening sections of the *Critique of Judgement*. 'The judgement is called aesthetical just because its determining ground is not a concept, but the feeling (of internal sense) of that harmony in the play of mental powers, so far as it can be felt in sensation.' Translated by J. H. Bernard (London: Collier Macmillan, 1951), p. 65.

intrinsically problematic because their basis is to be found in different realms of being. There is modern fragmentation in a nutshell.

Thus the outcome is even more serious than that charted by Craig. Because God no longer features as the one who provides the coordinates by which life's various activities are related, the fragmentation so characteristic of Western experience follows in the train of the developments we have followed. The legacies of Kant are now widely discussed, and I shall limit myself here to a summary of the main points. First, it can be said that in his articulation of human knowledge of the truth of being, Kant in effect limited himself to the justification of science. Other realms of culture, those of ethics and aesthetics, could not in the same sense be regarded as giving access to objective truth. This means that only in a limited sense could Kant have affirmed what is according to George Steiner the basis of the possibility of meaning. A brief digression to the latter's discussion will make clear the outcome of the Kantian critique. At the head of Steiner's discussion of the modern loss of meaning comes an affirmation 'that any coherent account of the capacity of human speech to communicate meaning and feeling is, in the final analysis, underwritten by the assumption of God's presence'.[35] He supports his thesis with a historical judgement:

> Does this mean that all adult *poiesis*, that everything we recognize as being of compelling stature in literature, art, music is of a religious inspiration or reference? As a matter of history, of pragmatic inventory, the answer is almost unequivocal. Referral and self-referral to a transcendent dimension, to that which is felt to reside … outside immanent and purely secular reach, does underwrite created forms from Homer and the *Oresteia* to *The Brothers Karamazov* and Kafka … Music and the metaphysical, in the root sense of that term, music and religious feeling, have been virtually inseparable.[36]

Kant is such an important transitional figure because, although he shared something of Steiner's view of the relation of theology and meaning, he played a major part in the process whereby the basis of that meaning was shifted from 'referral and self-referral

[35] Steiner, *Real Presences*, p. 3.   [36] Ibid., p. 216.

to a transcendent dimension' to self-referral alone. Those who worked out the underlying logic of Kant's theory of truth, heavily dependent as it was on the ideology of Newtonian mechanism, thus developed a continuing movement from the transcendent to the immanent location of the source of truth. The second aspect of Kant's legacy is to be found in the immense weight he placed on the will, and indeed a will conceived in abstraction from any foundation in other aspects of the person or in its broader environment. It was not in an absolute sense an arbitrary will, for its task was rational and universalizable legislation. But it was arbitrary in the sense that it was rootless, having no necessary reference except to itself: that is to say, no necessary reference to others except as those concerned in the ends of moral action, and no necessary reference to the world of facts, whose fate was, in the name of human autonomy, to be constrained to the requirements of the rational will.[37]

The outcome of the Kantian development, so far as the thesis of this chapter is concerned, was a radical disruption of the relation of the transcendental realms of truth, goodness and beauty, and so also of the unity of thought and culture. Before proceeding, I must become explicit about the constructive theological interest which will inform the remainder of the book. I believe that it is important for the health of culture, and in that I include what can be called the salvation or human flourishing in all dimensions of life of those who in various ways make and are shaped by culture (all of us), that we should be able to hold in some positive relation, yet without reducing one to another, the three central dimensions of human being: its formation by truth, goodness and beauty. Without a measure of integration of our knowledge, ethics and experience of beauty we are not fully what we might be. The writing of the third critique showed that Kant realized both the importance of all three realms of meaning and something of the failure of his first two critiques to provide a basis for the unity of culture. But it is also significant that, as the modern Plato, Kant shared his great

---

[37] We have thus reached, by another route, Charles Taylor's notion of disengagement. Alternatively, we may say that we have Ockham's voluntarist deity in human form.

predecessor's failure to integrate the three dimensions of culture. Plato's distinctive solution to the problem of the unity of culture, as is well known, was to integrate the realms of truth and of goodness at the expense of the realm of art, which he thought to be ontologically defective and morally destructive. Correspondingly, Kant helped to generate the fragmentation of modern culture by tending to identify science with truth, ethics with the will – although it is the rational will, it is reason operating at an ontologically different level from that of theoretical truth – and aesthetics with subjective judgement.

For a number of reasons, Kant's thought can be held to lie at the basis of the postmodernist subversion of community and rationality. The reasons concern his concepts of the person and of God. First, it can be argued that the absence of an adequate ontology of the person lays the groundwork for postmodernist denials of the existence of the subject. Here at the centre is Kant's attempted mediation of the positions of Descartes and Hume. Convinced by Hume's empiricist denial of the observability of the inner self on which Descartes had based his epistemology, Kant continued to seek a self in an inner region rather than in a broad human relationality. The outcome is an entity with little more ontological substance than something assumed for the sake of holding to the continuity of thought and experience. By attempting a transcendental bonding of what Hume had shown not to be discoverable empirically, Kant laid the foundation for the loss of the self which is so fashionable in some late modern thought, but which also appears in works of modern philosophy such as Parfit's *Reasons and Persons*.[38] Here we return to the theme of Chapter 2. When individual self-contemplation becomes the basis of the self, rather than the relation to the divine and human others on which our reality actually depends, the self begins to disappear.

But much must also be laid at the door of Kant's concept of the will. Here, however, we must tread carefully, for, as we saw in Chapter 2, it is often pointed out that the concept of the will, somewhat lacking in Greek moral philosophy, is one of the

---

[38] Derek Parfit, *Reasons and Persons* (Oxford: Oxford University Press, 1984).

contributions of Christian theology to the concept of freedom in general and to modern thought in particular. This is very important, for we encroach again on the tangled question of the rise of modern science. According to Michael Foster's thesis, modern science required a concept of the will of God as the basis for a sense of the distinction between God and the world. 'The *voluntary* activity of the Creator (i.e. that in his activity which exceeds determination by reason) terminates on the *contingent* being of the creature ... '[39] We can agree with Foster that many of the blessings of modernity derive from the space thus opened between God and the world. But as we have seen in other areas, the blessings of modernity are counterbalanced by its especial horrors. It is here that much harm may be seen to derive from Kant's conception of the absolutely self-determining finite will, which tends, as we have seen, to displace the infinite divine will from the centre of the universe. At the same time, Kant has divorced the will from certain essential dimensions of relationality. He is undoubtedly concerned with human social relatedness, as his social and political thought reveals. But his concept of autonomy tears the ethical will out of tradition and dissociates it from a reciprocity of human moral giving and receiving. Yet we must ask what is the source of Kant's concept of will. The answer is: Christian theology, or rather, as I wish to argue, the inadequate theology of the Christian West.

4 THE ORIGINS OF THE ROOTLESS WILL

We return to a much rehearsed theme of the book. What is the origin of the rootless will that is so disturbing a feature of modernity? Much light is thrown on the situation if we pause to examine concepts of creation in the Christian tradition, and it is here that we reach the third of the variations on the relation between Irenaeus' theology of creation and that of his successors. It can plausibly be held that the origin of the concept of

---

[39] Foster, 'The Christian Doctrine of Creation', in Russell, ed., *Science and Religious Belief*, p. 311. See also Michael Foster, *The Political Philosophies of Plato and Hegel* (Oxford: Clarendon Press, 1935), p. 192: '[The Christian] revelation as a whole is the source of almost all in modern philosophy that is distinctively modern ... '

will which freed the universe from logical dependence on God
and so opened the way for modern science is to be found at least
as early as Irenaeus.[40] In opposition to the plethora of
mythologies of the creation to be found in gnosticism, Irenaeus
stressed the absolute freedom of God to create. There must be
creation out of nothing, he argued, because if there is anything
coeternal with God, that would be a kind of deity for it would
impose necessity on the creator.[41] All things other than God
must, therefore, derive from the unconstrained will of the
creator. Irenaeus' conception of the will of God thus sees it as
free, but it is not therefore arbitrary and rootless. As important
as the concept of will for Irenaeus is that of love. As we saw in
Chapter 2, creation is for this theologian achieved through the
instrumentality of the Son and the Spirit, the 'two hands' of
God, by the form of whose agency an unrelational individualism
of will is ruled out. The will of God is realized through a kind of
community of love, so that the centrality of the trinitarian
mediators of creation ensure the purposiveness of the creation,
its non-arbitrary character. The creation has a purpose: the
world is made to achieve perfection through time and to return
completed to its creator.

At the fountainhead of the Western treatment of creation is
Augustine's subtly altered account of the matter. Again, I have
already argued that weaknesses in his theology of creation have
exercised a damaging influence on the Western tradition. Two
further problems come to light in this context. Because in his
theology, the mediation by Christ and the Spirit, as well as the
teleological directedness of the creation, play too limited a role,
a first effect is that the link, so beautifully maintained in
Irenaeus between creation and redemption, becomes weakened
to the point of disappearing, so that it is rarely adequately
treated in Western theology after this time. And second it comes
to be that the theme of love becomes subordinate to that of will.
If not in Augustine, certainly in those who learned from him,
creation becomes very much the product of pure, unmotivated

---

[40] Its basis is, of course, found in scripture. For an explicit reference to will, see
Revelation 4.11: 'thou didst create all things, and by thy will they existed and were
created'.   [41] Irenaeus, *Against the Heresies*, II. 10. 4.

and therefore arbitrary will, a will that operates equally arbitrarily in the theology of double predestination that became after him so much a mark of the Western tradition.[42]

In the matter of meaning and truth, Christian theology thus sowed the seeds of its own downfall. What is the link with the general question of meaning? We return to the relation between the concept of God and the founding of meaning in the thought of George Steiner. As we have seen, for Steiner, the communication of meaning and feeling presupposes the presence of God. But which God? In criticism of both Steiner and Peter Fuller, Brian Horne has pointed out the undifferentiated concept of God with which they operate.[43] That takes us to the very heart of our problem, for it suggests that the idea of the rootless will, whose anthropological form derives from Kant and has all the destructive effects outlined in the first section of this chapter, is of Christian theological provenance. One cause of our troubles is the will of God construed in terms of arbitrariness rather than in terms of loving freedom. Another is the unitary and restrictive conception of truth which is its correlative. Let me take that otherwise admirable theologian Anselm of Canterbury as an example of what has gone wrong. His conception of truth in the *De Veritate* is highly unitary and restrictive and becomes increasingly monistic as the treatise proceeds.[44] Beginning with a Platonizing definition of truth in purely mental terms, Anselm proceeds to develop a homogeneous conception of truth, in which any suggestion that its unity is compatible with some kind of plurality is vigorously rejected: 'for truth does not have its being *in* or *from* or *through* the things in which it is said to be'.[45] The implication of

---

[42] The form of Western election teaching is, as Barth realized, a function of an inadequate relating of creation and redemption. Barth's own relating of the two can be suspected of leading to a subsuming of creation into redemption, and so of repeating the characteristic Western weakness.

[43] B. L. Horne, 'Art: A Trinitarian Imperative', *Trinitarian Theology Today*, edited by Christoph Schwoebel, forthcoming.

[44] I owe this point to a thesis by David Adams, 'The Doctrine of Divine Person Considered both Historically and in the Contemporary Theologies of Karl Barth and Jürgen Moltmann', PhD, Fuller Theological Seminary, 1991.

[45] Anselm of Canterbury, *On Truth*, in *Works, Volume 2*, edited and translated by J. Hopkins and H. Richardson (Toronto and New York: Edwin Mellen Press, 1976), p. 102.

Anselm's way of putting the matter is that truth has its being in some single, transcendent and undifferentiated source. In view of the fact that it is the christological and trinitarian dimensions of Irenaeus' concept of creation out of nothing which prevented it from becoming rootless and arbitrary, we should note their complete absence from Anselm's discussion.

Thus it can be seen that just as ancient scepticism developed from a critique of the inadequate theology of the Greek tradition, so modern scepticism and fragmentation derives in part from the justified rejection of the arbitrary God and the limited concept of truth associated with that theology. Meaning is not well served if it is conceived to be founded in an essentially arbitrary will, whether divine or human, for arbitrariness suggests irrationality, instability and hence the subversion of meaning. Furthermore, the lack of differentiation returns us to the problem of homogeneity, for it may be that modernity is in justified revolt against conceptions of meaning and truth which impose upon it a premature closure or homogeneity. The matter at issue is therefore not merely a question of the relation of God and meaning, but also of the relation between different conceptions of God and their implications for the meaning of finite realities. A sense of meaninglessness may derive from the loss of a founding in a concept of God, but different conceptions of meaning may, undoubtedly do, derive from different conceptions of the relation of God to the world.

Modern relativism and scepticism are, then, in part the outcome of the failure of a doctrine of God, and particularly of a doctrine of God as creator. The modern development begins with a proper rebellion against the authoritarian theological homogenization of truth, and ends with the morally destructive homogenization of culture charted by Finkielkraut and others. In the process, the Parmenidean God of Christendom is replaced by the dispersed Heraclitean deity of individual human judgement. The chickens truly come home to roost when the attributes of the rejected deity are transferred to a multiplicity of individual and unrelated human agents. That is the reason why Edward Craig finds the doctrine of the image of God so destructive in effect. Modern fragmentation is the result of seeing human life in terms of the competition of unrelated and arbitrary wills. Where there is a multiplicity of gods there results not a genuine human plurality, but fragmentation. The point can be put otherwise: God is not so much replaced as displaced, and it is the displacement which is the source of the morally disintegrative paradoxes which have been charted in this chapter. The paradoxes I have isolated in Part One are the symptoms of the fragmentation that is so often remarked as being characteristic of modern culture.

5 THE SHAPE OF MODERNITY

What, then, in sum are we to make of the culture of modernity? First, we can say that as a historical phenomenon, modernity can be understood as the era which arises out of Christendom by making against its predecessor a charge of hypocrisy: that its freedom is a cloak for tyranny, its creed a pretext for the suppression of the authentic human quest for truth. Another way of putting the matter would be to say that it renders to Christianity account for its institutional, social and intellectual deficiencies, with interest. It is the interest that concerns us, because, if my analysis is right, modernity is parasitic upon the preceding Christendom in the sense that it takes its major orientation from its rejection of some of the latter's primary doctrines, and in particular its ontology of the transcendent basis of things. Yet, as we have also seen, the plight of the one delivered from possession by one devil is not in every respect improved.

Second, it has been argued that with respect to the content of its ideologies and assumptions, the deficiencies of the modern age are in certain respects similar to those of ancient thought and practice. Like antiquity, modernity can be understood as an era which has serious deficiencies in thought about and practice of relationality, particularity, temporality and truth, even though they are the values on whose behalf it rejected the inheritance of Christendom. In that respect, it is far less distinctive than its apologists suppose. What gives the deficiencies their distinctive unpleasantness – as well as much of their positive power – is the theological background against which they must be understood. There has been a displacement in which the characteristically monistic God of mediaeval antiquity has been displaced to the individual mind and will, producing a fragmentation that threatens the health of culture and social order. An attempt to wrest from God the prerogatives of absolute freedom and infinity leads to the inversion of Pentecost and what is in effect a new Babel. 'Postmodernism' represents that Babel perfectly, because when each speaks a language unrelated to that of the other – when language is not the basis of the communication that shapes our being – the only outcome can be fragmentation. In that sense, postmodernism is modernity come home to roost.

Third, the theological heart of the matter is to be found in the doctrine of creation. Much has been made of Václav Havel's image of the coordinates by which the relative importance of things may be judged. It has been argued that with the dismantling of the transcendent measure by which the world is understood, modernity has come to be marked by a loss of measure and balance: everything, both the good and the bad, is disproportionately magnified. But that is precisely where the doctrine of creation is so important, not simply as a teaching about the origin of things in the unconstrained freedom of God but as an articulating of the way things are by virtue of the relation they have with their creator. The deficiencies in thought about and practice of relationality, particularity, temporality and truth that have been uncovered in successive chapters derive in part from a deficiency of fundamental ontology. Parmenides and Heraclitus have called the tune and so have obliterated the trinitarian categories which enable us to think of the world – and therefore also culture and society – as both one and many, unified and diverse, particular and in relation. That is why the doctrine of creation as triune act is so important.

The question now is: what is to be done? The voices with which I began this chapter are for the most part stronger as laments for the disasters of modernity than prescriptions for its healing. So, indeed, is much of the content of the book so far. But we are only half way, and my hope in the second half will be to ask whether theology can contribute to the healing of modern fragmentation. Can there be found a vision of things which unifies without producing totalitarianism or homogeneity? Can Christianity find the means by which it can be renewed and contribute to the healing of the modern world? The lineaments of an answer to the question will be attempted in the second part of the book, where I shall hope to develop some of the concepts with the help of which new approaches can be made to the questions that have engaged our attention so far.

CHAPTER 5

The universal and the particular. Towards a theology of meaning and truth

I FOUNDATIONALISM AND RATIONALITY

In the first four chapters, a theological critique was essayed of some dogmas and practices of the modern world, the heart of the argument taking the form that major deficiencies of thought and practice have theological roots, in, on the one hand, the Christian tradition's inadequate theology of creation and, on the other, what I called the modern displacement of God. In Chapter 4, I argued that part of the responsibility for the modern fragmentation of culture, and especially its loss of a coherent sense of meaning and truth, is to be laid at the door of Christian theology's traditional tendency to a monolithic conception of God and of truth. By a kind of reflex or reaction, it has given rise to modernity's displacement of deity, as a result of which a plurality of competing wills has replaced the single will of the tradition, but in such a way that the basis of a diverse but coherent culture has been lost. In many, though not all, parts of modern culture the loss of the concept of truth, and with it, all the connotations of objectivity and universality that it once had for much of Western intellectual history, has generated various mutually related but overwhelmingly disastrous moral, social and political outcomes.

In the light of such analysis, the responsibility of the theologian – whose concern is with the universal dimensions of meaning suggested by the concept of God – is to seek for ways to rehabilitate or reinvigorate the concept of truth, without, however, ignoring the genuine weaknesses of that against which much modern thought has reacted. If, however, the root of the problem is theological – that is to say, if what is both right and wrong about the modern age derives in large part from our world's Christian past and its present relation to God – then the solution is to be sought in a renewed theological vision of truth that both does justice to the concerns of modernity and offers a way forward that is free of some of the weaknesses of the Western tradition. That will then lead into a treatment of the realms of creation that have been so inadequately conceived in the past. The structure of the work will take the form of a chiasmus, so that as this chapter takes up the theme of the fourth, the next will develop the theme of the third, until the final chapter returns to the problem outlined in the first.

A glance at one of the crucial stages in the development of modernity, the Enlightenment's critique of traditional Christian theology, provides a foothold. In so far as so widespread and complex a movement can be said to have a common theological direction, it lay in a certain use of reason both to undermine confidence in the authority of traditional institutions and to replace them by new ones. To a large extent the Enlightenment and its later representatives succeeded in the first but made a disastrous failure of the second, in unsurprising fulfilment of the truth that it is easier to demolish than to build. The success of Enlightenment criticism of the past and the failure of the Enlightenment project to establish by reason alone the necessary religious, philosophical and moral certainties upon which to reconstruct our culture have had in our time a double outcome. On the one hand, some of the inadequacies of the form Christianity had taken in the past were exposed, in particular its tendency to elevate the one above the many and make the eternal appear the enemy rather than the fulfiller of time. On the other, the renascent Hellenism of the modern tradition suffered from equivalent, and, in the end, more destructive, weaknesses, so that the putative new certainties have collapsed under the weight of their own inadequacies. There is a dialectic of Enlightenment[1] such that in due time

---

[1] The expression comes from the essentially Marxist analysis of the situation by T. W. Adorno and M. Horkheimer, *Dialectic of Enlightenment*, translated by J. Cumming (London: Verso, 1979). I have sought to treat the same dialectic theologically in

certain aspects of the Enlightenment programme have generated their own opposites.

The dialectic of Enlightenment comes into view in the
opposition expressed in Finkielkraut's *The Undoing of Thought*
between the universal claims of reason and the particular focus
of individual cultures. According to him, the universal claims of
reason have, when combined with elements of Romanticism,
been submerged by the elevation of the claims of any and every
particular, in this case the claims of particular national cultures.
Where the Enlightenment stood for the universality of truth, he
argued, postmodernism has adopted a pluralism of indifference
that is socially and politically disastrous.[2] But this is in effect an
imperious claim for truth which abolishes all other truth by a
process of homogenization. It is, despite appearances, a form of
universality.[3] The outcome can be summarized by saying that
the search for absolute rational truth led, through Kant's
critique and the work of his great successors, to a suspicion of the
very idea of objective truth and in turn to an insidious because
absolute and unrecognized form of the very thing that was
rejected. The first question which that development raises is
whether the whole programme was not mistaken, because it has
its basis in an impossible quest for an absolute truth whose
demand for certainty and omniscience displaces God and
generates a quest for what is humanly unrealizable. The quest
for the unrealizable leads to its own subversion, but at the same
time rules out a third possibility: that there may be a truth that
is in its own way universal and objective, while acknowledged to
be the work of fallible human minds.

The second question raised by the development is about that
third possibility. In the contest between modernity and late
modernity, we appear to reach an absolute opposition, that is,
between the exponents of universality and of particularity –

Enlightenment and Alienation. An Essay towards a Trinitarian Theology (London: Marshall,
Morgan and Scott, 1985), an intellectual ancestor of this book.

[2] Chapter 4, Section 1.

[3] Postmodernism's inability to avoid universal judgements, and hence its subversion of
its own basis, is one of the theses of Harvey, *The Condition of Postmodernity*. See, for
example, p. 117.

between those who would stress the claims of universal truth against all relativism and pluralism; and those who would argue the claims of the particular. Is there any way of developing a theory of meaning in which the rights of both can in some way be preserved; a conception of the universal which does not force the particular into a procrustean bed, but allows it still to be itself? That is the quest which begins in this chapter. Another aspect of the same quest will be for a conception of truth that is in its own way universal and objective, while acknowledged to be the work of fallible human minds. May there not be a concept of truth that is happy to acknowledge its limits, the limits both of those who seek it and of such universals as they might hope to find? They will be universals that are avowedly mediated through finite experience whose shape is in part determined by the historical and cultural contexts in which it takes place. Can there be, that is to say, an enterprise that is both realistic and yet more modest in its hopes than those, both ancient and modern, whose deficiencies it was the aim of the first four chapters to expose?

A new approach to the relation between the claims of the universal and the particular is offered in the recent debate about foundationalism. Foundationalism is a word describing one aspect of the Enlightenment's quest for universal truth. In general, it holds that a discipline's claim for rationality and truth must be based on some broadly accepted intellectual foundations, established by universal and certain reason. There are in recent times two rival candidates for being the foundations for thought, the rational and the empirical: universal and certain structures of concepts, on the one hand, and certain indubitable data of sense experience on the other. However, the search for universal and indubitable foundations has come into question because neither of the approaches has succeeded in delivering what it promised. There are no certain and indubitable sets of concepts, no certain and agreed reports of sense experiences. The Enlightenment project has failed to produce the certainty it sought, and indeed has often, as we have seen, replicated the disorder it sought to dispel. The burden of the previous chapter was to chart the intellectual and social disorder consequent upon the failure of the modern project and the irrationalisms that have been the reflex response to its failure.

The more measured responses to the failure of the project have taken the form of a quest for non-foundationalist rationalities. These responses take the form of arguing that the basis and criteria of rationality are intrinsic to particular human intellectual enterprises, which should not have imposed upon them in a procrustean way the methodologies which are appropriate for other forms of intellectual life. In particular, it is recognized that the tendency to take the natural sciences as models for intellectual respectability and to dismiss all enterprises which do not conform to their particular standards has led to reductionism and a constriction on free intellectual enquiry. In theology, two models for a non-foundationalist epistemology have been Barth and Wittgenstein, and their links are indicated by the fact that both tend to be labelled fideist by foundationalist opponents. In this light, the methodological aspects of Barth's attack on natural theology can be seen as attacks on foundationalism.

For theologians groaning under the oppression of demands to justify their discipline before the bar of what is supposed to be universally valid scientific method the appeal of non-foundationalism is immense. It liberates a celebration of the rights of particularity. It enables the theologian to say that theological method must be different from other methods because it shapes its approach from the distinctive content with which it has to do – just as, indeed, other disciplines shape their approaches in the light of their distinctive content. Non-foundationalism, that is to say, is a way of advocating the autonomy of distinct intellectual disciplines.[4] Theologically it also has much to be said for it. Foundationalism appears to derive from an excessive confidence in human intellectual powers, to be too titanic an enterprise. According a place to human particularity, fallibility and sin allows historical and cultural particularity to be friends rather than foes of an appropriate rationality. We can see only so far, and must limit ourselves to what we can handle rather

[4] It thus paradoxically derives an Enlightenment value from an otherwise anti-Enlightenment claim.

than attempt to roam in realms of speculation from which little reliable knowledge is likely to be forthcoming.

It must be realized, however, that the anti-foundationalist song is the voice of a siren. The allusion to fideism indicates the perennial weakness of non-foundationalist epistemologies. They may appear to be attempts to render their contents immune from outside criticism and so become forms of intellectual sectarianism. In other words, they may appear to evade the challenges of the universal and objective, and to run the risk of the rank subjectivism and relativism into which their extreme representatives have fallen. Theologically speaking, they evade the intellectual challenge involved in the use of the word God. If that word refers in part to the universal source of being, meaning and truth, then those who would use it must be prepared to take some responsibility for intellectual enterprises which impinge upon theirs from 'outside'. Here two illustrations bring out something of the point. The first is that although Barth is by no means subject to a temptation to play down the universal implications of his use of the word, he is most in danger of appearing to make unsupported assertions precisely where he evades the challenge of the links between theological and other epistemology.[5] The second is that a favourite move of postmodernists such as Cupitt is to withdraw some of the universalistic implications of the concept of God. *God* loses its ontological universality and becomes a word to express particular and therefore possibly incommensurably diverse modes of human experience of the world. When anything goes, then with it goes any notion of the overall unity and coherence of being and thought.

The quest must therefore be for non-foundationalist foundations: to find the moments of truth in both of the contentions, namely that particularity and universality each have their place in a reasoned approach to truth. If that appears to be a characteristically English quest for a middle way, it must be stressed that the underlying intellectual question is too im-

---

[5] Colin Gunton, 'No Other Foundation. One Englishman's Reading of *Church Dogmatics*, Chapter V', *Reckoning with Barth*, edited by Nigel Biggar (London: Mowbray, 1988), pp. 61–79.

portant to be construed merely in that way. What underlies the
quest is not a belief in some middle way so much as a conviction
that foundationalist and anti-foundationalist share certain
presuppositions believed to be false. On the one hand, it can be
argued that the problem is not the quest for foundations, that is,
for some understanding of the unity of the world and of the
thought with which we attempt to come to terms with it, so
much as the form the quest has taken from the Presocratics and
Plato to the present day.[6] There may be a quest for foundations,
but it must be recognized as one engaged in by fallible, finite
and fallen human beings. On the other hand, the anti-
foundationalist position, certainly in its extreme postmodern
form, must be understood largely as a reaction to the failure of
the discovery of certainties, and therefore to depend upon the
assumption that failure to find a particular kind of certainty –
that characteristic of 'Cartesian anxiety' – is a failure to
discover any truth at all. But if we are finite and fallible human
beings, should we not rather seek for a concept of truth that is
appropriate to our limits, both in capacity and in time and
space? For something that can be believed short of absolute
certainty? It is worth our while perpetually to remind ourselves
of what Michael Polanyi said of his great book on the nature of
human scientific and other knowing. 'The principal purpose of
this book is to achieve a frame of mind in which I may hold
firmly to what I believe to be true, even though I know that it
might conceivably be false.'[7] Although he would not have put it
like this, what Polanyi is seeking is a conception of created
rationality rather than the divine reason aspired to in the
tradition. It is a rationality appropriate to created knowers in a
world with which they are continuous.[8]

---

[6] The confusion of foundation with foundationalism may be at the root of the finally
unsatisfactory appeal in much recent theology to narrative, for example in Ronald
Thiemann, *Revelation and Theology. The Gospel as Narrated Promise* (Notre Dame:
University of Notre Dame Press, 1985). The problem with all such appeals is that
they either succumb to some form of subjectivism ('I have my story, you have yours')
or they introduce in 'narrativity' an implicit and not always acknowledged form of
foundationalism. Here again, universality will out.

[7] Polanyi, *Personal Knowledge*, p. 214.

[8] That is why for for Polanyi, all knowledge derives from a kind of faith. Faith, said
Calvin, not meaning quite the same thing, is 'a firm and certain knowledge of God's

2 THE ONE AS TRANSCENDENTAL

In the remainder of the lecture, I propose to begin a quest for the kind of 'fallibilist' foundations that are needed, and to pursue it in a way that may appear to be very old-fashioned indeed, as a quest for transcendentals. By transcendentals I mean those notions which we may suppose to embody 'the necessary notes of being', in the pre-Kantian sense of notions which give some way of conceiving what reality truly is, everywhere and always. Since Kant, the quest for transcendentals has come into disrepute, but Daniel Hardy, in a paper which will receive attention in the final chapter, has brought it to prominence again. 'As traditionally conceived, these are the forms through which being displays itself, through which being is determinate; they constitute an answer to the search for the fundamental features of the cosmos.'[9] Such notions provide thought with a way of conceiving both the unity and the diversity of being, for they enable us to seek both what kind of being is to be found everywhere and – if there are sufficient and various transcendentals – the complexity and richness of things. However, a new approach must also take account of the Kantian claim that the old quest was a failure, so that metaphysics became nothing more than a field on which empty and undecidable battles were fought. As we shall see, the transcendentals must be open transcendentals. The error of imposing a priori philosophical categories on the being of God must also be avoided. If there are transcendentals, they have their being in the fact that God has created the world in such a way that it bears the marks of its maker. They are not then the 'forms through which being displays itself', because that might suggest a priority of 'being' over God, but notions which can be

---

benevolence toward us, founded upon the truth of the freely given promise in Christ, both revealed to our minds and sealed upon our hearts through the Holy Spirit'. It is not, we might gloss, something established beyond all shadow of doubt by some form of infallible human enquiry. Yet it has its own proper certainty. Calvin, *Institutes*, III. ii. 7.

[9] Daniel W. Hardy, 'Created and Redeemed Sociality', *On Being the Church. Essays on the Christian Community*, edited by C. E. Gunton and D. W. Hardy (Edinburgh: T. & T. Clark, 1989), pp. 21–47 (p. 25).

predicated of all being by virtue of the fact that God is creator and the world is creation.

Before, however, we reach the positive development of the thesis, there is some need to review aspects of the history, taking particular versions of the theory of transcendentals as instances of what has been proposed at different times. The quest goes back to those Presocratics whose work culminated in Parmenides' view that there was only one necessary note of being: that is to say, being which is timeless, unchanging and absolutely unitary. There is no plurality in reality, and therefore plurality is only an appearance, an epiphenomenon, in no way part of the being of things.[10] Plato's achievement is to have modified this to some extent. Plurality is introduced by the doctrine of forms, which enables greater justice to be done to the variety of phenomena, but it is a limited justice: the ontological status of becoming is still dubious, the forms are all essentially timeless, and it is the function of the form of the good to unify the forms in a way that was to lead to the essentially Parmenidean synthesis of Neoplatonism. As we have seen in previous chapters, there remains a tendency both to elevate unity and intellect and to relegate to varying degrees of inferiority the plural and material, the deficiency of the latter being so often seen to lie in its manyness.

The signs of a Platonic transcendentality which denies or subverts the rights of plurality are to be found in many parts of the Christian tradition. For all of Origen's attempt to write plurality into the being of things through the concept of the eternal spirits, there is no doubt that for him the plurality that is the mark of the finite world is a defect of being. Plurality is inherently problematic. Further, the world of becoming, materiality and time is created in order to provide a place of punishment and correction for the fallen spirits, in some contrast to Irenaeus' celebration of the goodness of the created order which was created as blessing. The tendency to a rather gnostic

---

[10] In respect of transcendentality, process philosophy represents a direct inversion of Parmenides: the necessary marks of being are for it temporality, change and plurality, although it has to be said that there are also limitations, particularly on the extent of the plurality.

view of matter is to be found in Augustine too. Despite his averrals of the goodness and reality of the created order, the sensible world is for him manifestly inferior to the intellectual – that Platonic dualism is never long absent from his writing – while the oneness of God is manifestly elevated over the plurality of the Trinity. It is symptomatic of his suspicion of plurality that the material world is rejected as manifestly inferior to the spiritual in providing analogies for the being of God.[11] What we see in the Origenist-Augustinian tradition is an elevating of the one over the many in respect of transcendental status. Unity, but not plurality, is transcendental. The elevation of the one is most clearly visible in the thought of Aquinas, whom I shall use as my main illustration of the downgrading of the many.

The strengths of Aquinas' programme are to be found in the concept of analogy. By means of a carefully qualified doctrine of the way in which the world reflects the being of God, there is developed a form of transcendentality whereby the concept of being is adapted to Christian theological use. The relations between finite and infinite are made conceivable, while the otherness of God and the world is also preserved. If Christian theology is to engage in any kind of intellectual integration of the kind epitomized by the quest for transcendentals – and I repeat that the intellectually responsible use of the concept of God virtually requires such an engagement – something of that kind is inevitable. In some way, the relation of one God and plural world require conceptualization. There are, however, weaknesses in the Thomist programme which finally disqualify it. An approach to them can be made through the objection associated with Barth that the analogy of being makes the mistake than which none can be greater, of bracketing God and that which is not God under the same concept. In other words, it is idolatrous. The objection does not hold as it stands, in that any concept used analogously will attempt something of the kind. But it does hold for the form that Thomas' analogy tends to take. It is that which Michael Buckley has argued to underlie the development of modern atheism, the erection of theological

<hr />

[11] Augustine, *De Trinitate*, XV. 1ff.

structures independently of christology and pneumatology.[12] In that respect, the Barthian objection holds: a system of transcendentality is developed independently of the historical becoming on the basis of which Christian theology is distinctively what it is. Norman Kretzmann has observed that 'the medieval theory of [transcendental terms] appears to have developed independently of considerations of the Trinity'.[13] The objections to be raised to the analogy of being are, then, both that being appears to have been arbitrarily elevated above becoming as a transcendental concept, and more generally that it must be doubted whether the concept has been truly commandeered to theological service; that is, in this context, of whether it is not still essentially Parmenidean rather than trinitarian in content.

The weaknesses of the Thomist programme become further manifest in its content. While the concept of being does not necessarily have Parmenidean connotations, there is no doubt that in Thomas it does. The negative way, which is so important for the method, means that it is easy for Thomas to become liable to the critique associated with Feuerbach that the concept of God is projected from a negation of the marks of worldly being, so that the world appears to be negated in order that God can be affirmed. Thus the temporal is negated in order to provide the route to the (timeless) eternal, the material treated as the route to the immaterial. Far from being the source of transcendental insight, God appears to be derived from a process of negating the essential characteristics of the world of time and becoming. That judgement is confirmed when we come to see what Aquinas says explicitly about transcendentality. There are for him four transcendentals, so that 'the terms "one", "true", and "good" are, like "being", transcendent of

---

[12] 'In the *Summa theologiae*, Christ makes a central appearance only in the third part – after the doctrines of god, providence, the nature of the human person, creation and human finality have already been defined.' Buckley, *Origins*, p. 55. It is for reasons such as this that I do not find at all convincing John Milbank's thesis that the 'neo-Platonic/Christian infinitization of the absolute' adequately introduces a modification in Platonism by introducing 'the relational, productive and responsive into the Godhead'. *Theology and Social Theory*, p. 295.

[13] Norman Kretzmann, 'Trinity and Transcendentals', *Trinity, Incarnation and Atonement. Philosophical and Theological Essays*, edited by R. J. Feenstra and C. Plantinga (Notre Dame: University of Notre Dame Press, 1989), pp. 79–109 (p.87).

the categories and universally applicable – to God as well as to everything else'.[14] For our purposes, there are two related implications: true to the heritage of Plato and Augustine, neither beauty nor plurality is believed to be a necessary – transcendental – mark of being.

The logic of this claim is important for the general theme of this book, that the way in which we conceive human life in its fulness is closely bound up with the way we conceive its universal framework. The downgrading of plurality involves a downgrading of the beautiful, or certainly of materially embodied beauty. Material beauty, which the Augustinian tradition regards as of importance only as the route to a higher, immaterial beauty ('Heard melodies are sweet, but those unheard are sweeter'), is necessarily linked with plurality, with the manyness of created reality. It is the essential plurality and materiality of finite beauty that disqualifies it in so many epistemologies, including that of Augustine, from participation in true being. But if beauty is in some way both ontologically and epistemologically inferior to the other realms of being, to truth and goodness, is not the ground laid at the very heart of the theological tradition for what we saw in Chapters 2 and 4 to be the cultural fragmentation of Western life?

What, then, will be the basis of a new approach that enables the development of a theology in which both the one and the many have due place? As we have seen, Aquinas' analogy fails for the reasons marked out by Buckley and Kretzmann. Only a concept of relationality based from the outset in God's economic involvement in the world of the many will be adequate. But Aquinas' aim is right. We do need to be able to conceive the way in which created structures of relationality are marked by the hand that made and upholds them. In that respect, Barth's programme, too, falls short. He is right to develop his theology of analogy on the basis – foundation – of the implications of God's triune relatedness to that which is not God. But his quest is too limited, being mainly, if not solely, restricted to a theory of how language may be predicated of God. In distinction from

---

[14] Ibid., p. 88.

both of these paradigmatic theologians, my concern is to develop a trinitarian analogy of being (and becoming): a conception of the structures of the created world in the light of the dynamic of the being of the triune creator and redeemer.[15] Hence, this is a similar enterprise to the Thomist analogy, though with a form that is indebted to Barth. Put negatively, it can be said that the programme is unlike Aquinas' in being trinitarian in structure; it is unlike Barth's analogy of faith in being not just an approach to predicating qualities of God analogously, but to finding a way of speaking of all being. We approach the development by seeing something of what modern thought has made of transcendentality.

3 THE OPEN TRANSCENDENTAL

The Enlightenment quest for foundations must be understood as an attempt to discover a more adequate transcendentality than that bequeathed to it by its predecessors. Its main outcome, however, is that its sharing in the weaknesses of its predecessors, on the one hand, and its eventual loss of a concept of God, on the other, have together led to the scepticism about the quest that we have reviewed. Kant, as always, is a pivotal figure. As is well known, in despair of discovering a transcendentality qualifying the outside world, he sought it instead in the conceptual framework of the mind. There is much of value in the approach, for the thoughts of the human mind represent one side of the double enquiry which asks in what way they may reflect or represent that which lies beyond them. But Kant's was a disastrous limitation, for in effect he restricted true transcendentality to the concepts of Newtonian physics and excluded almost everything else. Furthermore, he exacerbated both of the weaknesses of the tradition that we met in Aquinas' conception

---

[15] I shall thus hope to avoid the pitfalls attributed by Robert Jenson to all programmes of analogy, that they involve 'religion', that is to say, a dialectic of time and timelessness in which the reality of life in time is evaded or negated by a flight to the eternal. The theme is almost universal in his writings, but see, for example, his critique of analogy in *The Knowledge of Things Hoped For. The Sense of Theological Discourse* (New York: Oxford University Press, 1969), chapter 3, and his several writings about Barth.

of the transcendentals. On the one hand, by his immense stress on the unifying action of the mind, Kant repeated at another level the traditional overemphasis of the one, so that a premature and excessive rational unification of being succeeds the previous metaphysical unification. On the other hand, with his divorce of the rationality of science and of ethics, and with his subjective view of aesthetics, he did nothing to heal the fragmentation of the three realms of truth, goodness and beauty that we have already met in Plato and Aquinas.

An alternative approach must essay the task of obviating the greatest weaknesses of the Western tradition, ancient and modern alike. Can we find a place for both the unity and plurality of being; for both the unity and plurality of the human cultural enterprises that would be true to the world of our experience? A beginning can be made by noting that the picture looks very different if we eschew the expectation of certainty, universality and infallibility in favour of something more limited, open and tentative; something more appropriate to the character of human being. Drawing on Wittgenstein, Sabina Lovibond has recommended a form of " transcendental parochialism " : a renunciation of the ... impulse to escape from the conceptual scheme to which, as creatures with a certain kind of body and environment, we are transcendentally related '.[16] I would prefer, in the light of that but taking it in a way less liable to a static or limited appeal to ordinary language – or to the postmodern idealizing of the particular – to suggest the idea of open transcendentals. An open transcendental is a notion, in some way basic to the human thinking process, which empowers a continuing and in principle unfinished exploration of the universal marks of being. The quest is indeed a universal one, to find concepts which do succeed in some way or other in representing or echoing the universal marks of being. But it is also to find concepts whose value will be found not primarily in their clarity and certainty, but in their suggestiveness and potentiality for being deepened and enriched, during the

---

[16] Sabina Lovibond, *Realism and Imagination in Ethics* (Minneapolis: University of Minneapolis Press, 1983), p. 210.

continuing process of thought, from a wide range of sources in human life and culture. What is thus needed is a dynamic: of ideas and of the operation of the active mind in its interaction with reality of such a kind that the process of thought is furthered, rather than possibilities being foreclosed, as has happened in some earlier approaches.

Something of what is being aimed at is suggested by Coleridge's notion of *idea,* which is neither a timeless Platonic abstraction nor the particular mental datum of empirical experience beloved of so many of the philosophers in Coleridge's recent past. It is like the innate idea of the rationalist tradition, but not such as to succumb to Locke's critique, for it is concerned more with common ways in which the human mind interacts with reality than with fixed or static concepts. For Coleridge ideas are not static, but dynamic, and are not abstracted or generalized so much as 'given by the knowledge of [the] *ultimate aim*' of something.[17] They are ontological rather than merely regulative in character, but that does not mean that they are easily apprehensible. As the product of reason, ideas often emerge only in apparent paradox.[18] It is possible in this connection so to stress the indefiniteness of the ideas that they appear to be vague and woolly,[19] but as instances will

---

[17] Samuel Taylor Coleridge, *On the Constitution of the Church and State. The Collected Works of Samuel Taylor Coleridge, Volume* 10, edited by John Colmer (London: Routledge and Kegan Paul, 1976), p. 12.

[18] 'Not ... that two contradictory positions always express an Idea; but that what the Understanding ... can convey by simple uncontradicted Affirmation, can *not* be an Idea.' *The Notebooks of Samuel Taylor Coleridge, Volume* 4, 1819–1826, edited by Kathleen Coburn and Merton Christensen (London: Routledge, 1990), 5294. I owe this reference to Mary Anne Perkins, 'The Logos Reconciler. The Search for Unity in the Relational, Logosophic System of Samuel Taylor Coleridge', PhD, University of London, 1991, p. 258.

[19] Speaking of Coleridge's uses of idea in *The Friend*, one commentator says that for Coleridge, 'Sublimely indefinite ideas ... can be adequately communicated by the obscure, periodic style, because only it does not fully divulge any meaning but always withholds some meaning, reserves a place meant for Being, Form, Life ... God.' Jerome Christensen, *Coleridge's Blessed Machine of Language* (Ithaca and London: Cornell University Press, 1981), p. 209. He cites a passage from *The Friend* – a relatively early work, it must be remembered – which shows that for Coleridge there is a distinction between, on the one hand, clear and distinct conceptions, which deal with objects which can be clearly conceived, and, on the other, deep and obscure ideas. Thus he wishes to '*reserve* the deep feelings which belong, as by a natural right

show, that is not the case. At the heart of the matter, rather, is the profundity and dynamic inexhaustibility of the ideas, for they give rise, as the mind interacts with reality, to possibilities for ever deeper involvement in the truth of things.

Coleridge himself says two things that are relevant to our theme. The first concerns the mediatory character of the ideas: 'in all [of the ideas] we contemplate the Particular in the Universal, or the Universal in the Particular, the Qualified (or determinate) in the Absolute, and the Absolute in the Qualified'.[20] That is precisely what we are seeking: the interaction of particular and universal in which neither the Parmenidean nor the Heraclitean, neither the absolute nor the relative, holds sway, but each is given its proper weight in a due conception of fallibilist rationality. The second point is that Coleridge on a number of occasions describes the Trinity as the 'idea of ideas', and therefore as being as at once basic to the human mind, most fertile of relevance and of deep impenetrability: 'that great truth, in which are contained all treasures of all possible knowledge ... the Idea itself – that *Idea Idearum*, the one substrative truth which is the form, manner and involvement of all truths'.[21] 'The Trinity is indeed the primary Idea, out of which all other ideas are evolved.'[22]

We should notice that there is a distinction to be drawn between *idea* and *transcendental*, and it will have continually to be borne in mind. The Trinity is not a transcendental, in the sense of being a mark of all being.[23] Rather, it must be maintained

---

to those obscure ideas which are necessary to the moral perfection of the human being ... for objects, which their very sublimity renders indefinite, no less than their indefiniteness renders them sublime ... ', p. 208.

[20] Coleridge, *Notebooks* 4, 5294.

[21] Coleridge, 'Notes on Waterland's Vindication of Christ's Divinity', *The Complete Works of Samuel Taylor Coleridge*, edited by W. G. T. Shedd (New York: Harper and Brothers, 1853), Volume 5, pp. 404–16 (p. 407).

[22] Coleridge, *Notebooks* 4, 5294.

[23] By being used as a kind of transcendental in the past the doctrine of the Trinity has been misused, so that ingenious minds have been led on a quest for *vestigia trinitatis*, traces of the Trinity in created being. These have usually taken the form of patterns of threeness in the world which have been supposed to reflect the Trinity, but which have, by reason of their essentially impersonal nature and by calling attention to the mathematics of the Trinity, had the effect of obscuring the real possibilities for a relational ontology inherent in the doctrine.

that the doctrine of the Trinity is in the first instance a way of characterizing the being of God, that is, of saying something of the kind of being that God is. It is thus idea rather than transcendental, for it is as a making known of something of the character of the source of all being, truth, goodness and beauty that the doctrine of the Trinity is important. But although it is not transcendental, not a mark of all being, it yet generates transcendentals, ways of looking at universal features of the world of which we are a part and in which we live. The expectation is that if the triune God is the source of all being, meaning and truth we must suppose that all being will in some way reflect the being of the one who made it and holds it in being.

So far as content is concerned, I believe that the new transcendentals will need to maintain the advantages of the classical tradition and preserve the otherness between God and the world.[24] Therefore we shall in that respect be of the tradition of Aquinas and Barth and against the immanentist theologies of such as Lampe[25] and the Process theologians. But in other ways, there will be differences. In particular, a more adequate account must be given of the transcendentality and interrelations of truth, goodness and beauty, and at the same time of the place of plurality. Such a process will be aided, I believe, if in place of the single, arbitrarily willing deity of so much of the Christian and anti-Christian tradition we consider further than has been the case the general implications of conceiving God trinitarianly.

I would repeat that it is on account of their dynamic and inexhaustible character that Coleridge's ideas are of interest. What he encourages is an approach which transcends the alternatives that recent philosophy has tended to present. It will thus be beyond the absolute opposition of objectivism and subjectivism (and of the related realism and idealism), for the

---

[24] As we have seen, the displacement of God to the immanent realm is one of the most damaging transformations that modernity has achieved, and is at the root of many of the ills of modernity.

[25] G. W. H. Lampe, *God as Spirit. The Bampton Lectures* 1976 (London: SCM Press, 1977).

hope will be of presenting a conversation between the subjective thoughts of the mind and the structures of the world to which they would answer. It will thus share something of the character of Putnam's 'realism with a human face',[26] and of Bernstein's concern to be 'beyond objectivism and relativism'.[27] It will also be beyond the absolute opposition of absolutism and relativism, because the transcendentals will be seen to involve a universal directionality, while taking shape variously in different times and places. The approach will try to hold in tension, similarly, two important theological doctrines. The first is that by creating the world good, God has made it of such a kind as to be a place in which the exercise of reason, as one among several properly human forms of activity, has a place and can therefore be expected to reap its own due reward in the achievement of a measure of understanding. The quest for open transcendentals is a *rational* quest, and continuous with the mainstream philosophical and theological tradition, for all of the disagreements with those who have come before. The second is that because of human limitation and sin we shall neither achieve the success nor find the agreement that the positing of the transcendentals might lead us to expect. All human action and thought shares in and exacerbates the fallenness of the universe, as well as, in Christ, taking place in the light of the promised perfection of all things. It is one of the responsibilities of theology to share in the enquiry as to which belongs to which.

Schematically, we can say that the quest for open transcendentals will be in certain respects for Kant and against Plato, particularly in accepting the dynamism of creative mind. It will be against Kant and for Plato, however, in making an 'objective' and metaphysical quest, which yet allows for the finitude, historicity and embeddedness in reality of the human mind. Transcendentals will then be provisional, 'finite' and 'open'. Here the quest will be against both Plato and Kant, and indeed against much of the direction of modernity. Therefore it

[26] Hilary Putnam, *Realism with a Human Face*, edited by James Conant (London: Harvard University Press, 1990).
[27] Richard Bernstein, *Beyond Objectivism and Relativism: Science, Hermeneutics and Practice* (Philadelphia: University of Pennsylvania Press, 1985).

will be against the whole tradition for its excessive veneration of unity and mathematical certainty. And that brings us to Hegel, to whom some reference must be made in a context such as this.

As we have seen, any modern quest for a concept of truth must take into account both the Enlightenment programme and its failure. It must therefore, as is often enough said these days, take account of the historicity of all forms of expression and claims for truth: everything that is said belongs in a historical and cultural context, and cannot therefore pretend to timeless validity. A modern quest must therefore seek no fixities, but an inner dynamic and direction within human thought. It must, therefore, take Hegel seriously, and by taking orientation from his programme seek the way in which to go. Hegel believed in both historicity and truth. Indeed, he believed that truth came to be within human culture. The key to what he did both right and wrong is to be found in his concept of Spirit. Spirit is that which at once unifies and gives meaning to what happens in the human cultural enterprise. It is a dynamic force, at once cosmic and human, individual and social. Hegel's cultural programme was to take quite seriously that which pre-modern culture, and particularly that of Christendom, had achieved.[28] He saw that the crisis of modernity was its inexorable directedness to fragmentation, and therefore he sought not so much a modernized Middle Ages as a theological basis for a renewed cultural unity. Kierkegaard rightly saw in this a form of paganism, not of Christianity, but, right or not, he can blind us to the real importance of Hegel's thought in this area, which is to teach that the historical relativity of cultural phenomena is no bar to their attaining truthfulness. As is well known, their truthfulness for Hegel consisted in their being part of the dialectical movement of Spirit. In so far as God realizes himself in time, there is truth.

The key to Hegel's programme is the way in which the 'in so far' is construed. How far can God be said to be present in and as culture in the way that Hegel supposed? The weaknesses lie in the immanentism and the eschatology. By conceiving of the

---

[28] Kierkegaard was right in seeing a kind of republication of Christendom in Hegel's social theory.

action of Spirit too immanently Hegel replicates what we have seen to be a feature of modernity's pathos: the failure to space God and the world in such a way that they can be understood to be distinct, though related, and so truly themselves. Hegel tends to confuse those which must be distinguished, and so represents in his near pantheism another tyranny of the One. The defective eschatology is likewise to be found in a mistaken conception of the relation of God and the world. Eschatology and the concept of spirit are inextricably related, but by interpreting culture, and especially modern culture, as the immediate product of the Spirit's operation, Hegel, as is often enough pointed out, tended to give modernity the status of the kingdom of heaven, of the finality that has been its undoing.[29] In sum, it can be said that Hegel presents a defective transcendentality: the Spirit displaces the Father and the Son, so that we have, at the root of a finally demonic immanentism, the inability truly to find room for plurality.

Yet there is much to be learned from Hegel, especially the notion of a truth to be sought and perhaps realized within the dynamic and temporal processes of human thought; and the shaping of this concept with the help of doctrine of God, the idea without a flaw. The defect is not the idea of Spirit, nor even the idea of Spirit realized within time and space. The problem with Hegel is the way in which his Trinity is conceived. First of all, his is a modalist account, in the sense that the three persons of the Trinity succeed each other in such a way that the third person of the Trinity in effect swallows up the others. The historical movement is all there is, so that God finally becomes lost in history. Second, it also appears that for Hegel history becomes swallowed up in God, as the pantheistic tendencies of his system assert themselves. In both instances, what is lost is the very feature of trinitarian thought that is required if a unification which abolishes particularity and individuality is to be avoided. Essential is the genuine distinctness and coeternity of the three persons of the Trinity in a conception which maintains their

---

[29] I cannot forbear to cite again Robert Jenson's dictum, that 'Hegel's only real fault was that he confused himself with the last judge; but that is quite a fault'. *The Knowledge of Things Hoped For*, p. 233.

community in together constituting the one God, but also establishes their otherness to one another and to the world. Without both of those, the identification of Hegel's thought with the thought, reality even, of God is finally unavoidable, as is the outcome as a republication of Parmenides.

From Hegel, then, as from his great contemporary, Samuel Taylor Coleridge, we shall take hints and guidance for a theology of transcendentality rooted in the doctrine of the Trinity. Perhaps, like the seekers for the *vestigia trinitatis*, Hegel misplaced it systematically, and that is the chief reason why he and Coleridge emerged with very different theologies, and therefore different cosmologies and social philosophies. Much, indeed everything, depends upon the way that that particular doctrine is articulated. Therefore an enquiry as to how the transcendentals emerge from the doctrine of the Trinity is of major significance for the enquiry. To that we now turn.

4 TRINITARIAN TRANSCENDENTALS

In a much cited passage, Gregory of Nazianzus writes of the triune God: 'No sooner do I conceive of the One than I am illumined by the splendour of the Three; no sooner do I distinguish them than I am carried back to the One.'[30] In itself, that might appear to be an instance of what makes trinitarian theology abstract and of little interest beyond its own internal convolutions: piety or theory without point beyond itself. There is a sense, of course, in which such a concern is right and proper: theology, in the patristic sense of the service of the glory of God for his own sake, should not be concerned to look perpetually and anxiously over its shoulder for marks of relevance. And yet there is a limit when conceptual convolutions become arid. Is that so of Gregory's formulation? Not, I believe, when it is expanded in the light of the foregoing discussion of transcendentals. If there are transcendentals, they will, as we have seen, be found in the dynamic interaction of the mind and that about which it thinks. The interesting point about Gregory is

---

[30] Gregory of Nazianzus, *Oration*, 40. 41.

that that is precisely what we find: a dynamic dialectic between the oneness and the threeness of God of such a kind that the two are both given equal weight in the processes of thought. Thinking about God denies his mind rest in either unity or plurality, in Parmenides or Heraclitus.

As we have seen, subsequent thought about the being of God and the nature of transcendentality failed to maintain the dynamic, so that the dogma of the transcendental status of the one came to dominate thought at the expense of the many. The result, as we have seen throughout the book, is not so much a holding in tension of the kind that Gregory desires, but an oscillation between Parmenides and Heraclitus that always tends to collapse into Parmenidean immobility. Suppose, however, that we take Gregory seriously. What possibilities for transcendental exploration emerge? They begin to appear when we develop some of the concepts which the Fathers used in order to hold together the one and the three in their doctrine of God. In the remainder of this chapter I shall outline some of them; future chapters will then be used to explore in more detail the possibilities they suggest for concrete thought about the human condition in the world. The point of the development is not simply, therefore, to generate concepts, however interesting, which will solve abstract problems about transcendental categories; rather the aim is to use them to throw light on those areas of human being in the world – intellectual, moral and aesthetic – that have been at the centre of our concern throughout this work. That is, I shall hope to use the trinitarianly developed transcendentals to throw light on the contested questions which the earlier chapters showed to have been so unsatisfactorily treated in both the ancient and modern worlds: relationality, particularity, temporality and the status and relation of what are sometimes called the three great transcendentals of truth, goodness and beauty.

Here it must be recalled that concern is very much with the doctrine of creation, and in particular with what light the doctrine of God throws on our understanding of created reality. In Part One I showed how the displacement of God that took place in modernity can be traced to a reaction against a deficient doctrine of creation, and in particular one that failed to develop the possibilities within Irenaeus' trinitarian theology of creation. The purpose was also to show that the same kind of conceptual problems are to be found arising in different areas of human culture. In Chapter 2, for example, similar difficulties emerged for the conception of particularity in both scientific and social thought. My corresponding positive point is that a renewed doctrine of creation is possible on the basis of a doctrine of God which in some way writes plurality into the being of things. If the new conception of transcendentals opens up possibilities for thought about the created order, the hope is that it will throw light on a range of phenomena similar to those treated earlier. I shall end this chapter by reviewing some of them, at this stage mainly sketching possibilities.

First, there is the question of the unity and diversity of human cultural enterprise, and in particular the relation in unity of the three classical realms of culture, truth, goodness and beauty (or science, ethics and art). Can the three be related in such a way that the distinctive character and importance of each may be guaranteed, without elevating it above the others; without that is to say, the one-sided elevation of one of the three against the others which has been in different ways so much a feature of modern culture? What should surely be the aspiration is a conception of the appropriate autonomy of science, morals and art – their genuine distinctiveness and diversity – which will yet not render them unrelated to questions arising within the other realms of meaning, so that they together contribute to a rich and diverse social culture.

Second, there is the matter of the way in which in social thought, for instance, the one and the many, society and the individual, may be held together without the submersion of one in the other. At the simplest level there is raised the question about whether the historical lurches between individualism and collectivism which so mark recent times can be transcended. Is there no mean between the kind of ethic of self-fulfilment – the quest for relations by the essentially unrelated – which is so dominant in the liberal democracies, and the subordination of the many to the needs of the collective that still marks many political systems in the world? [31] The matter of time and space gives a third focus to the enquiry. We have seen that from one point of view modernity is to be understood as the era in which existence in space and time has been elevated to the exclusion of the supposedly oppressive dimensions of eternity and infinity. This world has been chosen in preference to the alienating transcendent. Kant's programme, for example, in canonizing the Newtonian categories in effect made time and space, mechanically understood, the transcendental realities. But we have seen something of the price that has been paid in the constriction and alienation of so much of modern life. Can we then avoid the two tendencies which both impoverish culture, antiquity's belittling of life in this world and modernity's one-sided reaction against it? Can we again find transcendent coordinates which will enable us to find our place in and way around the world? In sum, does a development of trinitarian transcendentals enable us to contribute to a discussion of the nature of created reality?

Such a theology does enable new directions to be taken, for a number of reasons. Chief among them is that it provides concepts by which particularity and relatedness may both be given due right and due place in our thought and practice. Central here is the notion of perichoresis. In its origins, the concept was a way of showing the ontological interdependence and reciprocity of the three persons of the Trinity: how they were only what they were by virtue of their interrelation and interanimation, so that for God to be did not involve an absolute simplicity but a unity deriving from a dynamic plurality of persons.[32] The transcendental possibilities of this

---

[31] It is surely significant, as I have pointed out above, that one at least of the beneficiaries of the breakdown of Communism has no wish simply to adopt the forms of the former Western bloc, and, at the time of writing, there are to be heard many expressions of doubt about the benefits to the former East German state brought by the manner of its rapid embrace by the West.

[32] That is not quite accurate. As Prestige showed, the concept was first used (unsatisfactorily) in christology. But 'christological indiscretion' was the means of theological advance, for what led to an effectively monophysite christology became theologically a way to dispose both of Sabellianism and tritheism. Leonard Prestige, 'ΠΕΡΙΧΩΡΕΩ and ΠΕΡΙΧΩΡΗΣΙΣ in the Fathers', *Journal of Theological Studies* 29 (1928), 242–52 (243–4).

concept will be developed in the next chapter, where the central question will then be whether it enables us to to understand something of the interconnectedness of both persons and things. Does it, I shall ask, enable us to integrate our experience of our diverse and amazingly complicated world without depriving it of its very variety and multiplicity?

A concept polar to that of perichoresis is that of particularity, which in trinitarian theology is a way of pointing to the distinctness of the persons. According to the teaching of perichoresis, the three divine persons are all bound up with each other, so that one is not one without the other two. But what is there about the particular persons that prevents them from collapsing into or being reduced to each other? What may such a concept of particularity as emerges from the theology of the Trinity have to contribute to an understanding of the loss of particularity in the modern world, as happens, for example, in the pantheism which is so near to the surface in many aspects of modern culture, certain exponents of New Age and ecological ethics, for example, in addition to the realms discussed in Chapter 2? The programme of Chapter 7 will be to ask whether there is a better way of conceiving particularity than that of individualism, which, as we have seen, loses particularity even as it stresses individuality in terms of the unrelatedness of particulars. Can we have the particular in both the social and the natural world without losing it in the one direction or the other? In the final chapter I shall complete the chiasmus, by returning to the problem I raised in the first, about the one and the many in mutual interrrelation.

It is important that when these transcendental concepts are used as springboards for further thought, note should be taken of their extreme generality. They are, as in Coleridge's characterization of the most important ideas, both unfathomable and infinitely suggestive. They introduce a relational dynamic, but also bring with them all the problems associated with analogy. It is a complex process to consider in their light questions of particular application, so that the different realizations of the ideas must be considered at a number of levels. On the one hand it must be asked how the concepts may be considered to apply analogously to God and the world. On the other hand, the enquiry will concern the use that can be made of them in distinguishing between and relating the personal and impersonal dimensions of worldly existence. That question in its turn takes us back to the matter raised near the beginning of the book: in what sense are the institutions in which human living takes shape related to or rooted in the dynamic of cosmic process? How far are the structures of created relationality genuinely universal, and the transcendentality embodied in different ways and at different levels?

In the light of these and similar questions, there will be pursued in the remaining chapters a quest suggested by the Coleridgean conception of the Trinity, a conversation between the idea of ideas and the open transcendentals it generates. What he called ideas will act as heuristic devices, guides to possible lines of thought. Do they dynamically open up new possibilities for thought? If they do, then Christian theology will have a genuine contribution to make to the understanding and shaping of the modern world and enable us to probe some of the mysteries of what it is to be a human being living on earth before God and in varying structures of relations with our neighbour and with the universe in which we are set.

CHAPTER 6

'*Through whom and in whom ...*' *Towards a theology of relatedness*

I RECAPITULATION

In Chapter 3, I discussed the question of relationality, of the way in which things hold together in the world, by an examination of the way in which in the modern world we understand our habitation of the world of time. I argued that the displacement of God that is so marked a feature of modernity brought it about that we enter a tyranny of time which alienates us from our past and disrupts our present. In this chapter, I take up aspects of the theme adumbrated there. Can there be a rebuilding on the new theological foundations suggested by the trinitarian open transcendentals? Let me begin by saying that one of the functions of the concepts of time and space is to give a measure of unity to our experience of the world. By using the concept of time, we are able to relate things as before and after, and thus as belonging in some kind of order. Similarly, the concept of space enables us to conceive a different but related form of order and to understand the various realities we experience as belonging in some way together although they are distinct from one another. Some uses of the concepts take us into theology. For example Newton's conceptions of absolute space and time go beyond immediate experience into metaphysics. The changes in Newton's understanding of these concepts, as charted by Blumenberg, for example, suggest that he was not himself sure of the function the concepts were supposed to perform.[1] None the less, it seems at least likely that for him they

---

[1] It has been pointed out that he did not argue for their existence, but simply asserted it (Funkenstein, *Theology and the Scientific Imagination*, p. 92), and there is continuing

were something like transcendental concepts, which functioned as a system of analogy, so that absolute time and space provided both an ontological and a rational basis for the relative time and space that is the object of our apparent experience.[2]

The concepts of absolute space and time were subject to severe criticism by Newton's successors, sometimes – in Berkeley's case, for example – for theological reasons, and it fell to Kant to reassert the transcendental status of the *concepts* of space and time, in something like a Newtonian sense, if not their objectively real existence. Kant's programme involved a shifting of transcendentality, so that its location was not the objective structure of reality but the objective structure of human rationality. Along with the shift there went a displacement of divinity and a change in the ontology of space and time, so that they became functions more of human rationality than of the real world. It was not that there was a secularization, in the sense of the conceiving of space and time completely or largely non-theologically, so much as a displacement: the locus of the divine ordering of space and time was now the human mind rather than the eternal structures of being. (But perhaps that is what secularization means.) As we have seen in previous chapters, this led not to the opening of time but to a rigid spatializing of time and mechanizing of space, as well as to a loss of the coordinates by means of which human life gains its orientation. As in so many spheres, modernity's bid for freedom led to a form of slavery, in some respects a worse one than that from which escape was sought.

The theological lesson can be put thus: to give transcendental status to that which is simply part of the created order is to misplace the object of worship, and so to misconstrue the kind of being that it is. But here we reach the equal and opposite problem of pre-modern times. There, the tendency was to give to eternity and infinity the kind of theological status that

debate about the theological meaning for him of the doctrine that absolute space and time formed the divine sensorium: the *place* where God perceives the universe? For Blumenberg's discussion, see *Legitimacy*, pp. 80–3.

[2] It seems clear that the distinction between the two corresponds to Newton's Platonizing distinction between appearance and reality.

appeared to deny due reality to the created order. It was as if the former, as attributes of the absolutely simple, were the transcendentals, and the world of the many in some way or other largely epiphenomenal. That, at least, is the fashionable modern 'secular' interpretation. But if we are to resist the choice that is no choice, between a denial of the full reality of the world of space and time and their subjection to human idealizing, we must seek the true transcendentals, the true marks of being, within whose conceptual dynamic we may conceive both eternity and time in their interrelatedness. If the denial of God leads to the idolatrous confusion of time end eternity, the finite and the infinite, we must ask what theological proposals will allow for their appropriate integration, according to which their due order, eternity first and then time, may be asserted without the overwhelming of the latter by the former that has happened in some theologies, both ancient and modern.

In this and the two final chapters, then, I shall be seeking to rethink the framework within which human life is lived. To repeat Havel's expression, I shall be engaging in a quest for the coordinates the loss of which has led to the impoverishment of our culture. Or rather, the quest will be for a new set of coordinates which obviates both the weakness of those against whose felt inadequacy and cramping the modern world justly rebelled and the destructive effect of the inversion of them. In this, I shall be concentrating not on personal being, though that will always be in view, but on the framework, the context, or rather structural dynamic within which we think and have that being. The quest is for an open metaphysic, or rather for a theology of creation which enables us to locate ourselves in reality without taking away that freedom and openness to the new without which we are not truly human.

2 ECONOMY

The enquiry begins with a consideration of the concept of economy, though not that understood in the dismal and reductionist sense that characterizes so much of modernity. An interesting account of an early theological use of the concept has been given by Frances Young and David Ford in their study of the Second Letter to Corinth. From its simple and original meaning of the management of the home, the word comes to be used in the New Testament, particularly by Paul, as an explicitly financial metaphor to express forms of both human and divine action. Christology is the heart of the matter: 'You know the grace of our Lord Jesus Christ, that though he was rich, yet for your sake he became poor ... ' (2 Corinthians 8.9). Paul uses the idea of an economy of divine generosity to overcome human conceptions of economy based on mere reciprocity and prudence. Above all there comes into view 'the central, generative exchange of Christ's sufferings and death'. Through the divine economy a new human way of being in the world is realized: 'The exchange of Christ, his costly work, which involved suffering the most intractable realities of sin and death, has generated "the power of Christ" (12.9), a new creation, a new currency which can, through the downpayment of the Spirit, be spent now in living the sort of life which Christ's pattern of humility and weakness laid down.'[3]

After such a beginning, it happened that a household word, along with its transferred application to the organization of finances and the running of the state, was commandeered for theology by some of the early Fathers – Ignatius, Clement of Alexandria and Origen, for example – to express aspects of the divine dispensation. The concept of economy became a way of integrating a plurality, of maintaining the richness and diversity of the ways of the one God towards and in the world. Irenaeus has a rich conception of the divine economy. Against the gnostic divorce of creation from redemption, he argued that the different aspects of God's agency formed a unity through time and space: from beginning in creation to the final eschatological completion, which was, however, anticipated in Christ and in life in the Spirit. Creation, fall, redemption and eschatology all therefore had due part, thought together in their distinctness, but not separateness, and interrelatedness. By means of his

---

[3] Frances Young and David F. Ford, *Meaning and Truth in 2 Corinthians* (London: SPCK, 1987), p. 175.

trinitarian conception of the divine economy, Irenaeus was able to allow history to be itself, by virtue of its very relation to God. Because all that God does is achieved by means of his two hands, the Son and the Spirit, it is done both effectively and in due recognition of the integrity of created being. Von Balthasar, who sees that in Irenaeus there is a kind of aesthetic of the divine economy – one of the sections of his chapter on this theologian is entitled 'God's Temporal Art' – comments that 'there is no extraction of a permanent content from lost time as in the Platonists; *recapitulation gives time itself validity before eternity*'.[4] Putting the matter otherwise, we may say that Irenaeus is able to give a remarkably coherent and satisfying account of the divine constitution of and involvement in the created world's time and space. Time and space are given their distinctive dynamic of interrelatedness by God's creating, upholding, redeeming and perfecting activity.

It is arguable that few later theologies have achieved so adequate an integration of time and eternity, the one and the many, as Irenaeus. His work should not be idealized, for he also bequeathed problems to the tradition, but in general we shall not go far astray if we use him as a measure against which to assess prospective accounts of the economy. In contrast to him, some theologies are in danger of emphasizing creation at the expense of redemption, and the reverse. The typical Western theology, for example, tends to stress salvation to the neglect of creation, and this accounts for the fact that much recent discussion of christology – for example, in connection with the quest of the historical Jesus – abstracts it from its broader context.[5] This is important, because different conceptions of the

---

[4] Hans Urs von Balthasar, *The Glory of the Lord. A Theological Aesthetics, Volume 2, Studies in Theological Styles: Clerical Styles*, translation edited by John Riches (Edinburgh: T. & T. Clark, 1984), p. 51. The italics have been added.

[5] For reasons I have already recounted, the Western tendency to divorce creation and redemption took its direction from Augustine, whose discussion of creation is, with one exception, virtually abstracted from christology. Whether Aquinas' polarity of nature and grace is a successful attempt at integrating the two or whether it compounds the problem by treating the two in separate categories is a question that can be decided only in the light of whether his account of nature is adequate as a theology of creation. Similarly, despite the brilliant dialectic of creation and reconciliation as the outer and inner bases of one another, Barth's treatment of the

divine economy bring in their train different ways of understanding God's relatedness to time and space. Those different
emphases in their turn bring varying accounts of what it is to
live in the world.[6]

There are, then, different conceptions of economy, and their
differences mark major variations in theological teaching and
emphasis. But there is a general community of direction, so that
the notion of economy gives us (1) a conception of God's action
in and to the world which is diversified within fundamental
unity; and (2) along with it a conception of worldly happening
that is diversified and open because it is embraced by eternity.
A teaching of God's economic openness to the world walks hand
in hand with a view of the world that is open both to God and
within its own structures of being. Thinking economically thus
gives us richness and variety within a broadly unified way of
thinking theologically: we might say, relativity without relativism. 'Economy' embraces the being of the world in its
relations to God and the action of God in relation to the world.

The concept also has its limits. It cannot be considered to be
a universal mark of being, and so is not transcendental. Two
reasons should have become apparent from the foregoing

economy must be judged to be seriously unbalanced in the light of the subordination
of both to the strong protological, as distinct from eschatological, drive of his doctrine
of election. In fact, the heart of the Western weakness can be seen as a whole to derive
from a stressing of the protological over against the eschatological, the christological
against the pneumatological, as is evidenced by the fact that much Western
eschatology, in contrast to Irenaeus, sees the end essentially as a return to the
beginning. Irenaeus' conception of economy has a dynamic teleological drive which
conceives the end as something more than a return to the beginning. Much recent
theology, recognizing the imbalance, has tended to overbalance in an opposite
direction, stressing the eschatological at the expense of the protological, as for
example in Pannenberg's claim that creation is something that happens from the
future, a manifest leaning, if not more, to a disappearance of creation into
eschatology.

6 Thus an account of the economy, like modernized – and distorted – versions of
   Irenaeus such as those of Schleiermacher and, following him, John Hick, in *Evil and
   the God of Love* (London: Fontana, 1968), pp. 217–21 – will minimize or suppress the
   place of sin and its overcoming on the cross, and produce a rather unqualified
   affirmation of this world, the *saeculum*; in contrast, the Augustinian view against
   which they are in reaction tends to be more bleak, stressing the irredeemability of
   things finite, and locating salvation in an inner sphere or relegating it to a largely
   post-temporal eschatology. (Or both: the two are correlates, both deriving from a
   pessimistic disbelief in the redeemability of this material world.)

discussion. The first is that, as it stands, it does not contain within itself the resources to deal with the inconsistent ways in which it is conceived. It does not give us the transcendent coordinates that we need to be able to develop a theological critique of different theories of the economy, and, indeed, of different theories of time and space. Without uncritical or even fundamentalist use of Irenaeus' or some other scheme, there is no satisfactory way of deciding what is and is not an unbalanced construal of the economy, whose usage therefore requires a measure of theological control from without. The second reason takes us to the heart of the main theme of this book. Modernity, we may say, is from one point of view that era which has made the economy of time and space coincident with such divine agency as it decides to allow in its different constructions of reality. The objection to an attempt to restrict theology to the economy alone is not that it involves the world of becoming, decisively not, but rather that, as it stands, it does not allow for an ontological distinction between God and the world to be securely maintained. On that depends the maintenance of time and space, being and becoming, the one and the many, in their own most proper being. For space and time to be truly themselves, their own proper being and realm must be marked out, and that can only be achieved by distinguishing their being from the being of their creator. The common weakness of all merely economic doctrines, and that includes those that tend to reduce the Trinity to the economic Trinity, is that they lose the dynamic of what is the essence of economy as theologically construed: a structured though open embracing of time by eternity. A theology restricted to the economy loses that which it wishes to affirm, the positive but not exclusive or idolatrous valuation of the world of time and space.

In the previous chapter, I made something of Coleridge's *ideas*, and contrasted them with the notion of the transcendental. Ideas do not embody universal marks of being, but are fathomless concepts by which the mind and the deep things of existence come into relation. Ideas, and specifically the doctrine of the Trinity, the idea of ideas, may give rise to transcendentals as the result of the elaboration of their content, but without being of transcendental application themselves.[7] Of economy it could be said that it is an endlessly fruitful idea, giving rise to all kinds of possibilities for thought about the world.[8] We may say, then, that like all concepts, economy is one formed within the human mind, though we must remember that, in view of its provenance, that means the mind under the impact and guidance of revelation and inspiration.[9] As such, we can also accept its 'relative' status, that is to say that it is not uniform in meaning in all its uses, but it is a general concept which enables us to conceive something of the universal dynamic and interrelatedness of everything in time and space. In elaborating its meaning, we are free to draw upon the conceptual resources which modern relativity physics has made available, as well as that more recent cosmology which, in a way parallel to that of Irenaeus, would speak of the arrow of time, of cosmic evolution and the rest. But we shall reserve the right to question these speculations theologically, as we question different constructions of the economy of creation and redemption. The question now is: do all these things together enable us to go further, and explore on its basis things that are true of all reality? That is to say, do they enable the discovery of an open transcendental which will enable us to understand something of how things are with our world as the creation of God?

[7] It is of great relevance to our purpose that Coleridge himself gave as an instance of idea something that fits our theme perfectly. It is that of life, and according to him the idea of life incorporates into itself both oneness and the manyness of reality: 'By Life I everywhere mean the true Idea of Life, or that most general form under which Life manifests itself to us, which includes all its other forms. This I have stated to be the *tendency to individuation*, and the degrees or intensities of Life to consist in the progressive realization of this tendency ... this tendency to individuate cannot be conceived without the opposite tendency to connect, even as the centrifugal power supposes the centripetal, or as the two opposite poles constitute each other, and are the constituent acts of one and the same power in the magnet.' Samuel Taylor Coleridge, *Theory of Life*, cited by Perkins, 'The Logos Reconciler', pp. 152–3.

[8] What, for example, do we make of the notion of political economy, which undoubtedly, in its origins, had theological connotations? See John Milbank's discussion of its theological background and implications, *Theology and Social Theory*, Chapter 2.

[9] It is in ways such as this that we can avoid arid disputes between proponents of reason and revelation. In a topic such as this, both are involved all the time.

3 PERICHORESIS

We have seen that the original motor of the concept of economy was trinitarian, albeit an economic trinitarianism. For Paul it was the divine generosity in Christ and the downpayment that is represented by the gift of the Spirit which drove his use of the economic metaphor. In Irenaeus, too, the economy has a trinitarian shape. When we come to ask about the implications of the economic involvement of God for our understanding of his being, the most obvious patristic concept to which to turn is that of *perichoresis*. That may appear to be a surprising development. In those modern discussions of the doctrine of the Trinity in which its value has been doubted, the concept of perichoresis often appears as an example of the way in which the doctrine is most speculative and useless. I want to argue the opposite: that it opens up all kinds of possibilities for thought. The reasons are first that it is a concept heavy with spatial and temporal conceptuality, involving movement, recurrence and interpenetration; and second that it is an *implication* of the unity-in-variety of the divine economic involvement in the world. Because the one God is economically involved in the world in those various ways, it cannot be supposed other than that the action of Father, Son and Spirit is a mutually involved personal dynamic. It would appear to follow that in eternity Father, Son and Spirit share a dynamic mutual reciprocity, interpenetration and interanimation.[10]

The concept of perichoresis can thus be understood to be one which was developed by means of a movement in thought from the dynamic of the divine involvement in space and time to the implications of such an involvement for an understanding of the eternal dynamic of deity. It is one way of expressing the unity and plurality of the being of the God whose interaction with the world is unified and yet diverse; that is, of drawing out the implications of the economy. The central point about the concept is that it enables theology to preserve both the one and

---

[10] The Latinate derivative, coinherence, is less satisfactory, suggesting as it does a more static conception.

the many in dynamic interrelations. It implies that the three persons of the Trinity exist only in reciprocal eternal relatedness. God is not God apart from the way in which Father, Son and Spirit in eternity give to and receive from each other what they essentially are. The three do not merely coinhere, but dynamically constitute one another's being in what Coleridge called 'an ineffable cycle of Being, Intelligence and communicative Life, Love and Action'.[11] One of the things to be noted, in the terms which have dominated the argument so far, is that they allow a particular kind of relational diversity, or rather non-Heraclitean flux. Or rather we might say that it is Heraclitean in the sense that it is not aimless flux, but a flux which has a logos, or rather *is* a logos, the logic of its own being in relation.

As with economy, we have in the notion of perichoresis a human rational construct which has been developed under the constraints of revelation and inspiration, a process of thinking theologically under the impact of the economy of creation and redemption. That it is a human concept is quite clear: the going in and about is a way of speaking of the being of God by means of an analogy of movement in space and time. Here, if we are not to relapse into the tendency to a unitary concept of God that has dogged both Eastern and Western theologies of the Trinity, we must accept a movement of thought like that of Barth in his discussion of God's eternity and infinity.[12] Because God is involved economically in time and space, he cannot be conceived to be *merely* timeless and non-spatial. Perichoresis implies an ordered but free interrelational self-formation: God is not simply shapeless, a negatively conceived monad, but eternal interpersonal life. There is thus a richness and space in the divine life, in itself and as turning outwards in the creation of the dynamic universe that is relational order in space and time.

It is in such wise that perichoresis can be developed to serve as an analogical concept. On the one hand, it resists a merely

---

[11] Perkins, 'The Logos Reconciler', p. 195, citing the unpublished *On the Divine Ideas*.

[12] Karl Barth, *Church Dogmatics*, volume 2/1, translated by T. H. L. Parker and others (Edinburgh: T. & T. Clark, 1957), pp. 608–40 (on eternity) and pp. 468–90 (on spatiality and omnipresence).

negative and privative conception of eternity and infinity. God is not timeless and spaceless by negative abstraction from the qualities of finite being. On the other, however, we must also treat the concept apophatically if we are to prevent a simple equation between the use of temporal and spatial concepts of God and of finite realities.[13] Properly analogical thought is therefore essential if due allowance is to be made for the distinction in relation between God and the world. There is a difference in the *quality* of divine temporality and spatiality which is yet demonstrated by God's free and transcendent relationality revealed in the incarnation of the Son and the work of the Spirit. Nothing finite so completely shares in the being of other finite realities without the subversion or dissolution of its own or the other's proper being.

The possible developments of the analogy will concern us in the next section. It can here be concluded that in this one we have moved in thought from the divine economic involvement in the world to an outline of the conceptual implications of that involvement. To speak theologically of the economy is to speak of the way in which God constitutes reality: makes it what it is through the activities we call creation and redemption. To speak of divine perichoresis is to essay a conceptual mapping, on the basis of that economy, of the being of God: God is what he is by virtue of the dynamic relatedness of Father, Son and Spirit. The question now is whether we can make significant moves in the reverse direction. Can we use the concept of perichoresis not only analogically but transcendentally, to lay to view something of the necessary notes of being? If, as I am suggesting, the concept of perichoresis is of transcendental status, it must enable us to take a third step and begin to explore whether reality is on all its levels 'perichoretic', a dynamism of relatedness. Do we live in a world that can be understood relationally on all its levels? If things can be so understood, if to be temporal and

---

[13] We are not thus reading space and time upwards into God, as happens in some modern theology, for instance Process theology, but drawing out the implications of God's economic relatedness to time and space. In doing so, we must with the patristic tradition 'think away' the limitations of our spatiality and temporality, of which God is the eternal and infinite creator.

spatial is to echo in some way, however faintly, the being of God, may we not find in this concept a way of holding things together that modernity so signally lacks? Does the concept enable us to find a framework, or, better because more dynamic, coordinates for our human being in the world?

4 AN ANALOGICAL EXPLORATION

Let me begin with a proposal. It is that we consider the world as an order of things,[14] dynamically related to each other in time and space. It is perichoretic in that everything in it contributes to the being of everything else, enabling everything to be what it distinctively is. The dynamism of mutual constitutiveness derives from the world's being a dynamic order that is summoned into being and directed towards its perfection by the free creativity of Father, Son and Holy Spirit. That orientation of being is, of course, distorted and delayed by sin and evil, and returns to its directedness only through the incarnation and the redeeming agency of the Spirit. But evil distorts the dynamic of being, does not take it away. A theology of createdness is necessarily concerned with ontology: with the shape that things are given by virtue of their relation to their creator.

We have seen something of what is involved from an economic point of view: that the world's being – which includes its teleology, its determination to completedness – takes the shape that it does through God's activity in and towards it in Christ and the Spirit. In this section, we are not so much concerned with the elaboration of that set of relations with God in which the world is what it is and becomes what it shall be, as with its own internal relatedness: its way of being distinctively what it is. Without denying that the shape of the world is what it is in dependence upon the creating and redeeming activity of God, we shall now attempt, in relative abstraction from this relatedness, to understand something of what it is in itself. This is for a good theological reason. If the world is creation, then it has its own particular being, even if that being is not separable from its

---

[14] The status of these 'things' (*res*) will be the topic of the following lecture.

relation to its maker and redeemer. Our enquiry is whether the concepts generated by our consideration of the economy, particularly in this context the notion of perichoresis, have any light to throw on the being of that which is not God, but the creation of God.

Another way of describing the programme is to say that we shall be looking analogically at aspects of the world and the culture that takes shape within it in order to enquire whether the being of God and the concepts it encourages us to use have any light to throw on the being of the world. Such an enquiry is, of course, a perilous one, for it is free if guided speculation: looking at the world in the light of concepts whose primary usage is elsewhere. That will involve the conceptual exploration of the world while maintaining a strong awareness of the differences between God and the world, and in particular of the temporal and spatial limitedness of the creation. The difficulty will be eased by the fact that, as we have seen, perichoresis is a concept which, because it derives from reflection on the involvement of God in time and space, is not conceptually foreign to createdness. But the difference will remain nevertheless, particularly in view of the fact that theological concepts do not give us a confident inner view of the in one sense unknowable deity, but rather mark the parameters of thought about him, the kind of things that may be said of God.

The positive possibilities of the quest may be put in this way. If God is God, he is the source of all being, meaning and truth. It would seem reasonable to suppose that all being, meaning and truth is, even as created and distinct from God, in some way marked by its relatedness to its creator. Without wanting to ignore the fallenness that marks all created being apart from redemption, we should gladly affirm Paul's confession that 'Ever since the creation of the world [God's] invisible nature, namely, his eternal power and deity has been clearly perceived in the things that have been made' (Romans 1.20). Theology has often engaged in the quest for marks of the creator either by ignoring the Trinity altogether or by seeking instances of threeness in the natural world. But mathematics is not the game, which is rather to seek ways in which the structure (*taxis*) of relations in God is reflected in the world. We shall therefore, guided by the idea of ideas, seek some of the marks of createdness in the hope that the doctrine of the Trinity will prove the source of the open transcendentals we seek. Clearly, however, the reference to being, meaning and truth cannot mean that we are in the business of discovering the truth of everything. That is precisely the trap into which the titanism of much modern culture has fallen. Rather, the proposal is to examine some dimensions of being, meaning and truth, particularly those most ill-served in recent thought, in order to enquire whether our concept generates a measure of understanding.

Three realms of being and meaning can be isolated for our purposes. The first is the personal world, and the question to be asked will be whether the concept of perichoresis enables us the better to understand the being-in-relation of human beings. The second is the material world, both in itself and in relation to the human; and the third is what could generally be called culture, the realm of knowledge, action and art, or, expressed abstractly, of truth, goodness and beauty. I shall orient the discussion to the third, for two reasons. The first is that, as has been said a number of times, the chief concern in this book is to sketch out conceptual possibilities as a way of reconceiving the coordinates, created and uncreated, within which our personal being makes for death or makes for life. The second is that the heart of the concern is not the realms of person, matter and culture variously, but in their interrelationship. The hope is for an engaged theology to counter the ideology of disengagement that is the mark of so much modernity. It is in the way that we have failed to achieve an integrated understanding of the three realms that the deepest problems of modernity are to be found. That is not to deny that there are also serious inadequacies in the way in which we conceive the distinct dimensions of our being, but that questions for treatment are being selected in line with the main direction of the argument.

Because it has long been taught that to be human is to to be created in the image of God, the idea that human beings should in some way be perichoretic beings is not a difficult one to envisage. The sad truth is, however, that the notion has rarely been taken seriously. As we have seen, the individualist teaches that we are what we are in separation from our neighbour, the collectivist that we are so involved with others in society that we lose particularity.[15] In Chapter 2, I spelled out something of the origin and basis of this problem. If the notion of perichoresis helps us to rethink the matter, it is by virtue of the fact that, although it envisages close relatedness, it never does so to the detriment of particularity. Rather, it teaches that, as made in the image of God, we are closely bound up, for good or ill, with other human beings. It is not simply that we enter into relationship with them. It is possible to conceive of a relationality that does not shape our being. There are in circulation many non-perichoretic conceptions of relationality. The historian David Bebbington has suggested that one of the marks of modernism's view of things is a tendency to attempt to envisage relations apart from the persons who are related.[16] Charles Taylor has made a similar point in his study of modern moral philosophy. '[A] common picture of the self, as ... drawing its purposes, goals and life-plans out of itself, seeking "relationships" only insofar as they are "fulfilling", is largely based on ignoring our embedding in webs of interlocution'.[17] By contrast, a doctrine of human perichoresis affirms, after philosophies like that of John Macmurray, that persons mutually constitute each other, make each other what they are.[18] That is why Christian

---

[15] It might be said that what could be called mystical views of the God – or marriage – relationship, suggesting or aiming at a total union with or submersion in the other are doctrines related to collectivist conceptions, in that they involve, or are in danger of involving, a loss of personal particularity.

[16] 'In ethics the qualities of the individual or of the community became less important ... What has been central for Modernist moral theorists is interpersonal relationships ... There was in Modernism undoubtedly a tendency to downgrade humanity as such.' David Bebbington, 'Evangelical Christianity and Modernism', *Crux* 26 no. 2 (June 1990), 3.

[17] *Sources of the Self*, pp. 38–9, see also p. 106, where he speaks of 'the contemporary notion of a love "relationship" between two independent beings'. The same incapacity to envision the relationality of human beings is shown in examples I owe to Stanley Hauerwas, that modern ethical thought has no way that it can express the wrongness of sexual acts with children or of rape except by saying that they are performed without the consent of one of the parties.

[18] John Macmurray, *Persons in Relation* (London: Faber, 1961), pp. 17, 69. Despite the immense value of Macmurray's philosophy of the person, there are aspects to his thought which make it less convincing overall than some of its advocates suggest. See

theology affirms that in marriage the man and the woman become one flesh – bound up in each other's being – and why the relations of parents and children are of such crucial importance for the shape that human community takes. Our particularity in community is the fruit of our mutual constitutiveness: of a perichoretic being bound up with each other in the bundle of life.

It is at this stage of the argument, however, that we must be aware also of the way in which perichoresis is – only – an analogy. When used of the persons of the Godhead, it implies a total and eternal interanimation of being and energies. When used of those limited in time and space, changes in the intension of the concept necessarily follow. To be created involves spatial and temporal limitation, so that living autonomously within the bounds of the created order – living according to the law of spatial and temporal being – involves the acceptance of limitation, but not simply the limitation involved in not being God. Our non-divinity certainly involves renunciation of the Faustian and Promethean temptations that have so disfigured our world, but it also involves accepting gladly the limitations of being perichoretically bound up with other human beings and the non-personal universe. Such limitations are both spatial and temporal. There is no true freedom which does not also allow for the fact that we are passive as well as active in relation to others and the world: we are what we are in perichoretic reciprocity. Similarly, there is no true understanding of our being which attempts to resist the limitations of 'the seven ages of man' and of the death that brings them to an end. The limitations are thus spatio-temporal, involving our lives in both dimensions.[19]

To illustrate the point, we return to the positive aspects of the analogy and to the form of our temporal perichoresis with others – those who come before us – that we call tradition. In

John Aves, 'Persons in Relation: John Macmurray', *Persons, Divine and Human. King's College Essays in Theological Anthropology*, edited by Christoph Schwoebel and Colin Gunton (Edinburgh: T. & T. Clark, 1992), pp. 120–37.

[19] It is our attempts to evade the limitations of our finitude that lie at the root of the 'tyranny of time' (Robert Banks) and the 'time-space compression' (David Harvey) that we met in Chapter 3.

Chapter 3, I spoke of the destructive individualism of those modernists who believe that art or any form of culture can flourish only or mainly by denial of the past. Not only does this attitude proclaim arrogantly the alienated uniqueness of modernity, but it indicates the age's equally arrogant refusal to accept part of what it is from others whose human being and achievements are mediated to us by word and artefact from the past. The renunciation of a positive relation to tradition is a futile attempt at evasion of who and what we are: of our human spatial and temporal placedness. To proclaim the salutary nature of tradition, and in particular the possibility of conversation with the past,[20] is not the same as traditionalism, which is the assertion of one sector of time, the past, *against* the present. If there is a perichoresis of times, it should be necessary to treat none of the dimensions, past, present or future, as absolutely fallen or absolutely redemptive, but as all alike in potentially positive interrelation with us as we are.

The astonishing thing about modern human culture is that such things should be so little taken account of. Yet I believe that here we have an instance of Coleridge's belief that 'Ideas are their own evidence', so manifestly true that their self-evidence is the more apparent the more deeply they are considered. That is not to claim that there is no more to be said, for the unfathomability of the idea of personal perichoresis means that we have here but begun to harvest its fruits for thought and action. But an enterprise like this, involving as it does a survey of possibilities, must leave it there and move to an examination of the analogy as it concerns other aspects of being. Is it right to speak of perichoresis in the impersonal world also? Two examples will suffice to show that much modern physics and cosmology appear to teach the perichoretic character of the universe. Michael Faraday is one of the fathers of modern physics, and a recent study of his science and religion makes

---

[20] 'As regards theology ... we cannot be in the Church without taking as much responsibility for the theology of the past as for the theology of our present. Augustine, Thomas Aquinas, Luther, Schleiermacher and all the rest are not dead but living. They still speak and demand a hearing as living voices ... ' Karl Barth, *Protestant Theology in the Nineteenth Century*, p. 17.

clear that the two were intimately related.[21] According to Faraday:

> Like the members of the Sandemanian community who work in harmony for the common spiritual good, so the different material bodies and laws of nature cooperate with one another within the system of nature. Yet each type of force differed markedly from every other source in its mode of operation... The clear echo of the Christian tri-unity suggests both that the individual powers are mysteriously united and also that the different powers are the outward symbols of the invisible Godhead.[22]

From Michael Faraday in the nineteenth century until more recent relativity physics, many scientists have spoken the language of perichoresis in their descriptions of the universe. The way this is put in one recent study uses the conceptuality with which we are here concerned of the material universe. '[Physics] now recognizes that, for an interaction to be real, the "nature" of the related things must derive from these relations, while at the same time the relations must derive from the "nature" of the things.'[23] That is a statement of created, analogous, perichoresis. Everything in the universe is what it is by virtue of its relatedness to everything else.

It must, in conclusion of this section, be emphasized that perichoresis, properly understood, is the foe, not the agent, of homogeneity. Both things and relations are various, just as the Father, Son and Spirit are personally distinct and constituted so by the form of their relatedness. While the apparently chance movement of an electron the other side of the universe can affect the behaviour of a gas over this side, it does not follow that it affects my being in the same way as the meat infected by salmonella that I may have eaten. Just as relationships with parents, spouse and children shape our being more deeply than other human involvements, so it is generally true that things

---

[21] In some contradiction of the myth recounted by John Polkinghorne, *One World. The Interaction of Science and Theology* (London: SPCK, 1986), p. 97, that 'It was said, perhaps unjustly, of... Michael Faraday ... that when he went into his laboratory he forgot his religion and when he came out again he forgot his science.'

[22] Geoffrey Cantor, *Michael Faraday: Sandemanian and Scientist. A Study of Science and Religion in the Nineteenth Century* (London: Macmillan, 1991), p. 172.

[23] Prigogine and Stengers, *Order out of Chaos*, p. 95.

contiguous in space-time in general shape each other's being more deeply. But the general point, that we live in a perichoretic universe, remains. Everything may be what it is and not another thing, but it is also what it uniquely is by virtue of its relation to everything else.

5 THE HEART OF THE PROBLEM

So far, so good. We can argue more or less convincingly for the perichoresis of persons, and point to the perichoretic world revealed in some of the discoveries of modern physics. It may well be accepted that we are what we are by virtue of our perichoretic relations with other people; that the universe, too, is a perichoretic unity. But it does not follow that the two can be combined satisfactorily. Modernity has grave difficulties in construing the relation of people to each other, as we have seen. It has grave difficulties in accepting a perichoretic rather than mechanist view of the universe. But these difficulties are as nothing compared with its problems in coming to terms with the relationship of the one to the other: the personal to the impersonal. The ethics of the environment is one area where attempts are being made to heal the fragmentation, and indeed if the universe is to provide adequately conceived coordinates for human being, the character of our relation with the natural world will be at the centre of human concern. The danger here, so widely apparent, is of a failure to coordinate the two, to recognize the differences between person and the world, while respecting the proper being and status of the natural world. Serious though those problems are, however, there is a case for saying that at least as great a threat to human life is made by the fragmentation of human culture.[24] The world presented by much of the practice and philosophy of science is a rational place, to a degree open to human thought and language. The world presented in much ethical and aesthetic thinking, especially that which can be labelled modernist and post-

---

[24] ' ... we know too much about ecological systems to suppose that you can remove one element and leave the rest unchanged. There is, if you like, a God-shaped hole in our ozone layer. And it is time that we thought about moral ecology, too.' Sacks, *The Persistence of Faith*, pp. 26–7.

modernist, sees the human as deeply alienated from that world, so that ethics is in many approaches a study of action in a meaningless universe while some art shows symptoms of spiritual emptiness, as Peter Fuller remarked of the painting of Francis Bacon. Can we then see culture as an interrelated whole?

As we have seen, one apparent cause of the disarray is to be found in traditional dualisms of personal being: of seeing the human in terms of mind or will that is essentially different from nature (disengagement again).[25] Theories of evolution have called this model into question, but at the same time have thrown the baby out with the bathwater and encouraged an *identification* of the human with the natural, often the natural conceived mechanically. It is the latter point that is crucial. It is one of the many contradictions of modernity that side by side have developed a view of the person as essentially indistinguishable from, identical in being with, the non-personal universe, and a view of the person as so discontinuous with the matter of the world as to be an alien within it. Naturalistic views of the human, deriving from a view that everything, whatever it is, should be subject to the same kind of scientific theorizing, have encouraged an equally unbalanced stressing of subjectivity, consciousness, rationality, all those things which make us appear utterly different from the material world. In the next chapter, I shall attempt to call that dualistic picture of the particular person into question. Here, however, I want to approach the question of the interrelatedness of person and nature through a discussion of the perichoresis of culture and of meaning.

The problem presents itself to us through a discussion of the fragmentation of culture. It could be put crudely as follows. Science, except in the theories of those who approach it through scepticism engendered from other sources, for the most part celebrates the rationality and meaningfulness of the universe. According to relativity theory, for example, it would appear that the same laws of physics hold throughout the universe. By

[25] See Chapter 2, Sections 2 and 3.

contrast, modernist and late modernist art appears to celebrate the opposite: the meaninglessness of the world on to which the artist imposes individually or socially constructed 'meaning'. A similar point could be made, and has often been made, about the relation of science and ethics. Some conceptions of moral autonomy require the kind of disengagement from the natural environment that Charles Taylor has charted. But let us concentrate in the first instance on the relation of the true and the beautiful, and move thence to ethics. And let us also begin with Keats' famous line, from the *Ode on a Grecian Urn*, ' "Beauty is truth, truth beauty, " – that is all / Ye know on earth and all ye need to know.'

On the face of it, that is a typical if early piece of absurd nineteenth-century aestheticism, a symptom of that very fragmentation of culture that is the root of our problem. But at another level, may it not point to a profound truth? Is it not true that a scientist will sometimes use aesthetic criteria when choosing between alternative possible theories? Why should then the beautiful and complex world that is revealed by microscope and mathematics not in its turn encourage the artist to express the truth of the world in works that do not simply express social alienation and cosmic disillusion, but in some way reflect the deeper truth of things? The reason that it so often does not is, of course, both ontological and theological, or rather, as Peter Fuller has shown so clearly, anti-theological. He tellingly quotes William Morris: 'Modernism began and continues, wherever civilisation began and continues to *deny* Christ.'[26] But, as we have seen, the problem is not Christ but a God conceived apart from Christ and the Spirit.

The matter of ontology is closely related. For aesthetics, the chief question concerns in what sense art may be conceived to embody being, meaning and truth. Defenders of the autonomy of art argue rightly that it should not be compelled to serve some extraneous moral, and certainly not political, end; its task is to serve reality as it distinctively perceives it. But that raises the question of reality. Underlying much argument about

---

[26] Cited by Fuller, *Theoria*, p. 139.

modernism and postmodernism is a disagreement about the nature of the real. To suppose that meaninglessness, the evil and the discordant are the essentially real is to serve a Manichaean vision which holds that reality is irredeemable. To suppose otherwise, however, is to be involved in the question of whether art should incorporate some kind of redemptive vision, as for most of its history it has done. It is therefore inextricably involved with the question of moral good, which does not mean that it must be didactically moral, but rather must in some way or other come to an understanding of its relation to human moral reality.[27]

What, then, does the discussion of our concept contribute to the integration of the three focuses of human activity and thought, truth, goodness and beauty? Can we see perichoresis as a clue to the due integration of the three realms of meaning while maintaining their relative autonomy? Here we return to George Steiner's point about God as the basis of all meaning. It is worth citing again the crucial passage:

Does this mean that all adult *poiesis*, that everything we recognize as being of compelling stature in literature, art, music is of a religious inspiration or reference? As a matter of history, of pragmatic inventory, the answer is almost unequivocal. Referral and self-referral to a transcendent dimension, to that which is felt to reside ... outside immanent and purely secular reach, does underwrite created forms from Homer and the *Oresteia* to *The Brothers Karamazov* and Kafka ... Music and the metaphysical, in the root sense of that term, music and religious feeling, have been virtually inseparable[28]

Steiner's point can be developed to apply to the relation in distinction of different realms of culture, and specifically with the help of some words of Wittgenstein. 'The work of art is the object seen *sub specie aeternitatis*; and the good life is the world seen *sub specie aeternitatis*. This is the connexion between art and ethics.'[29] Despite its opacity, that is a beginning in conceiving the relation in difference between the two realms as being rooted in eternity. It is eternity that provides the coordinates

---

[27] Somewhere in this area is the answer to the question of where the portrayal of the erotic degenerates into pornography.   [28] Steiner, *Real Presences*, p. 216.
[29] Ludwig Wittgenstein, *Notebooks 1914–19*, edited by G. H. von Wright and G. E. M. Anscombe (Oxford: Blackwell, 1969), p. 83e.

that we are seeking. As we have seen, however, not any *aeternitas* will do, and a God conceived as creating possibilities for cultural meaning in an undifferentiated way only exacerbates the strife of the faculties, encouraging a choice between different unitary theories of meaning and truth – scientism, moralism or aestheticism – all of which demand adherence, against the claims of the other two, as the one key to life on earth.

But just as a unitarily conceived ultimate reality encourages fragmentation, so by contrast a God conceived trinitarianly, a God who contains within himself a form of plurality in relation and creates a world which reflects the richness of his being, can surely enable us better to conceive something of the unity in variety of human culture. Unitary conceptions of God militate against an integration of the three realms of culture, because they help to generate a premature unity, which in turn generates a drive to subordinate the realms of being to one of their number, usually the narrowly rational, but also often the moralistic and aesthetic. However, if the triune God is the source of all being, meaning and truth, we should be able to develop a theology of the unity of culture without depriving each of its dimensions of its distinctive approach and validity. It is in that respect that our concept enables us at least to consider the possibility that while the different areas of human thought, action and experience are each distinctive and to a degree autonomous, they cannot be understood without reference beyond themselves, for their realms impinge upon all others. Is that not what we should expect in the light of an understanding of the creation according to which they are human activities in the one various but single world?

Among all human concerns, it could be argued that the social is at present – and perhaps always – the most pressing and important. This book began with an outline of the social problem of the one and the many, and the theme will be at the centre of the final chapter. But the matter can be illustrated here in the light of the theology here attempted of the perichoresis of all things. The reciprocal and many-sided involvement of social and personal ethics, of culture and of environment is no more concretely embodied than in the human love affair with the internal combustion engine. The motor car shapes our relations with each other and the world for good or ill and in all dimensions of our being. It is a thing of beauty and the cause of ugliness and squalor. That it involves at least in part a misshaping of relatedness is evident from the facts, on the one hand, that the threat of injury and the defence of the honour of both driver and vehicle are the source of the disruption of human relatedness, involving both verbal and physical abuse; and, on the other, that the institution shapes our urban society – through town planning, noise, changed patterns of mobility, the decay of public transport – and our relation with the universe as a whole. It is often seen as the source of freedom, but like other technology it also determines large aspects of social and personal being. It is thus a symbol of our perichoresis for both good and ill with each other and the world: with the way in which all things are what they are in relations of mutual constitutiveness with all other things.[30]

6 CHRISTOLOGICAL CONCLUSION

It is to Paul and other New Testament writers that we owe the confession that all things cohere in Christ. There is a long and respectable tradition, beginning with the writer of the Fourth Gospel and reaching through Coleridge and Barth to our times, of identifying Christ with the Logos, the Word of the Father, and sometimes also with that rationality which the Greeks had discerned as underlying the structures and dynamic of material being. The dangers of making too much of the latter approach, of seeking an *underlying* rather than embodied rationality, have also been evident in the history of thought. They have encouraged too great a concentration on abstract reason at the expense of other features of being and a consequent depersonalizing of that through whom all things hold together. But its moments of truth should also not be denied. God comes into

[30] The illustration has its limits, for it begs the question of whether something that is individualistic, technocratic, wasteful and in many ways the subverter at once of truly personal relations and of our habitation of the world, is a vehicle of perichoresis or rather of its failure. Appropriately, it also provides another of the paradoxes of modernity that have bulked so large in the argument of this work.

relation with that which is not himself through his Son, the mediator between himself and the creation, and the Son is rightly conceived as Logos, not only the Word spoken to time from eternity, but the immanent dynamic of meaning which holds time and space together.

We do not need to accept all the rationalizing tendencies of our Hellenic inheritance to affirm that in its philosophy of the Logos can be found an echo of the transcendentality that I am seeking. It is no accident that in both Greek and Hebrew, as in other philosophies and religions of the world, the human mind seeks for a principle of unity, for that which holds things together. It is the almost unanimous conviction of the human race – certain strains of modernity apart – that there is something which holds things together, or would but for the catastrophic fragmentation brought about by sin and evil. For Kant, as I have said from time to time, that principle of unity is to be found in the concept of God. But which God? One conceived as merely abstract unity? An insistence on the importance of a trinitarian articulation of these matters is not designed to dismiss all other approaches to and theories of the unity of things, but to stress its essential contribution to our understanding of our world and our appropriate habitation of it. It is thus to supply that without which the true focus of unity and coherence is lost and with it the rooting of all that we are and shall be in the personal being of God, that is to say, in the love which creates and redeems freely, giving to the world a perichoretic reality which in different ways reflects within the structures of the temporal and spatial the perichoresis which is God in eternity. It is not therefore some*thing* which holds things together, but some*one*: the one through whom, in the unity of the Father and the Spirit, all things have their being.

CHAPTER 7

The Lord who is the Spirit. Towards a theology of the particular

I THE CONCEPT OF SPIRIT

In the second chapter I argued that one spectre at the banquet of the modern world was homogeneity, symbolized by the idea of a Coca Cola advertisement in every village in the world. The pressures for homogeneity are various: philosophical, political, social but above all perhaps commercial. Homogenizing pressures take away our individuality and particularity, and make us all alike. Despite all the aims of modern enlightenment, there is a pressure for homogeneity in which the distinctiveness of particulars is called into question or suppressed. In this chapter, I want to explore the notion of particularity – that which makes us distinctive and non-homogeneous – and would begin with a simple point. It is often said that one of the intellectual drawbacks of Christianity is its elements of particularity. The fact that so much of the faith's content is linked to a particular human figure, and behind him a particular national history, and indeed that neither of them has any manifest world-historical importance, generates what is called the scandal of particularity. It has often appeared to the rational mind that there is something inherently problematic about a faith that is, unlike so many of the philosophies and religions of the world, not a general teaching but the proclamation of historical particularities as the centre of an account of God's being and activity. That scandal is made worse in the light of that to which some of the first uses of the concept of scandal referred: the ignominious death of Jesus on the cross. It becomes morally as well as intellectually scandalous.

The burden of this chapter, indeed of the whole book, is that quite contrary to the received view that particularity is a disadvantage, a theology giving central place to particularity is precisely what the modern age needs. If I am right in arguing that the threat to our personal existence in the modern world derives from the drive to homogeneity embodied by so many influential currents of thought, action and culture, a desperate need is for a metaphysic – or rather a theology of being – in which the particular bulks large. This will not be achieved simply by reiterating the historical claims on which the faith has traditionally been based, or by recourse to theologies of narrative which beg the question of the meaning of things as a whole. We could, I believe, make far more of the narrative particularities than we do, and glory rather more in the scandal of the one crucified for the sins of the world. But that is not the chief concern of this chapter, which is to explore the possibilities of some of the *ideas* which Christianity's historic basis allows us to construe in unique and illuminating ways. As in the previous chapter, concentration will be centred on the framework within which human life must take shape.

Where might we find a theology of being which resists the pressures for homogeneity by giving due weight to the particular? A beginning can be found in a theology of the Spirit. That may appear to be a surprising claim. Is not the Spirit concerned with universal things, with making the action of God real throughout the universe? Not, I think, in the first place. There is biblical evidence to suggest that there are two main aspects to a theology of spirit in general. The first is that spirit is to do with the crossing of boundaries. Spirit relates to one another beings and realms that are opposed or separate. That which is or has spirit is able to be open to that which is other than itself, to move into relation with the other. It is particularly but not only used of God and the world. By his Spirit God comes into relationship with the world, creating and renewing, as in Ezekiel's vision of the valley of the bones, in Luke's story of the new act of creation whereby the child is formed in the womb of Mary, and in the resurrection of Jesus Christ from the dead. The result of this movement is that by his Spirit God enables the

182 *The One, the Three and the Many*

creation to be open to him. In the Old Testament, the word *ruach* founds a way of speaking of human empowerment by God, and so is relational and particularizing. 'Most of the texts that deal with the r[uach] of God or man show God and man in a dynamic relationship. That a man as r[uach] is living, desires the good and acts as authorized being – none of this proceeds from man himself.'[1] A similar relational way of speaking is to be found in some New Testament characterisations of the work of the Spirit. 'When we cry "Abba! Father!" it is the Spirit bearing witness with our spirit ... ' (Romans 8.15–16). Spirit thus brings God into relation to the world and, reciprocally, the world into relation with God. But it is not only a matter of God and the world: it has to do with human spirit, too. Paul's saying that he is absent in body but present in spirit is a way of suggesting that created beings may in a limited way transcend the space to which they are tied. That, then, is the first aspect of what it means to be or have spirit: it is to do with the crossing of boundaries, with opening out of people and things to one another.

The second feature puts the other side of the same matter. Spirit is that which, far from abolishing, rather maintains and even strengthens particularity. It is not a spirit of merging or assimilation – of homogenization – but of relation in otherness, relation which does not subvert but establishes the other in its true reality. This is especially evident in biblical characterizations of the work of the divine Spirit, the perfecting cause of the creation.[2] It is in terms of particularities that we can understand many of the ways in which the New Testament characterizes the relation of Jesus and the Spirit. To see the point of the particularizing function of the Spirit, we must put out of our minds the popular view that the Spirit was a homogeneous possession of Jesus, like a built in soul-stuff. The Spirit is the one, the personal other, by whom Jesus is related to his Father and to those with whom he had to do. The gospel narratives of the Spirit's relation to Jesus show the distinctive-

---

[1] Hans Walter Wolff, *Anthropology of the Old Testament*, translated by Margaret Kohl (London: SCM Press, 1974), p. 39.

[2] Basil, *On the Holy Spirit*, XV. 36 and 38.

ness of the different phases of his life. That the Spirit formed his body in the womb and enabled him to confound the doctors in the temple does not rule out the fact that at the baptism there is a new particularity in his life: a new human calling through a renewed relationship with his Father. The new endowment with the Spirit also brought Jesus into particular relation with his own people, a relationality subsequently worked out in temptation, teaching, works of power, suffering and death. It meant that he was this kind of messiah, not that, the instantiation of one way of being the holy people of God rather than another.

A similar function can be seen to be performed by the Spirit in the ministry of the church after the ascension, when, according to the theology of the Fourth Gospel, the Spirit takes up the work of Jesus by relating believers – particular believers – to the Father through him. The Acts of the Apostles is full of instances of how one course rather than another was chosen under the impact of the Spirit's guidance. Another focus is provided by Paul's conception of the Spirit of the Lord as the giver of human freedom. According to this conception, the freedom of Christians derives from their institution into a new – particular – network of relationships: first with God through faith in Christ, and then with others in the community of the church. Just as the Spirit frees Jesus to be himself, so it is with those who are 'in Christ', that is, in the community of his people. The church is a community, not a collective: that is, a particular community into which particular people are initiated by the leading of the Spirit.[3] It follows that as the liberating Other, the Spirit respects the otherness and so particularity of those whom he elects. That is why Paul's characterization of the various charismata, in 1 Corinthians 12, for example, is so

---

[3] 'The problem of our moral ecology is that we have thought exclusively in terms of two domains: the state as an instrument of legislation and control and the individual as the bearer of otherwise unlimited choices. But morality can no longer be predicated of the state, for we have become too diverse to allow a single morality to be legislated. Nor can it be located in the individual, for morality cannot be private in this way. We have neglected the third domain: that of community. But it is precisely as a member of a community that I learn a moral language, a vision and its way of life.' Sacks, *The Persistence of Faith*, p. 45.

seminal for our conception of what it is to be in community, for it implies richness and variety, not homogeneity. It is here that we find the nub of the difference between the gospel and the modern world. God the Spirit is the source of autonomy, not homogeneity, because by his action human beings are constituted in their uniqueness and particular networks of relationality.

It is by virtue of both of those features, the crossing of the boundaries and the preservation of particularity, that I would argue that the notion of spirit is so important for our understanding of ourselves and our world. It is therefore a candidate for being a Coleridgean *idea* in the sense I have been exploring. Without it, certain major dimensions of life in the world become incapable of adequate conception. It is when spirit is reduced to or replaced by reason or will that the disastrous inhumanities and irrationalisms of the modern age take hold. Particularity is drowned in homogeneity, or asserts itself as the denial of genuine and open human relations. But spirit is a word for the most part limited to the personal world, to God and human beings. It has to do with that unique feature of persons, their ability to transcend themselves, to think and act beyond the present and the place in which they are set. To see why this is so, it is worth our while to pause briefly and examine the contribution of G. W. F. Hegel to this topic. His view was that spirit is not merely of ideal, but also of transcendental, significance. According to him, the transcendental of transcendentals, the universal mark of being, was *Geist*, generally regarded as untranslatable, but perhaps best rendered as rational spirit. The former of the two English terms points to Hegel's orientation to the classical rationalist tradition, the latter points to the biblical origins of Hegel's usage, and in two of the main New Testament connotations of the word. Spirit is used there both of God's characteristic way of being – 'God is spirit' – and of the third person of the Trinity, the Spirit of God – meanings Hegel tends to conflate, with ambiguous effect. The main point for our purposes, however, is that the transcendental use of the concept of spirit in Hegel introduces notes of dynamism and interrelationship into the concepts of philosophy and theology. As we have seen, that which is or has spirit is able to be open to that which is other than itself, to move dynamically into relation with the other. Spirit enables a form of perichoresis to take place, between mind and world, world and God. If the most fundamental reality of all is spirit, we are able to understand something of the nature of, on the one hand, our distinctively human being, according to which our personal and rational dynamism belongs *in* the world; and, on the other, of our distinctively human form of action *towards* the world, which is able to shape the world in a way that is not entirely foreign to its being – something that the mechanistic philosophy, with its dire long-term effects on the way we treat the world, has never been able to encompass. The philosophies of mechanism or of materialism on the contrary conceive mind and matter as foreign to one another, opposites and incompatibles. The concept of spirit is the foe of the dualistic division of reality into incompatible or incommensurable spheres of being, and enables a link to be made between different dimensions of reality. As the opening chapters of Genesis teach, we belong in different ways in and over the world.

There is a case, then, for claiming the transcendental status of the concept of spirit. The notion is prominent in one of the few apparent biblical attempts to define the being of God, and also in the biblical understanding of human being. In the affirmation that the Spirit speaks to our spirit is to be found part of the mystery – the revealed mystery – of what it is to be a human being in relation to our maker. God's Spirit enables the human being to be open to him. We can also make links with the themes of the previous chapter. If all being is what it is by virtue of 'an ineffable cycle of Being, Intelligence, and communicative Life, Love and Action', to repeat Coleridge's definition of peri-choresis,[4] then what better concept than spirit to express something of its relational dynamism? Hegel's proposal is undoubtedly an improvement on traditional metaphysics of being.

To claim the transcendentality – the universal applicability

---

[4] See Chapter 6, p. 164.

– of the concept of spirit, however, does bring with it serious problems, certainly with respect to Hegel's philosophy. It is the problem of idealism: of the etherializing of matter and the subsumption of the world into God. If all is spirit, we appear to return to the difficulties we have already met in our account of the modern human treatment of the created world, whose sheer materiality becomes problematic, and is indeed no longer part of its real being. To make everything spirit is to bring about a loss of particularity, or so it would appear, because it is the material shape of the objects of our experience that is the means of their individuation and the mark of their particularity, so that I recognize someone by the shape of his head, the distinctive character of her walk. In Hegelian terms, however, matter, time and space are finally abolished as a result of Spirit's relentless movement. As I argued in Chapter 3, the outcome of Spirit's work is the abolition of time, so that there is a loss of the very dynamism and perichoresis which was the specific contribution to thought of the concept of spirit. A perichoresis which dissolves particulars is no longer perichoresis, being rather unrelational homogeneity.[5]

The underlying theological problem would appear to be found in the way in which the Hegelian Trinity is conceived. The modalist way in which Spirit succeeds the first two persons of the Trinity reveals a form of that bugbear of Western theology, the transcendentality of the one. Plurality is not elevated but abolished because it cannot be given transcendental status, and that in part because the plurality of the persons of the Trinity is merely 'temporary'.[6] And yet, as we saw in Chapter 5 in connection with the discussion of the historicity and temporal nature of truth, Hegel's contribution is very important. In some way or other, spirit is at the heart of the matter of reality. If spirit is not transcendental, may it not yet be one of the ideas without which we cannot come to terms with ourselves and the world? May it not be a means of obviating the

---

[5] The same is the case with the general Romantic tendency, with its pantheistic overtones, to project the spirit into nature.

[6] Hegel thus replicates in a kind of mirror image the traditional failure, of which so much was made in the first chapters, to articulate a truly trinitarian doctrine of creation.

monism of will that underlies so many of the most destructive developments of modernism and late modernism, so that with its help we may conceive a relational rather than fragmented plurality, a rich complexity rather than a warring Babel? Attention to the concept of spirit as the vehicle of openness to and respect for what is other than ourselves serves as a corrective to the depersonalizing trends of our time. If we understand ourselves as spirit as well as will, may we not find a way to overcome the individualism that underlies the modern abolition of the other?

The clue to a way forward is to be found in the doctrine that as a qualification of the person spirit is of wide and illuminating significance. Theologically, it is a way of speaking of the personal agency of God towards and in the world; anthropologically a way of speaking of human responsiveness to God and to others; cosmologically a way of speaking of human openness to the world and the world's openness to human knowledge, action and art. Another advantage is that spirit, as that which is conceived to open person to person and person to world, does not exclude the bodily and material dimensions of our reality, nor, of course, in reaction to the overrationalizing of humanity, does it allow merely mechanist or physicalist conceptions of the person. On the contrary, it encourages the development of the idea of the person as both a whole, with its own proper privacy – truly particular – and as relational, capable of genuine interaction with the other. Unlike what happens in so many philosophies, it allows that we are both bodies and souls, and so have our being in a wide range of activities and relations. Such features of our humanity that have sometimes been taken to represent the sole or chief quality of personhood, such as consciousness, subjectivity, conscience, will, reason, creativity are all capable of – indeed, positively encourage – individualistic and non-relational views of the person in society and the world. Subordinated to and controlled by a concept of spirit they all take their proper and strictly subordinate place in an anthropology and psychology.

As a qualification of the person, then, spirit is of wide and illuminating significance, and must therefore have a strong claim to be an idea in the Coleridgean sense. A further reason for arguing the ideal status of spirit is that, along with other of the ideas, it is an analogical concept which gives rise to thought on different levels. The main difference between the human and the divine is expressed in the claim that God *is* spirit, while finite persons *have* spirit – and things neither are nor have spirit. And that is where we come to the heart of the the difference between idea and transcendental. God *is* spirit by virtue of the unqualified openness of the triune persons to each other and his free and unnecessitated movement outwards in creation and redemption to that which is not God, to the finite and temporal. As finite and temporal, yet created in the image of God, human beings *have* spirit because they are open to God, each other and the world in the peculiar although limited way that characterizes personal beings. They are able to relate, to love, hate, cherish, exploit, to enter into relations that enslave them and to be redeemed for relations that do not by the love of God. That is not the case with the rest of the created world.

2 THE PROBLEM OF SUBSTANTIALITY

According to the view being developed, spirit is one of those ideas without which we are unable adequately to understand our place in the world. But it is not properly a transcendental, because it is not a universal mark of being, but qualifies only the world of persons as they exist in relation to each other and to the world. The concept of spirit does not, I believe, assist us to understand the structure of an atom or the evolution of the material universe, to eat or to grow a cabbage or appreciate a work of art, at least not from the point of view of the objects under consideration.[7] This is not to suggest that the way we treat the world of things and animals is unimportant, but that if we are to treat the world aright we must be aware of its own

---

[7] This in opposition to the advocates of the so-called creation spirituality. I agree that there are 'boundary cases' where there is room for dispute, for example in thinking of what we mean by a 'spirited' horse, but that in general it is essential to maintain the distinction between the personal and the impersonal for the sake of both orders of being.

specific character and status. Much of our ecological disorder stems from a mechanical or technocratic view of things; from treating the world as if spirit were in every way irrelevant to its being. That is not – emphatically not – what I mean by saying that non-personal things do not have spirit.[8] If we are to treat major realms of the world as not properly speaking qualified by spirit – as not being or having spirit – we must without doubt be aware both of the way in which the divine Spirit upholds the world and directs it to its proper perfection, alike in company with and without human agency, and also of the way human spirit is related to it. But that does not detract from the main point, which is that spirit is a concept used to denote something of the mystery of personal being.

Where, then, does that leave us in our quest for truly universal notions, for transcendentals? To pursue the quest, we must ask the same kind of question as was asked in the previous chapter. If a study of the economy of creation and redemption led us from economy to the truly transcendental perichoresis, what may we learn from the economic activity of the Spirit of such universal features of our world as it appears to imply? Much has so far been made of the orientation of the Spirit to particularity. Now it is time to make a general point about the Spirit's action, and with respect to our particular concern with the doctrine of creation. According to St Basil, the distinctive function of the Spirit is to perfect the creation, and we can interpret this as meaning to bring to completion that for which each person and thing is created. In that respect, the distinctive work of the Spirit is eschatological. One way of expanding such an insight theologically would be to say that the Spirit's peculiar office is to realize the true being of each created thing by bringing it, through Christ, into saving relation with God the Father.

Two moves can be made on the basis of this teaching. First, we can explore the implications it has for our doctrine of God. What does it mean for our understanding of God that the

---

[8] Some things have life, which is manifested at different levels, particularly in the difference between animal and plant, but that, although related to spirit, is not the same thing.

personal being of the Spirit is to be found in the work of perfecting the creation? Can we speak, by implication, of the Spirit as in some sense also the agent of the perfection of the being of God? I think that it is important in this context to beware of the apparently tritheist tendencies of some of what are called social theories of the Trinity. We are not licensed by revelation to speak of a social life; we are, however, to say that if the Spirit works in a particular way in the economy as the one who perfects the creation, it is reasonable to suppose that he has a similar kind of function to perform in relation to the being of God, to the communion that is the life of God. Therefore, not only must we say, with Augustine, that the Spirit is the unifying link between Father and Son; it is even more necessary to add that he is the focus of the distinctiveness of Father and Son – of their unique particularity. It is an important feature of the being of persons that they have the capacity to be themselves and not a function or clone of another. That is the point of the stress placed on particularity. Richard of St Victor argued that the third person of the Trinity is essential if there is to be true otherness in the Godhead. There must be three if there is to be a true outwardgoingness and diversity in God.[9] In that sense, we may say that the Spirit's function in the Godhead is to particularize the *hypostases* – and I shall show later why I have to use this technical term – or persons of Father and Son: to liberate them to be themselves, to be particular *persons* in community and as communion. Accordingly, the Spirit's distinctive mode of action in both time and eternity, economy and essence, consists in the constituting and realization of particularity. There is, then, and it is crucial for the argument, a form of particularity at the very heart of the being of God.

We now come to the second move that can be made on the basis of Basil's teaching that the Spirit is the one who perfects the creation. It can be contended that the concept of *hypostasis*, with its connotations of particular being, should be more at the centre of our thinking than historically it has been. Only so, I believe, shall we lay the intellectual basis for the liberation of the

---

[9] Richard of St. Victor, *De Trinitate*, 3, xix.

many from the submersion in the one that is so much the reality and threat of modern life. According to this teaching, what might be called the *substantiality* of God resides not in his abstract being, but in the concrete particulars that we call the divine persons and in the relations by which they mutually constitute one another. It could here be argued that when the Western tradition took the decision to translate the Greek *ousia* by *substantia*, which is in point of fact a literal translation of *hypostasis*, it effectively deprived the concept of the person of due weight because it introduced a stress on the *underlying* reality of God. On such a translation, the thought is encouraged that the real *substance* of God, what he substantially is, is the being that underlies the particular persons. What was lost was the force of the Cappadocian desynonymizing of ousia and hypostasis: of making what were synonymous terms into words of distinct meaning.[10] By using hypostasis to refer to the concrete particulars – the persons – and then proceeding to say that the *ousia* – general being – of God is constituted without remainder by what the persons are to and from each other in eternal perichoresis, these theologians made it possible to conceive a priority of the particular over the universal. God is what he is only as a communion of persons, the particularity of whom remains at the centre of all he is, for each has his own distinctive way of being or τρόπος ὑπάρξεως.[11] *Therefore* – and here we move from our understanding of the creator to a notion of transcendentality – the particularity of created beings is established by the particularity at the heart of the being of the creator.[12]

---

[10] For the concept of desynonymizing and Coleridge's part in its development, see Stephen Prickett, *Words and* The Word. *Language, Poetics and Biblical Interpretation* (Cambridge: Cambridge University Press, 1986), especially pp. 137–40.

[11] Barth's proposal to use mode of being or tropos uparxews as the equivalent for 'person', rather than as a way of referring to the way in which the persons are who they particularly are, not only makes it impossible to redeem the concept of person from its modern individualistic usage, but also replicates the Western tendency to make the Trinity practically redundant by depriving the persons of distinctive forms of agency. *Church Dogmatics* volume 1/1, translated by G. W. Bromiley (Edinburgh: T. & T. Clark, 1975), pp. 355–9.

[12] It is surely significant also that the Western tradition has also been notoriously weak in giving due weight, substance, to the third person of the Trinity.

The Western theological tradition, and almost certainly also the Eastern, failed to capitalize on the conceptual revolution that had taken place. As we have seen, abstractness rather than concreteness became the chief note of divine being, a note derived more from Greek philosophy than from the concrete particularities of biblical revelation, that is, more from a metaphysic of being than a theology of Spirit. Two citations from theologians influential in the West illustrate the tendency for God to be conceived in terms of abstraction and indeterminacy. Speaking of God, Pseudo-Dionysius writes that 'He has every shape and structure, and yet is formless and beautyless, for in his incomprehensible priority and transcendence he contains the sources, mean terms, and ends of all things and he undefiledly enlightens Being for them in one undifferentiated cause.'[13] Similarly, according to Aquinas, He Who Is 'is the principal of all names applied to God; for comprehending all in itself, it contains existence itself as an infinite and indeterminate sea of substance'.[14] The long-term impact of this on our Western culture was charted in Chapter 2, and our concern now is with the general problem of what I have called the substantiality of things. If God's existence is essentially abstract and indeterminate, as both of these citations suggest, whence comes determinateness and particularity? Only, it might seem, as the negation of God, either, as with Hegel, as part of a dialectical process or, in Hegel's atheist successors, as the denial of God in the name of human particularity and freedom.

Yet the paradoxical outcome of modern protests, as has been argued in earlier chapters, is not the confirmation of the particularity and substantiality of being in the face of theological negation, but the loss of substance in leading intellectual and artistic movements in the modern world. G. K. Chesterton is reported to have said of the paintings of the Impressionists that the world in them appears to have no backbone, and some analyses of late modernity appear to confirm the judgement that a loss of substantiality is at the heart of the matter. The

---

[13] Pseudo-Dionysius, *The Divine Names*, v, 824b. The translation is from *Pseudo-Dionysius. The Complete Works*, translated by Colm Luibheid (London: SPCK, 1987), p. 101.   [14] Aquinas, *Summa Theologiae*, I. 13. 11.

modern assertion of particularity has not saved concreteness, but undermined it, so that both relation and substantiality have been lost. Robert Pippin puts it thus:

One can thus already detect in Manet's choice of subject matter a fascination in modernism and ultimately in postmodern discussions with the radical particularity of existence, and so ... a denial of the 'dependence' of the intelligibility of objects or persons or moments on the universal categories or descriptions of science or philosophy or even language itself as originally understood. The implicit claim is that this ineffable, original, 'independent' matter of existence, can be properly captured in some form of radical experience, ranging from the apparently trivial, momentary scenes captured by impressionists, through the attack on traditional notions of coherence or order mounted by the cubists, to found-object or Pop art and the chance transformations of Cage. [15]

The point is this, and it cannot be put too strongly: that we have here not only a matter of painting but 'a modern metaphysical issue, an implicit assertion of the wholly transient, fragmented and perspectival nature of the real, a reality accessible only in contingent, individual "moments" of representation'.[16] That is to say, the modern positing of the particular loses that particular, for it deprives it of concrete subsistence and meaning. Particulars become insubstantial, because it is assumed that their substantiality can be affirmed only by means of underlying universals which are in modern thought no longer believed to exist. We appear to meet again the syndrome already much lamented in this book: of a particularity without relation and a relationality without particularity that are a coincidence of opposites – the very same thing variously considered.

The time has therefore come to raise again the question of substance – or, as I shall say in the hope of minimizing misunderstanding, of *substantiality* – and to claim that people

[15] Pippin, *Modernism as a Philosophical Problem*, p. 37.
[16] Ibid., p. 36. To concede an inch at this place to postmodern views of the world, as John Milbank appears to do, is to subvert the doctrine of creation, despite what he says: 'as for the finite world, creation *ex nihilo* radically *rules out* all realism in its regard. There are no things, no substances, only shifting relations and generations in time.' *Theology and Social Theory*, p. 426.

and things, in dependence upon a God understood substantially and not abstractly, are also to be understood as substantial beings, having their own distinct and particular existence, *by virtue of and not in face of their relationality* to the other. The times are not propitious, for the fashion in many a work, especially theological work, is to affirm the superiority of relational to substantial thinking, as an altogether alternative way of conceiving being.[17] The first question to this, however, as will be by now apparent, is whether it is possible to have the one without the other.[18] It will be the burden of the rest of the chapter to attempt a defence of the doctrine that the two, ontology and relation, stand or fall together rather than are opposed approaches to the way we understand things. The second question is similar, and it is whether we can do without the notion of substance if our world is not to lose the substantiality on which the meaning of our lives as particular human beings depends. Everything, however, hangs upon the notion of substance that we develop.

Let me say something of what I do not mean. The modern protest against the idea of God is in part a protest against a kind of notion of divine substance, and particularly of God as a changeless, unitarily conceived will or authority. Much is made of the unrelational character of this God, with some cause, but also with much exaggeration and oversimplification. It could even be argued that because, as the result of the work of Descartes, a similar notion of substance was transferred to human being, modernity has come to be in reaction not only against God, but against substantialist views of the human person, too. On such an account, the reaction against a wrongly conceived substantial God has led to a false concept of human substantiality, and that in turn to a further reaction in a concept

---

[17] For example, Sallie McFague, *Metaphorical Theology. Models of God in Religious Language* (London: SCM Press, 1983), appears to trade upon some such distinction.

[18] I want therefore to distinguish between two senses of 'relational' in this connection. The first, idealizing, sense is that according to which things can be known only in terms of their relation to us, or rather *as they appear to us*; the second, realist, sense, is that according to which things have their (objective) being in relation. According to the latter understanding, there is an ontology of relationality: things are constituted by their relation to other things. In the former case, ontology is, apparently at any rate, disclaimed.

of human being that is relational but unsubstantial. It is not then substantial thinking that is at fault – for what is wrong with saying that you are you and I am I in our own proper distinctness, concreteness and particularity? – but what has been made of it.

In this realm, however, perhaps more than in any other, all turns on what is meant by the term. Donald MacKinnon has pointed out that, despite all the complexities and difficulties of his discussion, there is one side of Aristotle's teaching which encourages us to suppose that he had somewhere in mind the notion of substance as referring to the things that we experience and speak of: particulars. '[His] indebtedness to Plato has its bearing … on the extent to which he wavers between identifying substance with the individual natural thing in its concreteness … and with the form that makes it what it is … '[19] What we make of it accordingly will depend on what we suppose those particulars *to be*. Whether we hold them to be unchanging or changing, in networks of relations or not, there is a prima facie case for saying that we know that they are there, because we are related to them: because we eat cabbages, bump into tables and hear tones. Nor is there any need to take literally the 'below' of the latinate word we use. We may use the word substance of the particular things of our experience without having to suppose any of the hidden essences of mythology, of something different below the surface. Let us take it to refer simply to the particular entities – things, people, creatures – of our everyday experience. The question is: do we have any reason to regard these supposed objects of experience as substantial, or must we with the late moderns come to believe that on examination they disappear like the Cheshire cat into insubstantiality, a mere haze of homogeneously insubstantial relationality?

[19] Much of the argument of Chapter 2 above is to suggest that the latter of the two views MacKinnon contrasts was the one that conquered. D. M. MacKinnon, '"Substance" in Christology – a cross-bench view', *Christ, Faith and History*, edited by S. W. Sykes and J. P. Clayton (Cambridge: Cambridge University Press, 1972), pp. 279–300 (p. 281).

3 OF PARTICULARS

At the heart of the matter, and of immense importance, is the concept of the person. The centrality of the personal is explicit in what has been written above about the fact that persons have spirit and thus their distinctively relational being in the image of God. Indeed, it is the loss of the centrality of particular personality that is the theme of many aspects of Part One of this book. The chief affirmation to be made here is that if persons are, like the persons of the Trinity and by virtue of their creation in the image of the triune God, *hypostases*, concrete and particular, then their particularity too is central to their being. It is not an unfortunate accident but our glory that we are other: each unique and different. The destruction of forces making for homogeneity can be achieved by finding ways of allowing persons to be particular, particular in relation indeed, but made by that very relationality unique and free.

While continuing to stress the personal, and to refer for support to recent work on the person that will supplement this brief affirmation,[20] I shall maintain concentration on the framework – we might say in this context the *inscape* – within which human life takes shape. The loss of personal particularity and therefore of human freedom is bound up with the loss of an adequate conception of the concreteness of the world within which personal life is lived. To rethink the personal particular involves also a rethinking of the material particular, the status of the cabbages, mountains, statues and melodies that surround us, for it is the loss of the concreteness of the latter that has contributed to the subversion of the personal reality of the former. We shall, then, return to the person only after discussion of the thing.

In the history of thought, various terms have been used to denote and characterize the particulars of which the world is

[20] See A. I. McFadyen, *The Call to Personhood*; Christoph Schwoebel and Colin Gunton, editors, *Persons, Divine and Human. King's College Essays in Theological Anthropology* (Edinburgh, T. & T. Clark, 1992); British Council of Churches, *The Forgotten Trinity Volume 1, The Report of the BCC Study Commission on Trinitarian Doctrine Today* (London: British Council of Churches, 1989).

supposedly constituted. They are in some complex way related to the ways in which the particularity of God has been conceived and expressed. As we have seen, on one interpretation of the Cappadocian theology the ultimate particulars constituting the being of God are the hypostases, or persons; by contrast, a traditionally Western approach to the particularity of God will tend to speak in terms of the single substance, or, more recently, with Barth and others, the single person. It is surely no accident that for the being of the particulars perceived or thought to exist in the created world, the word 'substance' has also been used.[21] As we have seen it is the Parmenidean quest for timeless and changeless underlying reality that is at the root of the divorce between concrete reality and material particularity, not the use of the concept of substance as such. The chief problems have arisen from taking the metaphorical 'below' literally, and in forgetting the way in which the Cappadocian use of hypostasis enables us to move from appearance to reality.[22] It is concreteness that is lost in most quests for a concept of substance, which has almost always been for that which *underlies*: either a timeless substance or a timeless and usually homogeneous plurality of underlying atoms. In that respect, it is very much the same with the Platonic forms, with Leibniz's monads, with Newton's dualism of relative and absolute time, with the Newtonian mechanical matter, with Locke's unknown substance and with Kant's category of substance.[23] Rarely has attention been focused on the particular that meets the senses, and, where it has

---

[21] It has not, to be sure, been the only word. In the distinction between thinking and extended thing according to Descartes, the Latin *res* – roughly the same but not entirely coextensive in its usage with the English *thing* – was used to characterize the two features of reality. How far this word in Descartes' usage refers to particulars is an interesting question: he certainly sees himself particularized as a thinking *res*, but it may equally be seen as characterizing the essentially homogeneous character of the mechanical world.

[22] The crucial conceptual development that was canonized in the Definition of Chalcedon was the making synonymous of ὑπόστασις and πρόσωπον. The former word lost its connotations of something underlying; the latter its suggestion of mere surface reality. In the person of Christ, the appearance was the reality, as Irenaeus never ceased to point out against docetists: what he seemed to be, that he was.

[23] Donald MacKinnon deploys the concept of substance against a similar absurdity, the view that things are 'logical constructions out of events', "Substance" in Christology', pp. 284–8.

been, thought has concentrated not on the constitutive relationality of other particulars so much as on underlying generalities. The former is too changing and unreliable, too limited to a particular time and a particular space. Two revealing and apparent exceptions to the rule have been Duns Scotus and George Berkeley. Scotus' philosophy of particularity, calling attention as it does to the *haecceitas*, 'thisness', of the individual, is justly celebrated. It appears to betoken a real concern for the unique reality of each thing: 'singularity belongs to a thing according to true existence, and so, from itself and unqualifiedly'.[24] The relation of this singularity to the generalizing concepts of late mediaeval philosophy is, however, obscure: 'this being is not matter, nor form, nor the composite, insofar as any of these is a nature; but it is the ultimate reality of the being which is matter, or which is form, or the composite...'[25] According to Copleston, 'The *haecceitas* does not confer any further qualitative determination; but it seals the being as *this* being. Scotus's view certainly cannot be equated with the theory that every nature is of itself individual...'[26] Despite the obscurity of the details, however, there is a clear move in the direction we are seeking. As David Knowles puts it,

This form or 'thisness' (*Haecceitas*) is a novel notion: it is the ultimate intelligible factor beneath the generic and the specific, the basis of individuality that makes a being different from all else... For Duns, the first attainment of the understanding is the singular, not the common, essence.[27]

The weakness of Scotus' account of particularity – apart from its obscurity – is shown by the fact that it was succeeded not by a strengthening of its case but by Ockham's non-relational nominalism. In other words, the metaphysical 'inscape' was not

[24] Duns Scotus, *Oxford Commentary* II. III. q. 1, in A. Hyman and J. J. Walsh, editors, *Philosophy in the Middle Ages. The Christian, Islamic and Jewish Traditions* (Indianapolis: Hackett, 1977), p. 582.   [25] Ibid., q. 6, p. 589.
[26] Frederick Copleston, *A History of Philosophy, Volume 2, Mediaeval Philosophy: Augustine to Scotus* (London: Burns, Oates and Washbourne, 1950), p. 517.
[27] David Knowles, *The Evolution of Medieval Thought* (London: Longman, 1962), p. 306.

strong enough to support it, and disappeared. Nothing in it suggests a relationality corresponding to and supporting the theory of particularity.

The aim of Berkeley's polemic against atheism and scepticism was in part to establish the concreteness of the particular. Things are as they are perceived to be because God sees to it that they are. The fact that Berkeley's theory of particulars was taken, for example by the foolish Dr Johnson, to be the opposite of what it set out to be is in large measure the fault of the terminology of *idea* that he inherited from the tradition of Descartes and Locke. The concrete particulars appear to be unstable and merely occasional moments of perception rather than the substantial entities that Berkeley intended.[28] There is also a major theological problem that emerges in the frequent discussions of the relation in Berkeley of archetype and particular. Berkeley's God is essentially the God of unitary traditional theism, so that the undifferentiatedness of his relation to the world appears to make necessary a choice between the loss of the otherness of the world and the loss of its substantiality. There is no way of establishing theologically the continuity of the tree in the quad without apparent special pleading. There is no hypostasis, but only idea. In sum, the weakness of the philosophies of both Scotus and Berkeley is that neither has an adequate doctrine of creation in which both the unity and diversity of things could be grounded.[29]

---

[28] '[I]s it not a sufficient evidence to me of the existence of this *glove*, that I see it, feel it, and wear it? Or if this will not do, how is it possible I should be assured of the reality of this thing, which I actually see in this place, by supposing that some unknown thing, which I never did or can see, exists after some unknown manner, in an unknown place, or in no place at all?' George Berkeley, *Three Dialogues between Hylas and Philonous, in Opposition to Sceptics and Atheists*, in *A New Theory of Vision and Other Writings* (London: Dent, 1910), pp. 259–60.

[29] The classical rationalist discussions of particularity are even more problematic than those of Scotus and Berkeley. Leibniz' atomistic theory of particularity is prey to equal and opposite difficulties. The problem with his monads is, as Charles Hartshorne never wearies of pointing out, that they are windowless, that is, that they lack relationality as integral to their being. They are self-contained substances, in the image of the self-contained monadic deity so characteristic of the Western tradition, and maintained in their harmony by him. Hartshorne's attempt to provide them with windows is, I believe, important, but finally fails to provide substantiality, most markedly in the doctrine that the unity of a series of events in time is merely

The modern problem of substantiality thus turns out to be the problem of God translated into the theory of finite realities. Corresponding to the deep-seated Western refusal to remain with the concrete hypostases in their relatedness, but to seek instead some underlying principle of deity, is the philosophical refusal to accept that a thing is primarily what it concretely is in its temporal and spatial relationality and limitedness. In contrast to that tendency, it must be argued that to be real, a being need not be supported by timeless monads or underlying substratum. It is here that Berkeley knew with such clarity the dragon that has to be slain. My suggestion is that something is real – what it is and not another thing – by virtue of the way it is held in being not only by God but also by other things in the particular configurations in space and time in which its being is constituted; that is to say, in its createdness. To take a simple example, we can say that a musical tone has its own proper being, given it for its brief time of existence by its relation to player, instrument, air movement and the rest; it has its own substantial being in space and time.[30] That is not to deny that

---

abstract. There is another problem with the Leibnizian approach, and it is Hartshorne's also: to suppose that the primary reality is not the particular that we experience, but the underlying constituent parts. The tendency to suppose that the reality is essentially other than the appearance is arguably at the root of the modern loss of substantiality, in which the failure to find the parts has led to a belief that there is no whole. Concreteness disappears because a basis for it is not discovered. As we have seen, Berkeley had long ago noticed that problem, and the realist side of his philosophy shows a concern to make the theological point that the concrete particulars of our experience are what they are by virtue of their constitution by God. Kant's analysis of substance is similarly indicative of the preoccupation of the tradition with an underlying unchanging basis for particularity: with the basing of what is spatial and temporal in the spaceless and timeless. Rightly seeing that under merely empirical analysis substance disappears, or loses substantiality, he attempts to establish it in terms of the categories. Kant's analysis reveals the same incapacity as that of Leibniz and Hartshorne to accept the concrete given as real on the ground that it lacks some quality supposed to be necessary for its acceptance, in this case a permanent underlying substratum. See, for example, *Critique of Pure Reason*, pp. 229–30.

30 Once again, Donald MacKinnon has made the point well in showing that the fact of degrees of substantiality does not deny the fact of what I am calling substantiality in general. 'The form of King's College Chapel remains relatively unaffected throughout the centuries; whereas a sandcastle is obliterated by the incoming tide and one can quickly mention entities (say successive waves of sound disseminated as the organ in King's College Chapel plays a Bach Prelude and Fugue) which never

there is often error in our perception and description of things, or that they can indeed be analysed into their constituent parts, nor is it to affirm that the surface is all there is. It is rather to deny the propriety of erecting a whole theory of being on the discovery that the sun does not go round the earth. More positively stated, it is to erect one on the implications of a theology of creation.[31] There is no need to deny that things, as much as – or rather, in different ways from – people, in some ways hide their true being. This is not a thesis about the transparency of things to the finite human mind but about the concreteness of things in their particular configurations in space and time: in their *haecceitas*.

To put it another way, I want to suggest that the crucial and concrete realities of our world are the particular things – substances – which are what they are by virtue of being wholes that are constituted indeed of parts but in such a way that they are more than simply the sum of the parts. In the natural world the thesis can be illustrated from the nature of crystals, of which it is sometimes said that they form spontaneously into the remarkable configurations of matter that they are. But the thesis has particular importance for man-made substances such as works of art. Modernism and late modernism tend to share the gnostic belief that because material particulars appear to be evanescent, they lack the kind of substantial reality that art has usually ascribed to them.[32] That is one cause of the tendency Fredric Jameson has noted to see works of art as disposable

---

coagulate to form a thing, while they yet possess a *Gestaltqualität* in their relations one to another which which makes them identifiable for what they are ... ', '"Substance" in Christology', p. 286.

[31] Once again, we must understand Genesis 1 as concerned to narrate the creation of particulars, not of timeless forms. Indeed, from one point of view, this book can be understood as a whole as consisting in an extended exegesis of that chapter in that way.

[32] The great achievement of Victor Zuckerkandl is to have shown that even those most apparently evanescent of realities, musical tones, have their own way of existing concretely. Music is a being in relation. 'Musical tones can be interpreted as events in a dynamic field ... The dynamic quality of each tone is determined by the dominant constellation of forces at the place where it sounded.' 'A piece of music is what it is, a particular meaningful entity made of tones, because its deep structure is organic in the exact biological sense of the term. To hear a composition is therefore directly to perceive organic structure ... ' *Man the Musician*, pp. 98, 195.

objects of consumer choice.[33] Such doctrines are in large measure anti-theological even if they also derive from a reaction against inadequate philosophies of substance coming from our past. If it is not believed that the world is the creation of God, it is hard to accept the goodness and rationality of the temporal and limited.[34]

It is by analogy with the inadequacy of the treatment of material particulars that we can realize also the failures of the philosophy of the human particular or person. For example, Hume's critique of the idea of human substantiality works only because it looks for the wrong thing, as, perhaps, do some modern proclamations of the loss of the subject. Because a timeless substratum has not been found, it is suspected that there is nothing to which substantiality can be attributed. Against this, a satisfactory conception of human particularity depends upon an acceptance of the fact that persons also are constituted in their particularity both by their being created such by God and by the network of human and cosmic relatedness in which they find their being. Here, the fact that the quest has been for some kind of internal characteristics parallels the quests for atomist or Leibnizian building blocks and for a timeless substratum underlying non-personal substances.[35] Another way of putting the point would be to say that the tradition is beholden to a false and essentially negative analogy between the person and the thing. We tend to see the thing as constituted by its externality or external relations, the person as internally constituted, largely, I suspect, because we believe that we know ourselves not by observing our relatedness with the other but by some kind of introspection, as a powerful tradition from Plato, through Augustine, Descartes, Kant to

---

[33] See above, Lecture 2, note 42.

[34] One must, indeed, wonder whether the very notion of a postmodern theology is not self-defeating.

[35] It is significant that Hume and Kant produce parallel critiques for both dimensions, and that when the object of the quest is not found the conclusion is that there is nothing at all to be found, so that the subject or the person disappears. The inner person can be saved by a number of moves, but whether the quest for the inner without the outer is any more successful in the case of persons than of things must be doubtful.

Freud has held.[36] If then we are to talk about the self, as I believe we must, it is essential not to neglect the external relations in which it is involved and through which it is constituted, nor, equally importantly, the analogy between personal and impersonal substance. It is in the analogy between the two, founded on the transcendentals, that is to be sought the true distinctiveness of the person as free but embodied spirit. A satisfactory conception of particularity depends upon an acceptance of the fact that persons also are constituted in their particularity both by their being created such by God and by the network of human and cosmic relatedness in which they find their being.

Thus despite, or rather for the sake of, the distinction of quality between the personal and impersonal, an analogy between the thing and the person can be developed. Both persons and things are hypostatic in the sense of being substantial particulars, and rendered such by the patterns of relations that constitute them what they distinctively are: with God in the first instance and with other temporally and spatially related particulars in the second. It is thus that *hypostasis*, meaning substantial particular, variously taking shape as person and thing and constituted relationally, acquires the status of a kind of transcendental. Everyone and every thing is what it uniquely is as hypostatic being; as we are often told, no two blades of grass are alike. It is our modern homogenizing culture that has tried to improve on the work of God. It is by developing the practical implications of such a transcendentality that the threatened and incipient homogenization of culture and reality can be counteracted. The importance of the particular person should not need to be stressed. Any society that subordinates persons to impersonal political or commercial philosophies offends against the divine image, confusing the creature and the creator, and will destroy itself. But the way we interact with nature in science, technology and art is closely bound up with our life in society, as we have already seen in the charge that

---

[36] Charles Taylor has argued, rightly I believe, that Augustine is the crucial influence on the modern conception of radical inwardness. *Sources of the Self*, chapter 7.

postmodernism represents the application to art of the philo-sophy of consumerism. Things are important as things, in all their concrete substantiality, as G. K. Chesterton perhaps uniquely among recent writers has reminded us.[37] Without that, there is no true philosophy of diversity – of true plurality within relation – as distinct from the kind of wet pluralism that assumes that deep down everything is really the same. Thus, it is crucial to the health of our culture that we pay attention to the transcendental status of particulars. Just as our reflections on the nature of perichoresis led to the conclusion that it is of transcendental significance, so here, it seems to me, must substance in the broadest sense, of a distinct – but not separate – particular, be seen to have the same status. I am related to you as a distinct person, to cabbages and stars and oceans as distinct beings, albeit as those whose substantiality takes a myriad of different forms.

4 THE LORD AND GIVER OF BEING

The theories of substance that I have criticized fail through lack of adequate theological support. In much of the Western intellectual tradition, the particularity of finite things has not been securely enough founded by particularity in the being of God. But with the help of the concept of the divine hypostases a theology of the many can be developed. We have seen that a case for the reality of particulars derived from experience alone is too weak, too subject to sceptical arguments derived from error and illusion. Barth is right in holding against Descartes and others that we can believe in the existence of the material world because we believe in God.[38] It is noteworthy how many philosophies and religions without a strong doctrine of creation do succumb to beliefs that the world is illusory or only half real.

---

[37] 'Thank God for hard stones; thank God for hard facts; thank God for thorns and rocks and deserts and long years. At least I know now that I am not the best or strongest thing in the world. At least I know now that I have not dreamed of everything.' Cited by Stephen R. L. Clark, 'Orwell and the Anti-Realists', p.149. Contrast this with John Milbank's ontology of creation, cited above, note 16, which concedes far too much to postmodernism.

[38] Karl Barth, *Church Dogmatics* volume 3/1, pp. 350–63.

But, as we have seen, there is a difference between the doctrine of creation classically conceived, as by Irenaeus, and its increasingly voluntarist and non-trinitarian expression in Augustine and his mediaeval successors. More is needed than asseverations that creation is *ex nihilo* because it comes from the free will of God. Without attention to the incarnational dimensions of the divine agency in creation, and the part played by the creator Spirit, the doctrine of creation comes to appear arbitrary and irrelevant.

In the Fourth Gospel there is laid a christological basis for an understanding of particularity in relationship which was later to be developed in the trinitarian theology of the church. In the language of mutual indwelling of, in the first instance, Jesus and his Father, we have a conception of relatedness without absorption. In it there is to be found the much noted and only apparent paradox that Jesus both claims a measure of equality with the Father and that 'the Father is greater than I'.[39] This is of immense importance for a conception of personal particularity, for it implies a variety of relatedness within the framework of an ontological equality. The particularity of persons does not imply their homogeneity. But the pneumatological determination of the relation of Jesus and the Father is also, as we have seen, important. The distinctive humanity of Jesus was constituted by his relation to the Father mediated by the Spirit. In his life, death, resurrection and ascension is to be discerned the eschatological action of God the Spirit, who thus perfects Jesus' particular humanity in space and time.

As we have also seen, we can infer from the economic activity a similar particularizing function in the life of the inner Trinity, but our interest now is on making that function universal. The Spirit's distinctive work in the world is, by relating the creation to God through Christ, to give direction to its being and beings. One of the ways – perhaps *the* way – that the Spirit thus perfects the creation may be seen in the constitution of particularity. We are accustomed – too accustomed – to speak of the Spirit as the

[39] John 14.28. 'Jesus' humiliation, whether we see that demonstrated in his birth, his washing of the disciples' feet or his sacrificial death, is a mark of his divinity and glory, not of his inferiority.' British Council of Churches, *The Forgotten Trinity*, p. 33.

unifier: bringing it about that in Christ we become one with the Father and each other, and so on. But trinitarian love has as much to do with respecting and constituting otherness as with unifying. As we saw in the previous chapter, it is the Son who is the unifier of creation, the one in whom all things hold together. By contrast but not in contradiction, we can understand the Spirit's distinctive mode of action as the one who maintains the particularity, distinctiveness, uniqueness, through the Son, of each within the unity. The stress here is on uniqueness. The mystery of existence is that everything is what it is and not another thing. That is the point of arguing for the transcendentality of hypostasis or substantiality.

The pneumatological dimensions of creation theology accordingly allow us to develop an ontology of the material particular as that which is destined to achieve a distinctively *finite* completeness or perfection in space and through time. ('It was the touch of the imperfect upon the would-be-perfect that gave the sweetness, because it was that which gave the humanity.'[40]) That is almost a definition of what I would want to call finite perfection, or rather, if the idea of perfection suggests something too static and given, it is a conception of finite realities as they are directed to the eschatological perfection that is promised, and sometimes realized from time to time in anticipation. Through the Spirit that which was and is will through Christ be in its own way completed, albeit, under the conditions of fallenness, only through redemption. If that is so, we can see also that divine creation is not, as it tends to be in Augustine, the creation of forms which are then embodied in dubiously real matter, but the constitution of particulars: not ideal and changeless forms but the one universe and the various things and persons within it – all those things that are so difficult of conception for the modern mind, as was

---

[40] Thomas Hardy, *Tess of the Durbervilles*, see also Shakespeare, *The Merchant of Venice*, 5. i. 108–9: 'How many things by season seasoned are / To their right praise and true perfection'; and 'A people sometimes will step back from war; / elect an honest man; decide they care / enough, that they can't leave some stranger poor. / Some men become what they were born for', Sheenagh Pugh, 'Sometimes', 100 *Poems on the Underground*, edited by G. Benson, J. Chernaik and C. Herbert (London: Cassell, 1991), p. 124.

argued in Chapter 2. The reading of Genesis 1 through Plato's eyes has obscured this point, that it does not celebrate the timeless being embodied in time but the richness and variety of life in matter: it celebrates the *haecceitas* that is the gift of the perfecting Spirit.[41]

If both *persons* and *things*, for all their crucial ontological differences, alike receive the shape of their being from the particularizing Spirit, we can no longer, in the tradition beginning with Descartes, treat matter as merely the intrinsically meaningless object of our instrumentality, as tends to be the way of both modernism and late modernism.[42] All particulars are formed by their relationship to God the creator and redeemer and to each other. Their particular being is a being in relation, each distinct and unique and yet each inseparably bound up with other, and ultimately all, particulars. Their reality consists, therefore – and this is the crucial difference from other theories of substance – not in the universals they instantiate, but in the shape of their relatedness with God and with other created hypostases. Their form is secondary to, because derivative of, their relation to the Other and to others. Thus it is that with the eyes given us by the doctrine of the Spirit we are enabled to see that substance is a kind of transcendental. Everything is what it is and not another thing. 'Substances', material particulars, are the most real things that there are, *because* the divine hypostases together constitute the being of God. Just as, therefore, we were free in the previous chapter to acknowledge the moments of truth in the apparently universal tendency of the human mind to discern a *Logos* holding together

---

[41] That such matters are of far more than merely theoretical importance has been the constant theme of this book. Here I can give two more examples. 'In a society which is really alive, something is always happening. The interplay of current activities and events, of overt and concealed movement, produces a constant succession of unique situations which provoke further and fresh movement.' Václav Havel, *Open Letters*, p. 72. The question for our culture, imprisoned in the tyranny of time, is how much of the life of our media is devoted chiefly to a shallow pretence that something is always happening. On the importance of richness rather than homogeneity, see also Bunge, *The Myth of Simplicity*, p. 48, for the conclusion of an argument for scientific theories that 'may yield an increasingly faithful and rich picture of the universe such that, to the extent to which it succeeds in combining diversity with unity, and in avoiding ontological reductionism (whether mechanistic of spiritualistic), it could be called *integrated pluralism*'. [42] Taylor, *Sources of the Self*, pp. 148–9.

the being of things, so here we can recognize the elements of truth in quests for a theory of substance, for the objects of the references and predications we attempt. The quest for substantiality is witness to the universal human relatedness, however suppressed and distorted by our sin, to the creator who gives us a substantial world in which to live, love, raise children, learn, grow plants, build houses and produce works of art.[43]

Substantiality is the gift of the creator, given in Christ in whom all things cohere. But, considered in the light of the Spirit's distinctive form of action as the perfecting cause of the creation, that substantiality is not fully given from the beginning but has to achieve its end. It is something that by divine and human agency is to be perfected through time and in space, and so is given from the concrete future that constitutes the promise of particular perfection.[44] That is the way in which the creation forms the framework, inscape, for science, art and morality. Human activity in and with the world becomes in that way part of the broader process in which human life as a whole may be offered to the Father in Christ and through the Spirit. It is here that the notion of art and science as the perfecting of the material world is important, but also and more important is that of human life as that which is to be offered to the Father in Christ and through the Spirit, agents alike of divine creation, redemption and perfection. If all that has been said so far is anywhere near to the truth, the created world in its teleology

---

[43] This means that we recognise the elements of truth in the complaints of, for example, Pannenberg that traditional conceptions of substance define it from the past, and thus enclose it in static changelessness. As we have seen, the point of a Coleridgean as distinct from a Platonic definition of idea is that a reality is understood in terms of its ultimate aim rather than of its statically defined past. To repeat Coleridge's definition from *Church and State*, p. 12: 'By an *idea*, I mean ... that conception of a thing, which is not abstracted from any particular state, form, or mode, in which the thing may happen to exist at this or at that time; nor yet generalized from any number or succession of such forms or modes; but which is given by the knowledge of *its ultimate aim.*' Thus there is no need to play, after the early Pannenberg, with unconvincing claims that the reality of something comes to it from the future, or even with Barthian ideas that the reality of things is to be understood as event. The dynamic is of a temporal substantiality, of a being completed through and in time rather than of a being from the abstract future.

[44] On such a view, substantiality and relational dynamic are not contraries, but correlatives.

CHAPTER 8

The triune Lord. Towards a theology of the one and the many

I RECAPITULATION

In the first four chapters, the theological determinants of salient aspects of modern culture were traced, and it was argued that certain crucial values have been lost, or submerged, in leading currents of thought and action. The result is a defective conception and practice of what I have called relationality, so that central dimensions of our created being are ignored, suppressed or distorted. In particular, the personal values on which so much depends have been endangered by an inadequate grasp of the way in which human life belongs in, and is shaped by, its habitation in wider reality. I argued also that a double movement underlies the problematic. On the one hand, it is possible to understand the ills of modernity as arising from a displacement of God and the replacing of the creator by the creature, with the only superficially paradoxical result that a movement aiming to give central importance to life in time and space has as a matter of fact cramped and distorted that which it claims to preserve. On the other hand, the leading thinkers of the modern world had some cause for the direction they took. The development of theology in the West had been strongly monistic, stressing the oneness and arbitrary will of God in such a way that the reality and importance of the created world appeared to be called in question. Modernity's protest against bad theology is therefore in large measure justified, although its displacement of the divine has been catastrophic in its effects.

In Part Two of the book, an alternative vision is being

adumbrated, alternative not only to the atheism of modernity but to the deficient theology against which it justifiedly protests. In the light of the claim that the problems on both sides derive from deficiencies of trinitarian thought, I have attempted to build some theses on Coleridge's conviction that the Trinity is the idea of ideas, in some way at once the clue to all thought and to all reality. This has had the following advantages. It has enabled a measured rather than dismissive response to some central categories of modern thought, while suggesting that they have been construed wrongly. In particular, the notion of *idea* has assisted in the development of aspects of Platonic thought – chiefly those suggested by Coleridge's adaptation of the Platonic tradition – without the drawbacks of the apparent disparagement of life in time and space which have nearly always been a mark of the form that Platonized theism has taken. The approach has also generated, I hope, new ways of thinking about the framework within which life is lived, and therefore gone some way to healing the divorce of the human from the world, which is perhaps the most disastrous outcome of the modern project.

Finally, the way of Coleridge has contributed to a non-authoritarian approach to a trinitarian theology of being, meaning and truth. It was his own view that there should be no absolute distinction between revelation and reason, and the position taken here is similar: that what can be learned from revelation, in this case the trinitarian concepts generated by the economy of salvation and understood apophatically of the eternal being of God, can be shown to correspond to the structures of universal human rationality. By this is meant that, because the trinitarian concepts reflect the being of God, we should be prepared to find them echoed in some way in human thought and in structures of the created world. Barth is right in arguing that by reason of human finitude and sin there is need for revelation if God is to be known as he truly is. He is also right, I believe, in arguing that such knowledge cannot be merely a human achievement, but rather must, as a human achievement, also be the gift of the Holy Spirit. But I believe that we can go further and hold that links can and may be drawn between the articulated theological implications of revelation and all other intellectual, moral and aesthetic concerns.[1] Revelation speaks to and constitutes human reason, but in such a way as to liberate the energies that are inherent in created rationality. It was in response to such a conviction that the fifth chapter was designed to take up the question of meaning and truth as it emerged in the discussion of the fourth.

Correspondingly, the sixth chapter took up the theme of the third, showing that christology, in the context of the whole Trinity, has an important contribution to make to the development of a distinct conception of the unity of things: a oneness which is not at the expense of the many. It did so by generating the first of three open transcendentals, perichoresis, which offers a way of articulating the oneness of things without derogating from their plurality. A perichoretic unity is a unity of a plural rather than unitary kind. In Chapter 7, the pneumatological contribution is shown to answer to this in a celebration of a particularity that takes shape in space and through time. The second open transcendental is thus substance or substantiality, and it suggested a new approach to the problems related in the second chapter. The many are truly many because everything is created by God to be and become what it is and not another thing. While it is the distinctive function of the eternal Son or Word to hold things together, the Spirit's characteristic form of action is the eschatological one of perfecting the particulars by relating them to their source and destiny.[2] We can also say that the Word is the focus of rationality, enabling us to conceive the relatedness of man and nature; while within that structure, the Spirit is the focus of freedom – of what Hardy and Ford call non-order[3] – of the non-determination of things that enables them to become determinate each in its own way.

---

[1] There can thus take shape a claim for the truth and distinctiveness of Christianity which is also truly open to conversation with other cultures and religions.

[2] As we shall see, the Spirit achieves this by bringing created realities to the Father through the Son.

[3] D. W. Hardy and D. F. Ford, *Jubilate. Theology in Praise* (London: Darton, Longman and Todd, 1984), pp. 96–9.

What becomes conceivable as a result of such a development is an understanding of particularity which guards against the pressure to homogeneity that is implied in modern relativism and pluralism. Both cosmologically and socially, we may say, there is need to give priority neither to the one nor to the many. Being is diversity within unity. By making it possible to show that there is a continuity and analogy between the universe as a framework and the human life which takes shape within it, christological and pneumatological emphases together enable us to understand the world as the context within which free personality and open society may develop. The human is *like* the non-human in being spatio-temporally particular, while it is also continuous with it in being bound up perichoretically with all of being. Thus can be found a framework which liberates rather than imprisons human life on earth, and which enables a symbiotic conception of the relation of man and nature, of a kind of community which makes us neither wholly active and dominant nor wholly passive and receptive in relation to the rest of the creation.

In this final chapter, we shall return to one of the concerns of the first, which opened with a discussion of the way in which the one and the many are treated in modern thought and culture, especially social thought. Using Heraclitus and Parmenides as symbols, I argued that antiquity and modernity alike are deficient in their tendency to drive towards unitary conceptions of social being and order. Modernity rightly suspects the monist tendencies of pre-modern theologies of encouraging a conception of unity which would suppress human particularity and freedom. But our world has its versions of the alienation, so that the modern world has tended to lurch between the one and the many and, through lack of an adequate mediating concept, has failed to do justice to the interests of both society and person, one and many. It has its own drive to repression, in the pressures it reveals not only in the repeated appearance in recent history of viciously totalitarian forms of government, but also in the drive to the herd society that has long been remarked to be characteristic of modern conditions. The twin spectres, which in many respects amount to the same thing, are totalitarianism and the culture of homogeneity. In this final chapter I complete what has been a chiasmus, by taking up the theme again in the light of the theology that has been developed in the latter half of the book.

2 COMMUNITY

The trinitarian conception suggested by the two transcendentals we have examined in the previous chapters – perichoresis and substantiality – is that of sociality. That is not the same as what has come to be called a social theory of the Trinity, with its suggestions of three almost independent deities. It is certainly closer to such a theory than the individualistic theories of the Trinity on the analogy of a single psychology. Rather, its central concept is that of shared being: the persons do not simply enter into relations with one another, but are constituted by one another in the relations. Father, Son and Spirit are eternally what they are by virtue of what they are from and to one another. Being and relation can be distinguished in thought, but in no way separated ontologically; they are rather part of the one ontological dynamic. The general point, to use the words of John Zizioulas, is that the being of God is not a blank unity, but a being in communion.[4] To adapt Gregory of Nazianzus, we may say that to think of divine being is to have one's mind necessarily drawn to the three persons, to think of the three to be led ineluctibly to a concept of shared, relational, being.

When we come to speak of human sociality, we once again speak by analogy. We are not what we are eternally because we are, as has been pointed out in previous chapters, constituted in a network of relations that takes shape within our boundedness in time and space. And yet we too are particulars in relation, both with respect to the primary constitution of our being by God and by its secondary constitution, in patterns of created sociality, by human society. Let us first look at the two poles of the analogy as it takes shape in the economy of divine action in

---

[4] It cannot be stressed too strongly that what we are concerned with here is a new kind of ontology, an ontology of communion. See J. D. Zizioulas, *Being as Communion. Studies in Personhood and the Church* (London: Darton, Longman and Todd, 1985).

time, particularly as it bears upon human community. It will take us to what can be broadly called ecclesiology, as the discipline concerned with human being together under God.

The crucial biblical and biblically derived concept is *koinonia* or communion. When speaking of the action of God, the New Testament, under the impact of the action and passion of Jesus, spoke of distinct forms of divine relation, being and action which yet in no way implied a loss of divine unity. To be sure, in some of the writing there is not always a strict demarcation between the actions of what later came to be called the persons of the Trinity, particularly between those of Christ and the Spirit. But the general point remains, and the Fourth Gospel is rightly considered as the completion of a process in which a conception of the divine being-in-relation comes strongly into view. The Father gives the Son, whose being and will is inseparable from his. He and the Father are one, while he is also sent to do the will of the Father on earth. After his glorification, the Son will ask the Father to send the Spirit who will perform towards the church and the world similar and yet distinct functions, again without a suggestion that anything is *individual* action. God appears to be conceived neither as a collectivity nor as an individual, but as a communion, a unity of persons in relation. If that is anachronistically to characterize the New Testament language in terms developed in later times, that is because I believe the later terms to be an appropriate generalization of the hints and pointers of the scriptures. If later theology also read the pattern back into the Old Testament - sometimes naively, it is true – that is because the being and action of God there are rightly adjudged to be those of a God whose being is more fully and personally defined in the light of the incarnation and the sending of the Spirit.

With the second phase of the analogy, we begin with the Old Testament, and especially with the opening chapters of Genesis, of which this book as a whole can be understood as an articulation. There it is made clear that creation is of beings in relationship, and in three distinct but related senses. First, the world is what it is by virtue of its createdness, which means a calling into otherness to and relation with its creator. The denial of that is the underlying reason why the misconstruals of human and worldly being that were charted in the first four chapters take the form that they do. In attempting to see the creation apart from the creator, they fail in important ways to see it at all. Second, the human creation is what it is as a being in relationship. That we have our true being in communion, and especially in the communion-in-otherness that is male and female, is the message of Genesis on both its positive and negative sides. Positively, humankind is social kind. Adam can find no true fellow creature among the animals, none that will enable him truly to be himself. It is only when he can rejoice in the fellowship of one who is a true other-in-relation that he is able to transcend the merely *individual* state that is a denial of human fullness. Negatively, the Fall leads to ever more disastrous breaches of communion, culminating in murder, the most serious sin against the image of God. The centrality of the two dimensions of communion is symbolized especially by Babel, according to which breach of communion with God leads to the depotentiation of that most central means of communion and communication, language. With the Fall, language divides rather than relates, and it is no accident that in the Acts of the Apostles one of the first actions of the Holy Spirit, the giver of communion, is symbolically to reverse Babel by restoring communication and so communion between the divided nations of the earth.

Third, and this is the conception with which we are chiefly concerned in this chapter, the world is what it is by virtue of its relation to those who bear the image of God. The shape that the world takes is in large part determined by what we, the human creation, make of it. Again, we can say that many disasters of all eras, but especially of modernity, derive from a misconstruction of that relation. The image has been understood individualistically, rather than in terms of a being in relation, so that patterns of alienation in relation to other human beings, of domination over rather than dominion of the rest of the creation, have eventuated. Yet despite the distortions, we must maintain a point that will recur, that the created world is not truly itself without us, its most problematic inhabitants. Without us, there is suffering and death but not pollution and moral evil; without us there is no science and art, none of the essentially moral action which enables the world to be itself. In summary, it can be said that the created world, as that which is what it distinctively is by virtue of its createdness, reflects in different ways the being of God in communion. The human creation, made in the image of God, reflects most directly the divine being in communion. But by virtue of its relation to both God and man, the rest of the created order, too, is brought into the relation of one and many that all this entails.

To begin to unpack the significance of all this for our topic, I shall begin with human community, and move from there to a discussion of the rootedness of that community in the rest of the created order. According to the New Testament, human community becomes concrete in the church, whose calling is to be the medium and realization of communion: with God in the first instance, and with other people in the second, and as a result of the first.[5] Of course, to bring in reference to the church is immediately to call attention to those institutions which play so ambiguous a part in Western history and society. I believe that it is a piece of foolish romanticism to believe that we can be human without our institutions. But it is also true that for much of our history the church has been an institution *rather* than a community,[6] and that is a matter we must take rather more seriously. The point of referring to the New Testament is therefore chiefly to remind ourselves of the centrality of

[5] It should scarcely require repetition that communion depends upon atonement: upon the reconciliation of relations lost at the Fall. That is one reason why both christology and pneumatology are essential to an understanding of communion. Where community is breached, it cannot be restored without the healing or extirpation of that which occasioned the breach. That is why Christ dies under the law, on the altar and in conflict with the demons. Communion, the will of the creator for his people, is the shape of their being in relation, but of a being that apart from redemption is destined for the relationlessness that is death. As we have seen in the illustration from Acts, the communication that is essential to communion must first be restored. But reconciliation is a restoration, and not the gift of new being: the reintegration of the disintegrated, the restoration by the Spirit of a directedness to the other rather than to the self. The need for reconciliation, the redirection to community, is also the reason why ecclesiology must be at the centre of our understanding of the human condition.

[6] Perhaps it would be better to say, 'fellowship of communities', in view of the fact that the local church is the first place where community is to be sought and found.

communion – of sociality – to the writers. We can here glance only at a number of aspects: at John's insistence that relations within the church must in some sense be analogies of those between the persons of the Father and the Son; at Paul's understanding of the relation between being in Christ, who for him is the instantiation of the image of God, and the breaking down of barriers to community and communication.

The notion of communion provides an important focus for understanding many of the themes characteristic of the theology of Paul. To look at his thought in its light is to show how concern for it pervades his writings. The claim that 'in Christ' there is no Jew or Greek, male or female, etc., is an obvious place at which to begin, along with the possibly deutero-Pauline conception of the breaking of the historic walls of partition. In 1 Corinthians 11 clear links are drawn between the holy communion and ecclesial community, while the succeeding chapters spell out some of the theology and ethics of the matter. The extended metaphor of the body and its members is a theology of being-in-relation, and it seems clear that Paul's talk of being in Christ is not to be construed in terms of Christ-mysticism but relationally, of being in communion. Thus, for example, the baptized are brought into relation with God and with each other in the same act, by virtue of sharing in communion with the one Father, mediated by the Son and realized by the Spirit. Those who are in Christ are in the church: brought into relation to God through him and into community simultaneously. Paul's near identification of Christ and the church derives from his theology of community. And it brings with it implications for human community in general, reinforcing what we saw to be a possible interpretation of Genesis, that to be human is to be created in and for community.

Despite what is often said, and despite the distinctive situation of the New Testament church as a minority community unsure of its place in the world, there is some evidence that its setting in the wider world was of interest to it. The confession of Christ as mediator of creation and the narratives of Jesus' authority over the created order witness a widely held conviction that the gospel was not merely one of human sociality, but with that in its cosmic context. The much-cited eighth chapter of Romans depicts some form of community with the created order as a whole, as does Revelation's promise of a new heaven and new earth as the context for the community of the new Jerusalem. Community is not context-less: it takes shape in a world which is not irrelevant to its being, as the garden was in some way integral to the being of Adam and Eve. Thus we return to the two themes adumbrated in the first chapter: of the one and the many of the social order, and of the relation of that order to the one and the many of cosmic order. In this chapter, the two questions will form the framework for the next two sections.

3 SOCIALITY

How much may we make of such summary remarks on biblical ecclesiology in a discussion of whether sociality is a transcendental? One could respond to the biblical teaching by agreeing that it is a good thing to be in community, but that it is a different matter to claim that human being is being in communion. That is to say, it is one thing to speak of what is the best way to live with others in community, another to develop what amounts to a *metaphysic* of persons in communion. For reasons that should be apparent, I believe that metaphysics, or, if that word carries too many negative associations, ontology, a theology of being, is important. The patterns of alienation set out in the first four chapters show that there is in some patterns of modern thought a denial of metaphysics that amounts to a metaphysic. Underlying much modern dogma there is the implicit belief that the prime reality is the human will which is ontologically either so distinct from the rest of the world or so continuous with it that the only conceivable orientations are the alternatives of dominance or resignation. It is in such a light that the fragmentation of the modern world can be questioned with the help of a theology of being which seeks to be true to the nature of human being in the world and in community. It is the justification of such a personal metaphysic that is here in question.

The background to the topic in modern thought is found in

Hobbes' view, which was in part a revival of that of Thrasy-machus reported in the *Republic*,[7] of the essentially individu-alistic and predatory nature of the human being. The view makes an ontology of human fallenness or sin, saying that certain forms of anti-social behaviour reveal us as what we essentially are, so that any form of social order is of chiefly negative purpose, to protect the weak from the effects of unrestrained domination by the strong. A similar view emerges later in what is called social Darwinism,[8] and in Nietzsche.[9] On such an account, a society is a form of social contract entered into for the sake of convenience or safety. Social existence is not essential to our being as humans, but a more or less unfortunate necessity. A similar, though more optimistic, view of the social contract was to be found in Locke, who is, none the less, strongly individualistic. Sir Ernest Barker claimed that 'The figure of the Individual – seated on his desert pillar – this, in brief, is the symbol with which we are left, alike by the *Essay* and the *Two Treatises*'.[10] Both Hobbes and Locke found their concepts of the social contract on a deficient sociality, a failure to consider the essentially social nature of human being. On such a conception, the very notion of a social contract is easy game. Not only is there no historical basis for such an idea, there is no positive basis in human nature either. Accordingly, it is not even an appropriate metaphor with which to approach the nature of human social order because that is an imposition upon or distortion of essential individuality.

A major agent in the criticism of such a view in modern times is G. W. F. Hegel. Hegel has already appeared in previous chapters as an essential catalyst in the history of thought. It is

---

[7] Plato, *Republic*, 336–46.

[8] It is becoming increasingly clear that what is now called social Darwinism was one of the forces driving the thought of Darwin himself, as his recent biographers make plain. Adrian Desmond and James Moore, *Darwin* (London: Michael Joseph, 1991).

[9] Reinhold Niebuhr's anthropology shows some of the marks of this tradition, and shows the theological roots of such a theory. In its extreme form, it is an ontology of fallenness or sin in which alienation is made an all but essential defining characteristic of the human being. In that respect, it is a social version of the gnosticism that is so marked a feature of some modernist art. See above, Chapter 3, Section 5.

[10] Cited by Sir Ernest Barker from an article he had himself written in 1932, 'Introduction' to *Social Contract. Essays by Locke, Hume and Rousseau* (London: Oxford University Press, 1947), p. xxiii.

clear, as Robert Solomon has pointed out, that he marks a clear advance on the individualism of Kant. 'It is worth noting that there is no social element in [Kant's] picture, no community of scientists, public opinion, or pressures from colleagues, employers, or research-granting agencies. Knowledge is purely a relationship between the autonomous individual and the world of nature, and morality is a relationship between the individual and universal law, a product of pure practical reason.'[11] In contrast to this, Hegel has a theory of sociality, of human being as social being. The weakness of Hegel's conception of social being, however, is that it so easily collapses, as in Marxism, into a form of society in which the particular is suppressed.

We would therefore be better advised to seek the basis of a theology of sociality in the thought of Coleridge. Early in his career, Coleridge had attempted a critique of the Hobbesian view of social order. Hobbes' theory fails because 'a million of insulated Individuals is only an abstraction of the mind ... '[12] In response, Coleridge developed the view that the idea of the social contract in some way represents a fundamental possibility for human social thought. It is not that the social contract is a historical reality, but that thought of human being in its light is a permanent possibility, a continuing way of conceiving human being in relatedness.

Now, if this be taken as the assertion of an historical fact, or as the application of a conception ... to an actual occurrence in the first ages of the world; ... I shall run little hazard ... in declaring the pretended fact a pure fiction, and the conception of such a fact an idle fancy ... For what if an original contract had actually been entered into, and formally recorded? Still I cannot see what addition of moral force would be gained by the fact. The same sense of moral obligation which binds us to keep it, must have pre-existed in the same force and in relation to the same duties, impelling our ancestors to make it ...

But if instead of the *conception* or *theory* of an original social contract, you say the *idea* of an ever-originating social contract, this is so certain and indispensable, that it constitutes the whole ground of the

[11] Robert Solomon, *Continental Philosophy since 1750. The Rise and Fall of the Self* (Oxford: Oxford University Press, 1988), p. 40.
[12] Samuel Taylor Coleridge, *The Friend: A Series of Essays to aid in the Formation of Fixed Principles in Politics, Morals, and Religion. With Literary Amusements Interspersed* (London: William Pickering, 1844), p. 224.

difference between subject and serf, between a commonwealth and a slave-plantation. And this, again, is evolved out of the yet higher idea of *person*, in contradistinction from thing ... [13]

If we are to develop these thoughts, we must bear in mind the metaphorical and personal character of the idea of contract. We are no more bound by it to a merely juridical view of human relations than we are by the teaching that Christ died under the law. The language of contract is a metaphorical way of speaking of the social.

The idea of social contract becomes the basis for a contention that ecclesiology, in the general sense of the word, is the basis of human being. That does not entail an authoritarian view, sometimes entertained in the history of Christianity, that all should be 'compelled to come in' to the ecclesiastical institution – and it should be noticed that it is no part of Coleridge's view – but that social being, of the kind embodied in a true *ecclesia*, is the deepest expression of human reality. It is significant here that the Bible has given us a word for social relations which allows neither a purely individualist nor a merely legal construal. It is that of covenant. *Covenant* expresses above all the calling of the human race into free and joyful partnership with God, and so with each other. [14]

In an important paper, Daniel Hardy has argued that in that sense ecclesiology can be regarded as the form of all created human being. He argues that sociality is a transcendental, and therefore pertains not just to redeemed being – being in the church – but to created being as a whole. While accepting the danger of ideology, in which 'universal human solidarity is too often based on the notion of assimilation to a particular social

[13] Samuel Taylor Coleridge, *Church and State*, pp. 14–15. Paul Johnson cites, from *Letters, Volume* 2, 1197, a saying that shows Coleridge's awareness of the relational character of those made in the image of God. 'A male and female Tyger is neither more nor less whether you suppose them only existing in their appropriate wilderness, or whether you suppose a thousand pairs. But Man is truly altered by the coexistence of other men; his faculties cannot be developed in himself alone, and only by himself.' *The Birth of the Modern*, p. 826.

[14] I owe this point to Christoph Schwoebel. In the covenant with Abraham, the promise is made that in him all the nations of earth shall be blessed; in the covenant realized through the death and resurrection of Jesus, all are called into the community of reconciliation made possible by his atonement.

group', he yet argues for the necessity of the social transcendental. 'The aim is to establish an element which will justify a true society, and thus inform the pragmatics of human society.'[15] The quest for him too is for what I have called open transcendentals, possibilities for thought which are universal in scope yet open in their application.[16] Hardy's contention is that 'ecclesiology', as sociality made explicit, is the true form of human being. To be a human being is to be created in and for relationship with God and with other human beings. The particular character of that being is defined and realized christologically and pneumatologically, by Christ the creator and the Holy Spirit, the one through whom the perfection of the creation is promised and from time to time realized. A theology of sociality teaches that those whose being is constituted by relation to the triune God should succumb to the ideology neither of the one nor of the many. Communion is being in relation, in which there is due recognition of both particularity and relationality. But that does not make sociality a transcendental, and here I depart from Hardy's vocabulary. It is a doctrine of the personal, and leaves unresolved the question of the relation of human society to the material context within which it takes shape. It is therefore ideal rather than transcendental. To see something of what is required for a true transcendentality that will embrace also the non-social world, we turn to another famous conception of the social contract, one indeed which pivots on the notion of a dualism of social order and nature.

4 SOCIALITY IN CONTEXT

As we have seen in the reference to Coleridge, the notion of the social contract, in some of its forms, enables us to see something of the point of the claim that sociality is of ideal status. It is one of those notions without which we cannot understand who and

---

[15] Daniel W. Hardy, 'Created and Redeemed Sociality', p. 34.
[16] Hardy illustrates the transcendental theory with a parallel from the philosophy of science. '[T]he social transcendental is like what is called a "generic semi-interpreted theory" in science, such as general classical field theory ... Like such a theory, it is comprised of notions which are assigned no factual interpretation ... ; and is testable only conceptually [if] it is given further specification ... ' Ibid., p. 29.

what we are. But we have not yet engaged with the second question raised at the end of the outline of the biblical background of the topic, the relation of social being and material environment. The characteristically modern problem is indicated by the thought of Rousseau, one of the proponents of that very social contract theory with which we have seen Coleridge engage so fruitfully. Just as for Hobbes the human condition is one of internecine strife, so for Rousseau it is one of a strife with nature which is the fruit of an essentially unnatural social order. As Solomon puts it, 'the infamous contrast of Rousseau's work, between happy individuals in the state of nature and the miserable creatures in modern society, is never very far from consideration'. He cites the crucial passages:

Savage man, when he has dined, is at peace with nature, and the friend of his fellow creatures ... The case is quite different with man in the state of society ...

Nature made man happy and good, and society depraves him and makes him miserable.[17]

It is in the dualism of man and nature that Solomon finds the basis of what he calls the transcendental pretence, that which I have argued theologically to result from the displacement of God. Kant, who was deeply influenced by Rousseau, shared with him:

a spectacularly self-centred image of the moral world ... Rousseau's 'inner self' becomes Kant's noumenal self, and the difference is more one of method than substance. The transcendental pretence begins with this extraordinary self-confidence that one is in touch with the absolute principle of Goodness ... Instead of morality we have cosmic self-righteousness – the transcendental pretence.[18]

The shift in the source of transcendentality, from God to the human will, I might gloss, is the root of the characteristically modern forms of alienation. In this case, it founds the deep modern unease with living in the world, in which we swing between a Kantian ethic of dominance to a Rousseau-esque

---

[17] Cited by Solomon, *Continental Philosophy since* 1750, pp. 20–1 from *Second Discourse and Emile*.   [18] Ibid., pp. 40–1.

worship of nature. But how may we escape it for a more wholesome way of living in the world? The key is once more to be found in a trinitarian doctrine of creation and theory of transcendentality.

We saw earlier, by reference to the theology of the Fourth Gospel, that God appears to be conceived neither as a collectivity nor as an individual, but as a communion, a unity of persons in relation. The theology of the Trinity as a dynamic personal order of giving and receiving is, in the idea of sociality that it suggests, the key to the matter of transcendentality that we are seeking.[19] Because there is a diversity of relations, the triune giving and receiving is asymmetrical rather than merely reciprocal, and is the key to the transcendentality that we are seeking. Like the other Coleridgean 'ideas', this can be seen to generate analogies of universal application, and, as it does, to lay open the following features. First is that the heart of human being and action is a relationality whose dynamic is that of gift and reception. Because human relationality is analogous to that revealed in the self-giving of Christ, sacrificial imagery appears in Paul's development of a non-reciprocal ethic of gift and response in the opening of the ethical section of the Letter to the Romans: 'present your bodies as a living sacrifice, holy and acceptable to God' (Romans 12.1). The realization of such an ethic is necessarily, as its development in Romans shows, communal and social: praise and righteous action are forms of human being that take place primarily in the church, under

---

[19] This is one of those places where the theology of creation is inextricably bound up with the economy of salvation, which provides its noetic basis. Trinitarian biblical talk of the saving action of God draws heavily on the language of sacrifice, and it is this that forms the gateway to the theology of the Trinity here outlined. God the Father 'gives up' his only Son, allows him to be delivered into the hands of sinful men. Jesus lays down his life, and, particularly but not only in the theology of the Letter to the Hebrews, offers his humanity, made perfect through suffering to the Father. So it is with the Spirit. As the gift of the Father he is the *aparchai*, first fruits, of the perfecting action of God in Christ. Although, under the conditions of the Fall, the sacrifice of Jesus must take the form of the spilling of blood, that aspect is not of the essence of sacrifice, which is rather to be found in the notion of gift. It is the Father's giving of the Son, the Son's giving of himself to the Father and the Spirit's enabling of the creation's giving in response that is at the centre. It is by such a means that we move from the economy to the heart of the being of God. It is as a dynamic of giving and receiving, asymmetrical rather than merely reciprocal, that the communion that is the triune life must be understood.

Word and through sacrament. It is important to note in this respect the forms of human relationality that are involved. In both the gospels and epistles, the chief ethical emphasis is in contradiction of mere reciprocity. Creative subordination to others in conformation to Christ and replication of his manner of being towards others is the form of humanity that lives out the transcendental dynamics of things.[20]

It is important to emphasize that we have in this an ethic of transformation and not of submission, or a glorifying in suffering of the kind that Nietzsche believed to be the heart of Christianity. As we have already seen, the use of sacrificial imagery in this connexion does not imply suffering in the first instance. The transcendental reference is not to that, but to the free offering to God, perfected, of that which he has created: a giving in praise of that which was given to be used for the praise of God. That this must often involve sacrifice in the popular sense of a giving up or suffering is a function of the fallenness of things, not of our fundamental createdness. Jesus' sacrificial recapitulation of human life is achieved for the purpose of a completing of the creation, of a setting free for the living out of creaturely being. That living out which is the offering to God of redeemed human action undoubtedly involves a carrying of the cross and the experience of toilsome and often unrewarding labour – of what we call failure – but the primary end is a giving in praise of that which is given to be used for the praise of God.

But it is also true that a Christian view of life will here come into sharpest conflict with modernity and what Lesslie Newbigin has called its 'myth of fulfilment'. The doctrine that the calling of the person is to fulfil himself or herself is both individualist and a characteristic fruit of the transcendental pretence that would make the world circle around the sun that is the individual. The false transcendentality that is the ideological basis of modernism mistakes the character of human relationality. Because in modernity individual self-fulfilment

---

[20] So it is that in 2 Corinthians Paul uses the language of economics that we have met elsewhere. In the triune economy, there is, by virtue of the priority of giving, no calculation of quantities and ends.

has displaced God from the centre of the world, it makes itself the centre of things, and so uses both person and world as means to its ends. Here it is appropriate to allude again to the observation that while modernism excludes the other, postmodernism seeks to render it irrelevant.[21] The logic of sociality as gift and reception, however, shows that the other is central for our being. What we receive from and give to others is constitutive: not self-fulfilment but relation to the other as other is the key to human being, universally.

As with human life in its specific directedness – and it will be noticed that the transcendental category is open to many distinct and particular forms of embodiment in different lives – so it is with the modes of human response to God and the world in thought, moral action and aesthetic shaping. And so we come to the second feature of the analogy: its implication for our relation to the non-personal world. It is through the logic of gift and reception that the links between the human quests for truth, goodness and beauty – between the diverse forms of human action in and towards the world – can be sought. If the true end of all human action is praise of the creator, of rendering to him due response for his goodness, we have here a common light to illuminate all the dimensions of human culture. To say that all action should take the form of the sacrifice of praise is to say that action toward the world is action directed to allowing that world truly to be itself before God. That will not prescribe in advance the form that any particular cultural enterprise should take, but rather place it within the framework of a universal transcendentality, which, as the remark of Daniel Hardy, cited above, showed, imposes no specific empirical shape. Charles Taylor cites to similar effect a saying of the seventeenth-century divine, William Perkins, that 'if we compare worke to worke, there is a difference between washing of dishes and preaching of the word of God: but as touching to please God none at all'.[22] It is the relatedness of everything to God, realized in the free offering of things to him, that is the basis for a universal and open transcendentality.

---

[21] Above, Chapter 2, p. 69.   [22] Charles Taylor, *Sources of the Self*, p. 224.

It is for such reasons that the practice of both art and the proper dominion of the natural order are trinitarian imperatives, for both are ways of fulfilling the command of the creator to those created male and female in his image. It is at that place that both Rousseau and Kant misconstrued the human relation to the natural world. Their approaches are two sides of the same dualism of spirit and nature, mind and thing, that alienates person and world. According to the logic of relationality, we may neither, with Rousseau and his modern New Age successors, romanticize nature in such a way that it becomes the main criterion for thought and action, nor with Kant and the mechanists impose on nature an entirely external ethic of domination. They both in the same measure deny the relationality which is the law of our being, tending in the one case to a pure receptivity, and corresponding conservatism, and in the other to a pure ethic of action, and corresponding revolutionary mentality. Such destructive modern tendencies can be obviated only by developing a different theology and ontology from that against which modernity reacted.

And that returns us to another of the themes of the first chapter, where there was promised the development of a non-Platonic conception of the transcendence of God. Transcendence means, among other things, otherness. As we have seen, modernity rebelled against an alienating otherness, but in such a way as at once to deny divine transcendence and to threaten the true otherness of the world, thus making the cure worse than the disease. The loss of otherness-in-relation, both personal and cosmic is its characteristic nemesis. In response to the crisis of modernity, the trinitarian logic of gift and reception modifies the logic of pure will that has so dominated the tradition, ancient and modern alike, because it frames that which drives human thought and action within a *social* metaphysic of gift and reception. In the first place, the theology of the Trinity enables us to conceive the utter *ontological* otherness of God and the world. It is one thing to be God, quite another to be the creation. All forms of ontological continuity, whether they express an assured link between divine agency and that of a church or the automatic divine involvement in forms of created being, must be excluded, *a limine*, as Barth liked to say, as a form of the transcendental pretence which claims divinity for the merely created. But, in the second place, because it generates a theology of free and open relations, such a logic is not necessarily alienating. God's relation to the world is personal and free, and so also liberating. The teaching that the creation is what it is by virtue of the real relation of God to it both in its absolute beginning out of nothing and in its being continually upheld and directed to perfection is not the offence that it has been taken to be. Because the world has its 'inscape' provided by the Son, the one who became part of the world for the sake of the world, and the Spirit, whose characteristic form of action is to enable the world to become itself, a trinitarian theology of creation offers that which neither antiquity – for the most part – nor modernity adequately achieved.

5 CONCLUSION

What, then, is the nature of the transcendentality that we are seeking? In the light of the foregoing discussion, we should conclude that sociality is of ideal status, in the Coleridgean sense. It is an essential concept if we are to understand the distinctive character of personal beings, but does not apply to everything. Personal beings are social beings, so that of both God and man it must be said that they have their being in their personal relatedness: their free relation-in-otherness.[23] This is not so of the rest of the creation, which does not have the marks of love and freedom which are among the marks of the personal. Of the universe as a whole we should conclude that it is marked by relationality rather than sociality. All things are what they are by being particulars constituted by many and various forms of relation. Relationality is thus the transcendental which allows us to learn something of what it is to say that all created people and things are marked by their coming from and returning to the God who is himself, in his essential and inmost being, a being in relation. And it is a transcendental which at

---

[23] Therefore, despite all that I have learned from Daniel Hardy's paper, I cannot with him speak of the 'social transcendental'.

the same time enables us to incorporate the insights gained from the discussion of the other two transcendentals, perichoresis and substantiality.

Accordingly, of both God and the world it must be said that they have their being in relation. In the case of God, the transcendentals are functions of the eternal and free relations of the persons, each of whom has, in inseparable relation to the others, his particular manner of being and acting. This does not mean that we have a private view into the being of God, but that the general characteristics of God's eternal being, as persons in relation, communion, may be known from what he has done and does in the actions that we call the economy of creation and salvation. In turn, the doctrine of God derived from the economy enables us to see that the creation bears in different ways the marks of its making, so that the transcendentals qualify people and things, too, in a way appropriate to what they are. In sum, the transcendentals are functions of the finitely free relations of persons and of the contingent relations of things.

To be created is to have a direction, a dynamic, which derives from the createdness of all things by the triune God. That dynamic can be subverted, reversed, even, so that that which is directed to its own particular perfectedness instead participates in dissolution and death. But such disorientation does not, at least not this side of eternity, deprive of being, for only the creator can do that. What can be brought about is not the deprivation of being but its involvement in patterns of relationship which make for its loss of ontic integrity. Ontologically, the creature is ordered to the completion of its particular end in space and time; ontically, it is caught up in a history and dynamic that would subvert its orderedness. Redemption thus means the redirection of the particular to its own end and not a re-creation. The distinctive feature of created persons is their mediating function in the achievement of perfection by the rest of creation. They are called to the forms of action, in science, ethics and art – in a word, to culture – which enable to take place the sacrifice of praise, which is the free offering of all things, perfected, to their creator. Theologically put: the created world becomes truly itself – moves towards its completion – when through Christ and the Spirit, it is presented perfect before the throne of the Father. The sacrifice of praise which is the due human response to both creation and redemption takes the form of that culture which enables both personal and non-personal worlds to realize their true being.

Bibliography

Adams, David, 'The Doctrine of Divine Person Considered both Historically and in the Contemporary Theologies of Karl Barth and Jürgen Moltmann', PhD, Fuller Theological Seminary, 1991.

Adorno, T. W., and Horkheimer, M., *Dialectic of Enlightenment*, translated by J.Cumming (London: Verso, 1979).

Auty, Giles, 'Prosaic Pontificators', *The Spectator*, 27 April 1991, 34–5.

Aves, John, 'Persons in Relation: John Macmurray', *Persons, Divine and Human. King's College Essays in Theological Anthropology*, edited by Christoph Schwoebel and Colin Gunton (Edinburgh: T. & T. Clark, 1992), pp. 120–37.

Bailey, Derrick Sherwin, *The Man-Woman Relation in Christian Thought* (London: Longman, 1959).

Balthasar, Hans Urs von, *The Glory of the Lord. A Theological Aesthetics, Volume 2, Studies in Theological Styles: Clerical Styles*, translation edited by John Riches (Edinburgh: T. & T. Clark, 1984).

Banks, Robert, *The Tyranny of Time* (Exeter: Paternoster Press, 1983).

Barrow, John D., *Theories of Everything. The Quest for Ultimate Explanation* (Oxford: Clarendon Press, 1991).

Barrow, J. D. and Tipler, F. J., *The Anthropic Cosmological Principle* (Oxford: Clarendon Press, 1986).

Barth, Karl, *Church Dogmatics*, translation edited by G. W. Bromiley and T. F. Torrance (Edinburgh: T. & T. Clark, 1957–1969), volumes 2/1, 2/2, 3/1, 3/2 and 3/3.

Protestant Theology in the Nineteenth Century: Its Background and History, translated by B. Cozens and J. Bowden (London: SCM Press, 1972).

The Christian Life. Church Dogmatics, Volume 4/4, Lecture Fragments, translated by G. W. Bromiley (Grand Rapids: Eerdmans, 1981).

Bebbington, D. W., 'Evangelical Christianity and Modernism', *Crux* 26 no. 2 (June 1990), 2–9.

'Evangelical Christianity and Romanticism', *Crux* 26 no.1 (March 1990), 9–15.

'Evangelical Christianity and the Enlightenment', *Crux* 25 no. 4 (December 1989), 29–36.

Beck, Lewis White, 'Kant's Theoretical and Practical Philosophy', *Studies in the Philosophy of Kant* (Indianapolis and New York: Bobbs Merrill, 1965), pp. 3–53.

Berkeley, George, *Three Dialogues between Hylas and Philonous, in Opposition to Sceptics and Atheists*, in *A New Theory of Vision and Other Writings* (London: Dent, 1910).

Berlin, Isaiah, *Two Concepts of Liberty. An Inaugural Lecture delivered before the University of Oxford on 31 October 1958* (Oxford: Clarendon Press, 1985).

Berman, Marshall, *All that is Solid Melts into Air. The Experience of Modernity* (New York: Verso, 1983. 1st edition 1982).

Bernstein, Richard, *Beyond Objectivism and Relativism: Science, Hermeneutics and Practice* (Philadelphia: University of Pennsylvania Press, 1985).

Bloom, Allan, *The Closing of the American Mind. How Higher Education Has Failed Democracy and Impoverished the Souls of Today's Students* (London: Penguin Books, 1987).

Blumenberg, Hans, *The Legitimacy of the Modern Age*, translated by R. M. Wallace (Cambridge, MA, and London: MIT Press, 1983).

Booth, Wayne C., *Modern Dogma and the Rhetoric of Assent* (Chicago and London: University of Chicago Press, 1974).

Bouwsma, William J., *John Calvin. A Sixteenth Century Portrait* (New York and Oxford: Oxford University Press, 1989).

Bradshaw, Timothy, *Trinity and Ontology. A Comparative Study of the Theologies of Karl Barth and Wolfhart Pannenberg* (Edinburgh: Rutherford House, 1989).

British Council of Churches, *The Forgotten Trinity, Volume 1, The Report of the BCC Study Commission on Trinitarian Doctrine Today* (London: British Council of Churches, 1989).

Brown, Peter, *Augustine of Hippo. A Biography* (London: Faber and Faber, 1969).

Buckley, Michael, *At the Origins of Modern Atheism* (New Haven and London: Yale University Press, 1987).

Bunge, Mario, *The Myth of Simplicity. Problems of Scientific Philosophy* (Englewood Cliffs, NJ: Prentice Hall, 1963).

Cantor, Geoffrey, *Michael Faraday: Sandemanian and Scientist. A Study of Science and Religion in the Nineteenth Century* (London: Macmillan, 1991).

Christensen, Jerome, *Coleridge's Blessed Machine of Language* (Ithaca and London: Cornell University Press, 1981).

Clark, Stephen R. L., *God's World and the Great Awakening. Limits and Renewals* 3 (Oxford: Clarendon Press, 1991).

'Orwell and the Anti-Realists', *Philosophy* 67 (1992), 141–54.

Clarke, Paul A. B., 'On Modernity', *Theology, the University and the Modern World*, edited by P. A. B. Clarke and Andrew Linzey (London: Lester Crook, 1988), pp. 91–136.

Coakley, Sarah, *Christ without Absolutes. A Study of the Christology of Ernst Troeltsch* (Oxford: Clarendon Press, 1988).

Coburn, Kathleen, *In Pursuit of Coleridge* (London: The Bodley Head, 1977).

Coleridge, Samuel Taylor, 'Notes on Waterland's Vindication of Christ's Divinity', *The Complete Works of Samuel Taylor Coleridge*, edited by W. G. T. Shedd (New York: Harper and Brothers, 1853), volume 5, pp. 404–16.

'On the Prometheus of Aeschylus', *The Complete Works of Samuel Taylor Coleridge*, edited by W. G. T. Shedd (New York: Harper and Brothers, 1853), volume 4, pp. 344–65.

On the Constitution of the Church and State. The Collected Works of Samuel Taylor Coleridge, Volume 10, edited by John Colmer (London: Routledge and Kegan Paul, 1976).

The Friend: A Series of Essays to Aid in the Formation of Fixed Principles in Politics, Morals, and Religion. With Literary Amusements Interspersed (London: William Pickering, 1844).

The Notebooks of Samuel Taylor Coleridge, Volume 4, 1819–1826, edited by Kathleen Coburn and Merton Christensen (London: Routledge, 1990).

The Philosophical Lectures of Samuel Taylor Coleridge, edited by Kathleen Coburn (London: Pilot Press, 1949).

Copleston, Frederick, *A History of Philosophy, Volume 2, Mediaeval Philosophy: Augustine to Scotus* (London: Burns, Oates and Washbourne, 1950).

Cowling, Maurice, *Religion and Public Doctrine in Modern England* (Cambridge: Cambridge University Press, 1980).

Craig, Edward, *The Mind of God and the Works of Man* (Oxford: Clarendon Press, 1987).

Cupitt, Don, *Creation out of Nothing?* (London: SCM Press, 1990).

Desmond, Adrian, and Moore, James, *Darwin* (London: Michael Joseph, 1991).

Einstein, Albert, *The World as I See It*, translated by Alan Harris (London: John Lane the Bodley Head, 1935).

Feuerbach, Ludwig, *The Essence of Christianity*, translated by George Eliot (New York: Harper and Brothers, 1957).

Feyerabend, Paul, *Against Method. Outline of an Anarchistic Theory of Knowledge* (London: Verso, 1978. 1st edition 1975).

Finkielkraut, Alain, *The Undoing of Thought*, translated by Dennis O'Keeffe (London: Claridge Press, 1988).

Foster, Michael, 'The Christian Doctrine of Creation and the Rise of Modern Natural Science', *Mind* 43 (1934), 446–68, reprinted in C. A. Russell, ed., *Science and Religious Belief. A Selection of Recent Historical Studies* (London: Open University, 1973), pp. 294–315.

The Political Philosophies of Plato and Hegel (Oxford: Clarendon Press, 1935).

Fuller, Peter, *Theoria. Art, and the Absence of Grace* (London: Chatto and Windus, 1988).

Funkenstein, Amos, *Theology and the Scientific Imagination from the Middle Ages to the Seventeenth Century* (Princeton: Princeton University Press, 1986).

Gill, Stephen, *William Wordsworth. A Life* (Oxford: Oxford University Press, 1990).

Graf, F. W. 'Die Freiheit der Entsprechung zu Gott. Bemerkungen zum theozentrischen Ansatz der Anthropologie Karl Barths', *Die Realisierung der Freiheit*, edited by T. Rentdorff (Gütersloh: Gerd Mohn, 1975), pp. 76–118.

Griggs, E. L., editor, *The Collected Letters of Samuel Taylor Coleridge* (Oxford: Clarendon Press, 1959), volume 4.

Gunton, Colin E., 'No Other Foundation. One Englishman's Reading of *Church Dogmatics*, Chapter V', *Reckoning with Barth. Essays in Commemoration of the Centenary of Karl Barth's Birth*, edited by Nigel Biggar (London: Mowbray, 1988), pp. 61–79.

Christ and Creation. The 1990 Didsbury Lectures (Exeter: Paternoster Press, 1993).

Enlightenment and Alienation. An Essay towards a Trinitarian Theology (London: Marshall, Morgan and Scott, 1985).

The Promise of Trinitarian Theology (Edinburgh: T. & T. Clark, 1991).

Guthrie, W. K. C., *A History of Greek Philosophy, Volume 1, The Earlier Presocratics and the Pythagoreans* (Cambridge: Cambridge University Press, 1971).

The Sophists (Cambridge: Cambridge University Press, 1971).

Hamilton, Kenneth, 'Doctrine and the Christian Life: Reflections on Kingdom and Triumph of the Will' *Theological Digest* 5 no. 2 (July 1990), 14–17.

Hardy, Daniel W., 'Created and Redeemed Sociality', *On Being the Church. Essays on the Christian Community*, edited by C. E. Gunton and D. W. Hardy (Edinburgh: T. & T. Clark, 1989), pp. 21–47.

'Rationality, the Sciences and Theology', *Keeping the Faith. Essays to Mark the Centenary of Lux Mundi*, edited by Geoffrey Wainwright (London: SPCK, 1989), pp. 274–309.

Hardy, Daniel W., and Ford, David F., *Jubilate. Theology in Praise* (London: Darton, Longman and Todd, 1984).

Harvey, David, *The Condition of Postmodernity. An Enquiry into the Origins of Cultural Change* (Oxford: Blackwell, 1989).

Harvey, Van A., *The Historian and the Believer. The Morality of Historical Knowledge and Christian Belief* (London: SCM Press, 1967).

Hauerwas, Stanley, *A Community of Character. Toward a Constructive Christian Social Ethic* (Notre Dame and London: University of Notre Dame Press, 1981).

Havel, Václav, Open Letters. *Selected Prose, 1965–1990*, selected and edited by Paul Wilson (London: Faber and Faber, 1991).

Hegel, G. W. F., *The Phenomenology of Mind*, translated by J. B. Baillie (London: George Allen and Unwin, 1949).

Hick, John, *Evil and the God of Love* (London: Fontana, 1968).

Hooykaas, R., *Religion and the Rise of Modern Science* (Edinburgh: Scottish Academic Press, 1972).

Hopkins, J., and Richardson, H., editors, *Anselm of Canterbury. Works*, volume 2 (Toronto and New York: Edwin Mellen Press, 1976).

Horne, B. L., 'Art: A Trinitarian Imperative', *Trinitarian Theology Today*, edited by Christoph Schwoebel, forthcoming.

Hyman, A., and Walsh, J. J., editors, *Philosophy in the Middle Ages. The Christian, Islamic and Jewish Traditions* (Indianapolis: Hackett, 1977).

Jaki, Stanley L., *Cosmos and Creator* (Edinburgh: Scottish Academic Press, 1980).

God and the Cosmologists (Edinburgh: Scottish Academic Press, 1989).

Jameson, Fredric, *Postmodernism, or, the Cultural Logic of Late Capitalism* (London and New York: Verso, 1991).

Jencks, Charles, *What is Post-Modernism?* (London: Academy Editions, 1989).

Jenson, Robert W., *The Knowledge of Things Hoped For. The Sense of Theological Discourse* (New York: Oxford University Press, 1969).

The Triune Identity. God According to the Gospel (Philadelphia: Fortress Press, 1982).

Johnson, Paul, *A History of Christianity* (London: Penguin Books, 1978).

The Birth of the Modern. World Society 1815–1830 (London: Weidenfeld and Nicolson, 1991).

Kant, Immanuel, *Critique of Judgement*, translated by J. H. Bernard (London: Collier Macmillan, 1951).

Critique of Pure Reason, translated by Norman Kemp Smith (London: Macmillan, 1933).

Kierkegaard, Søren, *Two Ages. The Age of Revolution and the Present Age. A Literary Review, Kierkegaard's Writings*, volume 14, edited and translated by H. V. and E. H. Hong (Princeton: Princeton University Press, 1978).

Knowles, David, *The Evolution of Medieval Thought* (London: Longman, 1962).

Kolakowski, Leszek, *Main Currents of Marxism, Volume 1, The Founders*, translated by P. S. Falla (Oxford: Oxford University Press, 1978).

Kretzmann, Norman, 'Trinity and Transcendentals', *Trinity, Incarnation and Atonement. Philosophical and Theological Essays*, edited by R. J. Feenstra and C. Plantinga (Notre Dame: University of Notre Dame Press, 1989), pp. 79–109.

Kuhn, Helmut, 'Personal Knowledge and the Crisis of the Philosophical Tradition', *Intellect and Hope. Essays in the Thought of Michael Polanyi*, edited by T. A. Langford and W. H. Poteat (Durham, NC: Duke University Press, 1968), pp. 111–35.

Lampe, G. W. H., *God as Spirit. The Bampton Lectures* 1976 (London: SCM Press, 1977).

Lewis, C. S., *The Abolition of Man* (Oxford: Oxford University Press, 1944).

Lewontin, R. C., 'The Dream of the Human Genome', *New York Review of Books* 39 (28 May 1992), pp. 31–40.

Lloyd Jones, Hugh, *The Justice of Zeus* (London: University of California Press, 1971).

Lovibond, Sabina, *Realism and Imagination in Ethics* (Minneapolis: University of Minneapolis Press, 1983).

Luibheid, Colm, translator, *Pseudo-Dionysius. The Complete Works* (London: SPCK, 1987).

MacIntyre, Alasdair, *After Virtue. A Study in Moral Theory* (London: Duckworth, 1981).

Whose Justice? Which Rationality? (London: Duckworth, 1988).

MacKinnon, D. M., '"Substance" in Christology – a Cross-Bench View', *Christ, Faith and History*, edited by S. W. Sykes and J. P. Clayton (Cambridge: Cambridge University Press, 1972), pp. 279–300.

Macmurray, John, *Persons in Relation* (London: Faber, 1961).

Markus, Robert, *Saeculum: History and Society in the Theology of St Augustine*, (Cambridge: Cambridge University Press, revised edition 1988).

Maxwell, Nicholas, *From Knowledge to Wisdom. A Revolution in the Aims and Methods of Science* (Oxford: Blackwell, 1984).

McFadyen, Alistair I., *The Call to Personhood. A Christian Theory of the Individual in Social Relationships* (Cambridge: Cambridge University Press, 1990).

McFague, Sallie, *Metaphorical Theology. Models of God in Religious Language* (London: SCM Press, 1983).

Midgley, Mary, 'Strange Contest: Science versus Religion', *The*

Gospel and Contemporary Culture, edited by Hugh Montefiore (London: Mowbrays, 1992), pp. 40–57.

Milbank, John, *Theology and Social Theory. Beyond Secular Reason* (Oxford: Blackwell, 1990).

Mill, J. S., *On Liberty and Other Essays*, edited by John Gray (Oxford: Oxford University Press, 1991).

Moltmann, Jürgen, *The Trinity and the Kingdom of God*, translated by Margaret Kohl (London: SCM Press, 1981).

Monod, Jacques, *Chance and Necessity. An Essay in the Natural Philosophy of Modern Biology*, translated by Austryn Wainhouse (London: Collins, 1972).

Neuhaus, Richard John, *The Naked Public Square* (Grand Rapids: Eerdmans, 1984).

Newbigin, Lesslie, *The Gospel in a Pluralist Society* (London: SPCK, 1989).

The Other Side of 1984. Questions for the Churches (Geneva: World Council of Churches, 1983).

Nicholls, David, *Deity and Domination. Images of God and the State in the Nineteenth and Twentieth Centuries* (London and New York: Routledge, 1989).

Parfit, Derek, *Reasons and Persons* (Oxford: Oxford University Press, 1984).

Pater, Walter, *The Renaissance. Studies in Art and Poetry*, edited and introduced by Adam Phillips (Oxford: Oxford University Press, 1986).

Penrose, Roger, *The Emperor's New Mind. Concerning Computers, Minds and the Laws of Physics* (London: Vintage, 1990).

Perkins, Mary Anne, 'The Logos Reconciler. The Search for Unity in the Relational, Logosophic System of Samuel Taylor Coleridge', PhD, University of London, 1991.

Peterson, Erik, *Der Monotheismus als politisches Problem. Ein Beitrag für Geschichte der politischen Theologie in Imperium Romanum* (Leipzig: J.Hegner, 1935).

Pippin, Robert B., 'Blumenberg and the Modernity Problem', *Review of Metaphysics* 40 (1987), 535–57.

Modernism as a Philosophical Problem (Oxford: Blackwell, 1990).

Polanyi, Michael, *Personal Knowledge. Towards a Post-Critical Philosophy* (London: Routledge, 2nd edition 1962).

Polkinghorne, John, *One World. The Interaction of Science and Theology* (London: SPCK, 1986).

Popper, Karl, *The Open Society and its Enemies, Volume 1, Plato* (London: Routledge, 4th edition 1962).

Prestige, Leonard, 'ΠΕΡΙΧΩΡΕΩ and ΠΕΡΙΧΩΡΗΣΙΣ in the Fathers', *Journal of Theological Studies* 29 (1928) 242–52.

Prickett, Stephen, *Words and* The Word. *Language, Poetics and Biblical Interpretation* (Cambridge: Cambridge University Press, 1986).

Prigogine, Ilya, and Stengers, Isabelle, *Order out of Chaos. Man's New Dialogue with Nature* (London: Fontana, 1985).

Putnam, Hilary, *Realism with a Human Face*, edited by James Conant (London: Harvard University Press, 1990).

Rawls, John, *A Theory of Justice* (Oxford: Oxford University Press, 1972).

Ritschl, Dietrich, *Memory and Hope. An Enquiry Concerning the Presence of Christ* (London: Collier-Macmillan, 1967).

Rorty, Richard, *Philosophy and the Mirror of Nature* (Oxford: Blackwell, 1980).

Rose, Gillian, *Hegel Contra Sociology* (London: Athlone Press, 1981).

Rosen, Stanley, *The Ancients and the Moderns. Rethinking Modernity* (New Haven: Yale University Press, 1989).

Sacks, Jonathan, *The Persistence of Faith. Religion, Morality and Society in a Secular Age* (London: Weidenfeld and Nicolson, 1991).

Schama, Simon, *Citizens. A Chronicle of the French Revolution* (London: Penguin Books, 1989).

Schmid, H., 'Creation, Righteousness and Salvation: "Creation Theology" as the Broad Horizon of Biblical Theology,' in B. W. Anderson, editor, *Creation in the Old Testament* (Philadelphia: Fortress Press, 1984), pp. 102–17.

Schumacher, E. F., *Small is Beautiful. A Study of Economics as if People Mattered* (London: Sphere Books, 1974).

Schwoebel, Christoph, and Gunton, Colin E., editors, *Persons, Divine and Human. King's College Essays in Theological Anthropology* (Edinburgh, T. & T. Clark, 1992).

Shanks, Andrew, *Hegel's Political Theology* (Cambridge: Cambridge University Press, 1991).

Sober, Elliott, *Simplicity* (Oxford: Clarendon Press, 1975).

Solomon, Robert, *Continental Philosophy since 1750. The Rise and Fall of the Self* (Oxford: Oxford University Press, 1988).

Steiner, George, *Real Presences. Is There Anything in What We Say?* (London: Faber and Faber, 1989).

Stout, Jeffrey, *The Flight from Authority. Religion, Morality and the Quest for Autonomy* (Notre Dame and London: Yale University Press, 1981).

Taylor, Charles, *Sources of the Self. The Making of the Modern Identity* (Cambridge: Cambridge University Press, 1989).

Thiemann, Ronald, *Revelation and Theology. The Gospel as Narrated Promise* (Notre Dame: University of Notre Dame Press, 1985).

Torrance, Thomas F., *Divine and Contingent Order* (Oxford: Oxford University Press, 1981).

Transformation and Convergence within the Frame of Knowledge. Explorations in the Interrelations of Scientific and Theological Enterprise (Belfast: Christian Journals, 1984).

Toulmin, Stephen, *Cosmopolis. The Hidden Agenda of Modernity* (New York: Free Press, 1990).

Weinberg, Steven, *The First Three Minutes. A Modern View of the Origin of the Universe* (London: Flamingo, 2nd edition 1983).

Wittgenstein, Ludwig, *Notebooks* 1914–19, edited by G. H. von Wright and G. E. M. Anscombe (Oxford: Blackwell, 1969).

Wolff, Hans Walter, *Anthropology of the Old Testament*, translated by Margaret Kohl (London: SCM Press, 1974).

Young, Frances, and Ford, David F., *Meaning and Truth in 2 Corinthians* (London: SPCK, 1987).

Yu, Carver T., *Being and Relation. A Theological Critique of Western Dualism and Individualism* (Edinburgh: Scottish Academic Press, 1987).

Ziman, John, *Reliable Knowledge. An Exploration of the Grounds for Belief in Science* (Cambridge: Cambridge University Press, 1978).

Zizioulas, John D., 'On Being a Person. Towards an Ontology of Personhood', *Persons, Divine and Human. King's College Essays in Theological Anthropology*, edited by Christoph Schwoebel and Colin E. Gunton (Edinburgh: T. & T. Clark, 1992), pp. 33–46.

'Preserving God's Creation. Three Lectures on Theology and Ecology. I', *King's Theological Review* XII (1989), 1–5.

Being as Communion. Studies in Personhood and the Church (London: Darton, Longman and Todd, 1985).

Zuckerkandl, Victor, *Sound and Symbol. Music and the External World*, translated by Willard R. Trask (Princeton: Princeton University Press, 1969).

Man the Musician. Sound and Symbol Volume 2, translated by Norman Guterman (Princeton: Princeton University Press, 1973).

Index